Urban Poverty in India

Dedicated to
My Beloved Parents

Urban Poverty in India

SEEPANA PRAKASAM

KALPAZ

First Published, 2017

Published by

Kalpaz Publications
C-30, Satyawati Nagar,
Delhi – 110052
E-mail: kalpaz@hotmail.com
Ph.: 9212142040

Printed at: G. Print Process, Delhi

Cataloging in Publication Data—DK
Courtesy: D.K. Agencies (P) Ltd. <docinfo@dkagencies.com>

Prakasam, S. (Seepana), author.
Urban poverty in India / Dr Seepana Prakasam.
pages cm
Includes bibliographical references and index.
ISBN 9789351282938

1. Urban poor—India. 2. Urban poor—Government policy—India. I. Title.

HV4139.P73 2017 DDC 362.50954 23

Contents

Foreword

I am happy to write the foreword for this book. This volume is known the vulnerabilities of urban poor and also for understanding the status of implementation and impact of the major anti-poverty programmes in India. Growing landlessness and underemployment forces distress migration of economically and socially backward sections of the society towards urban areas. The incidence of poverty in urban areas is more among the informal labour working in formal and informal sectors.

The migrant urban poor are vulnerable in many matters viz. earnings, credit, education, housing, health, sanitation and other civic amenities. Public distribution system introduced in India to provide food security to the poor people, but they are facing problems like waiting longer time in queue, irregular and untimely distribution, low quality of grains etc. Mid-day meal scheme is implemented to increase, enrollment, attendance and attention towards studies. There are problems in implementation viz. low quality of food, repetition of the same menu, and improper timings. At some extent this scheme has solved the class room hunger but malnutrition remained a major problem among the school going children. Rashtriya Swasthya Bima Yojana is introduced to provide health security to poor people by reducing out of pocket expenditure. The registered intended beneficiaries under this scheme as per the study are facing problems like inadequate information about the scheme, and improper attention by the hospital staff etc.

Dr Seepana Prakasam has to used in detail through field level study about the vulnerabilities of the urban poor and also evaluated the implementation and impact of Public Distribution System,

Mid-Day Meal Scheme, and Rashthriya Swasthya Bima Yojana. The study is not only relevant in Chandigarh but throughout urban India, because it gives true picture of the perceptions of different stakeholders in implementing the anti-poverty programmes.

Yoginder K. Alagh Ph.D
Chancellor
Central University of Gujarat
Former Minister of Power, Planning
and Science and Technology

Preface

The idea of this book originated while I was associated with my work on Post–Doctoral Fellowship (PDF) at Panjab University, Chandigarh. A good number of studies have been conducted on the incidence of rural poverty, which is obviously important; however, not many studies exist on urban poverty, although an increasing need is being felt for such studies in view of widespread urban poverty in India. This study examines the vulnerabilities of migrant urban poor and also the implementation of Public Distribution System, Mid-Day Meal Scheme, and Rashtriya Swasthya Bima Yojana, which has not examined in detail in any earlier studies with large size sample.

Though there is a dent on global poverty, still the existence of extreme poverty and widening inequalities are the matter of discourse. Rural-urban distress migration of poor and natural growth of poor population is causing the increase in urban poverty. In cities across the globe, millions of people suffering due to lack of adequate shelter, clean water, and basic sanitation. Most of the poor are living in slum areas are unskilled and semi-skilled, depend upon precarious employment in the informal sector, characterised by low pay and poor working conditions.

In India there is no uniform method and the formula has been developed by the economists and experts for poverty estimation as per time and situation of the country which is most suitable and generally acceptable. Anyhow, rural poverty is more than urban poverty and the overall poverty level is decreasing. The prevalence of incidence of rural poverty is more than urban poverty and the rate of decrease in urban poverty is lesser than the rate of decrease in rural poverty.

Indian planners believed (trickle-down theory) that, the continuous increase in national income would eventually remove poverty and raise the standards of living of the masses, but it is not realised. Moreover, globally it is recognised that the removal of poverty not only increases social harmony but also increase political stability and economic development. Our planners realised that increase in national income is necessary to reduce poverty but not sufficient so that the objective of planning from Fourth Plan onwards (all most all the plans) kept removal of poverty is one among the objectives. A large number of poverty alleviation programmes have been launched by central and state governments with a view to reducing poverty. Among the Anti-poverty programmes, Public Distribution System, Mid-Day Meal Scheme, and Rashtriya Swasthya Bima Yojana are crucial, from the point of view of this study.

Food occupies the first rank in Maslow hierarchy of human needs. Food security at the national level may be a necessary but not sufficient condition to secure food security at a household level unless poor people capable with adequate purchasing power. People who have no purchasing power cannot buy food grains at market prices, hence there should be some mechanism to provide food security. In India, the maximum proportion of people spent more than 50 per cent of their income on food items, an increase in food prices hit them very hard and pushes them to the point of starvation.

Right to adequate food is the human right under international law; hence ensuring food security totally should not be left to the market forces. In India, keeping in view the existence of market imperfections (price fluctuations, scarcity, low quality, black marketing, exclusion) government took initiatives to distribute certain quantities of essential commodities (mainly food grains) such as rice, wheat, pulses, sugar, kerosene oil etc at subsidized prices (issue price less than market price) at regular intervals to the vulnerable sections through public distribution system by the means of fair price shops to ensure food security at household level.

Education is thought to play a major role in capital formation and economic development leading to higher living standards. The literature says that the economic returns to investment in primary education are greater than those arising from other levels of schooling. Most of the children from low socio-economic strata suffer from undernutrition, more often they drop out from schools at an early age, which directly affects their personality development and human capital formation of the nation. By recognising the importance of healthy human resources for faster economic growth, advanced nations introduced school meal programmes much earlier than the developing nations.

Next to public distribution system, cooked mid-day meal scheme is the second largest food security programme in India, envisaged to support one-third of the daily nutrient requirement of school going children by providing hot cooked mid-day meal at free of cost. It is expected that mid-day meal will enhance enrollment, attendance, retention and attention towards studies. By and large Mid-day meal scheme became relatively successful in reducing classroom hunger than that of reducing malnutrition among the school going children.

The maximum proportion of the workers working as informal workers are not covered under social security benefits, they are vulnerable at the workplace and at the place of residence. Keeping in view the risk and no affordability of the vulnerable sections to meet the growing healthcare expenditure, Government of India has started a National Health Insurance Scheme (Public Private Partnership model) in the year 2008, for unorganised sector workers and Below Poverty Line (BPL) population; it is called as Rashtriya Swasthya Bima Yojana.The operation of the scheme involves three stages – enrollment, hospital transactions and monitoring.

The objective of RSBY is to provide protection to BPL households from financial liabilities arising out of health shocks that involve hospitalisation. Beneficiaries under RSBY are entitled to hospitalisation coverage up to ₹ 30,000 for most of the diseases that require hospitalisation. The insurer will get the smart card every year by paying ₹ 30 as registration fee. The smart card is divisible in use, portable and valid all over the country in all the empanelled hospitals; it is more convenient to migrant workers.

Along with identifying the vulnerabilities of the urban poor, evaluation of implementation and impact of the tri programmes i.e Public distribution system, Mid-day meal scheme, and Rashthriya Swasthya Bima Yojana has done in Chandigarh Union Territory by selecting large size sample, by following clustered systematic random sampling method. Beneficiaries of Public distribution system, school going children and their respective parents, mid-day meal in-charge teachers and the poor, registered under Rashtriya Swasthya Bima Yojana and government officials of the schemes implementing agencies are the respondents of this study. The perceptions of the respondents were analysed and discussed extensively by using statistical tools and rational interpretations was derived.

Acknowledgements

At the outset, I am thankful to ICSSR (New Delhi) administration for awarding Post-Doctoral Fellowship, the work under reference is based.

I am very much thankful and deem it a great privilege to thank my worthy and noble supervisor Professor Gurmail Singh for his valuable guidance, constructive suggestions, and motivation.

I am very much indebted to Professor Y.K. Alag, Professor Sukhadeo Thorat, Professor R. Radha Krishna and Professor S. Indrakant for their blessings, motivation and valuable suggestions.

I would like to express my profound respects and sincere thanks to Professor Upinder Sawhney chairperson of the department of Economics and teaching faculty of the Department of Economics, Punjab University, Chandigarh.

My profound gratitude to Professor Anita Kaushal Principal of the College, head PG Department of Economics Mrs Gurpreet Kaur and my learned colleagues for their inspiration and valuable suggestions, stimulating discussions, analysis and critical evaluation of the work under reference.

I am very much thankful to my friend and well wisher Dr Thomas Ongaro senior lecturer School of Economics University of Nairobi for his valuable suggestions.

I would like to thank the staff of the Commissioner of Labour, Food and Consumers Affairs Chandigarh, RSBY Nodal officers of Govt hospitals, District Education Office, Principals and Mid-Day Meal in-charge teachers of different schools in Chandigarh for giving me valuable inputs for the completion of this task.

Special mention needs to be made here to the staff of the office of the Department of Economics, Panjab University Library, Registrar Panjab University for their support at every stage of completion of this task.

My heartfelt appreciation goes to my interviewees who took time out of their busy schedules for participating in this research.

I am indebted to my parents and thankful to my wife Mrs Tejeswari and my children Prasanth and Surya the great for their support during the busy hours of my work.

Above all, I thank god for always showering blessings upon us.

Seepana Prakasam

List of Tables

List of Figures

Acronyms

AAY	:	Antyodaya Anna Yojana
ADB	:	Asian Development Bank
AIHM	:	Ambedkar Institute of Hotel Management
APL	:	Above Poverty Line
APC		Agricultural Price Commission
APM	:	Administered Price Mechanism
APY	:	Atal Pension Yojna
BSUP	:	Basic Services to the Urban Poor
BMI	:	Body Mass Index
BPL	:	Below Poverty Line
BOCW	:	Building and other Construction Workers
CALA	:	Casual Labour in Agriculture
CCR	:	Chandigarh Capital Region
CITCO	:	Chandigarh Industrial and Tourism Development Corporation Ltd
CIHM	:	Chandigarh Institute of Hotel Management
CPR	:	Chronic Poverty Report
CRRID	:	Centre for Research in Rural and Industrial Development
CMDM	:	Cooked Mid Day Meal
CPI	:	Capability Poverty Index
CDS	:	Current Daily Status
CSS	:	Centrally Sponsored Schemes

DBT	:	Direct Benefit Transfers
DFID	:	Department of International Development
EAS	:	Employment Assurance Scheme
EGS	:	Education Guarantee Scheme
EG-GOI	:	Expert Group Govt of India
EQI	:	Employment Quality Index
EPS	:	Employees Pension Scheme
EUS	:	Employment-Unemployment Survey
EWS	:	Economically Weaker Sections
FWP	:	Food for Work Programme
FPS	:	Fair Price Shops
FCI	:	Food Corporation of India
GDP	:	Gross Domestic Product
GMR	:	Global Monitoring Report
GOI	:	Government of India
GSDP	:	Gross State Domestic Product
HPI	:	Human Poverty Index
HCR	:	Head Count Ratio
ICSSR	:	Indian Council of Social Science Research
ILO	:	International Labour Organisation
ICMR	:	Indian Council of Medical Research
IMF	:	International Monitory Fund
LIG	:	Low Income Groups
LPG	:	Liquid Petroleum Gas
MDG	:	Millennium Development Goals
MNP	:	Minimum Needs Programme
MPCE	:	Monthly Per capita Consumption Expenditure
MPI	:	Multidimensional Poverty Index
MRP	:	Mixed Recall Period
MSP	:	Minimum Support Price
MDMP	:	Mid Day Meal Programme

MME	:	Management, Monitoring and Evaluation
MHRD	:	Ministry of Human Resource Development
NCEUS	:	National Commission for Enterprises in Unorganised Sector
NSSO	:	National Sample Survey Organisation
NFSA	:	National Food Security Act
NPNPSE	:	National Programme of Nutritional Support to Primary Education
ODI	:	Overseas Development Institute
OBC	:	Other Backward Classes
ORM	:	Other Religious Minorities
PH	:	Priority Households
PPS	:	Probability Proportionate to Size
PGI	:	Poverty Gap Index
PMJDY	:	Pradhan Mantri Jan Dhan Yojna
PMSBY	:	Pradhan Mantri Suraksha Bima Yojna
PMJJBY	:	Pradhan Mantri Jeevan Jyoti Bima Yojna
PMAY	:	Pradhan Mantri Awas Yojna
PPP	:	Public Private Partnership
PPP	:	Purchasing Power Parity
PRS	:	Poverty Reduction Strategy
PDS	:	Public Distribution System
RWSE	:	Regular Workers and Self Employed
RSBY	:	Rashtriya Swasthya Bima Yojana
RPDS	:	Revamped Public Distribution System
SEMP	:	Self Employed
TO	:	Tide Over
TPDS	:	Targeted Public Distribution System
UT	:	Union Territory
WCSDG	:	World Commission on Social Dimensions of Globalisation
WBG	:	World Bank Group

WDR	:	World Development Report
WHO	:	World Health Organisation
UGC	:	University Grants Commission
UN	:	United Nations
UNDP	:	United Nations Development Programme
UPR	:	Urban Poverty Report
URP	:	Uniform Recall Period
USAID	:	United States Agency for International Development

1

Introduction

"No society can surely be flourishing and happy, of which by far the greater part of the numbers are poor and miserable."

(Adam Smith, 1776)

During the last three decades, there is a dent on global poverty, but humanity still faces urgent and complex challenges of destitution and hunger. Moreover, rising inequality and social exclusion accompanied with rising prosperity in many countries are the matter of discourse. Poverty is a multidimensional and complex phenomenon in which a section of society is unable to fulfill even the necessities of life, (World Development Report, WDR, 2000-01).

Poverty can be defined as a deprivation of basic necessaries of life by certain sections of the population in the society. The poverty threshold or poverty line is the minimum level of income deemed necessary to achieve an adequate standard of living in a given country. All the households whose consumption level was less than what this line requires are considered to be poor. Humanity is facing mainly two dimensions of poverty: income poverty, which is the lack of income necessary to satisfy basic needs, whereas human poverty which is the lack of human capabilities viz. poor life expectancy, low maternal and child health, illiteracy, malnutrition, lack of access to safe drinking water, transport, communication, information, housing and credit, in addition to social discrimination, physical insecurity and political exclusion (Chronic Poverty Report, 2008-09).

Global Poverty

According to the 2011 estimates, just over 1 billion people remained in extreme poverty ($1.25 a day 2005 PPP), around (14.5 per cent) of the world's population (declined from 1.25 billion (18.6 per cent) in 2008). Sub-Saharan Africa and South Asia account for about 80 per cent of the global poor. Extreme poverty in Sub-Saharan Africa was around (47 per cent). Almost three-fifths of the world's extreme poor are concentrated in just five countries: Bangladesh, China, the Democratic Republic of Congo, India, and Nigeria. Adding another five countries (Ethiopia, Indonesia, Madagascar, Pakistan, and Tanzania) would comprise just over (70 per cent) of the extreme poor. World Bank Group kept a target to reduce global extreme poverty to the single digit level (nine per cent) by 2020 and (three per cent) by 2030. The target will be achieved by making greater investment in human capital, judicious use of safety nets, and development efforts environmentally sustainable. Reduction of poverty will be possible if the annual per capita consumption growth of four per cent in every country around the world, combined with no change in income distribution in each country (World Bank, 2015).

Table 1.1 indicates the extreme poverty status among different regions of the world. As per projections, Sub-Saharan Africa is far behind from achieving the target, while East Asia and Pacific, Eastern Europe, Central Asia, Middle East and North Africa and South Asia regions are the early achievers.

Poverty can be measured in absolute and/or relative terms. Absolute poverty is perceived as subsistence below the minimum requirements for wellbeing, generally based on the quantitative proxy indicator such as income or calories, but sometimes taking into account a broader package of goods and services. Alternatively, relative poverty views poverty as socially defined and dependent on social context. The relatively poor are those whose income or consumption level is below a particular fraction of the national average, income inequality is a relative measure of poverty.

The measurement of poverty involves two distinct problems, the specification of the poverty line and determining the index of poverty. There is no unanimity among the economists about the suitable method

Table 1.1: The Status of Global Extreme Poverty by Regions

Share of Population Below US$1.25 a day (2005 PPP)						*Projections*		
Region	*1990*	*2005*	*2008*	*2010*	recent	*2015*	*2020*	*2030*
East Asia and Pacific	58.2	16.7	13.7	10.3	7.9	4.1	1.5	0.1a
Eastern Europe and Central Asia	1.5	1.3	0.4	0.6	0.5	0.3	0.2	0.1b
Latin America and the Caribbean	12.0	7.4	5.4	4.8	4.6	4.3	3.8	3.1
Middle East and North Africa	5.8	3.0	2.1	1.7	1.7	2.0	1.8	2.4
South Asia	53.2	39.3	34.1	29.0	24.5	18.1	13.8	2.1
Sub-Saharan Africa	56.6	52.8	49.7	48.2	46.8	40.9	34.2	23.6
Total (developing world)	43.5	24.8	21.8	19.1			10.5	5.7
Total	36.4	21.1	18.6	16.3	14.5	11.5	9.1	4.9
Millions of people below US$1.25 a day (2005 PPP)						*Projections*		
Region	*1990*	*2005*	*2008*	*2010*	*2011*	*2015*	*2020*	*2030*
East Asia and Pacific	957.1	324.1	272.3	207.1	160.8	86.4	31.3	2.5
Eastern Europe and Central Asia	7.1	6.0	2.0	2.9	2.3	1.3	0.8	0.3
Latin America and the Caribbean	52.7	41.0	31.0	28.3	27.6	26.8	24.8	21.7
Middle East and North Africa	13.1	9.0	6.5c	5.5c	5.6c	7.3	7.0	10.3
South Asia	603.2	589.0	532.7	465.3	399.0	310.6	249.6	42.5
Sub-Saharan Africa	287.1c	399.1	406.8	416.4	415.4	403.2	382.9	334.6
Total	1,920.2	1,368.1	1,251.4	1,125.5	1,010.7	835.5	696.4	411.8

Source: World Bank calculations on poverty and poverty projections from Povcal Net database, the on-line tool for poverty measurement developed by the Development Research Group of the World Bank.

See http://iresearch.worldbank.org/PovcalNet/index.htm for additional information and data. The source of growth projections used to generate the poverty projections for 2015, 2020, and 2030, is World Bank calculations (World Bank 2014-15).

a. The statistic for 2030 is 0.11 for East Asia and Pacific. It has been rounded to 0.1 in the table.

b. The statistic for 2030 is 0.06 for Europe and Central Asia. It has been rounded to 0.1 in the table.

c. Refers to the numbers that are provisional because survey coverage is less than 50 per cent of population in the region.

to measure poverty. The most commonly accepted measures of poverty are; Head Count Ratio (HCR), Poverty Gap Index, Sen Index, Foster Greer – Thorbecke (FGT), Human Poverty Index (HPI), Capability Poverty Index (CPI) and Multidimensional Poverty Index (MPI) etc.

Millions of people stay in the state of poverty, generations together because of individual reasons, a subculture of poverty, social structure, natural, economic and demographic reasons. Some of them for the short period come out of poverty but in the course of time again slip into poverty. Short-term measures taken by the government are inadequate or improperly planned are the reasons for the persistence of chronic poverty in India (The Chronic Poverty Report, 2008-09).

Causes of poverty have been identified in a wide variety of sources, ranging from deficiencies in the administration of the income support to the injustice of the economic and social system. Essential assets may not be available to the poor because of the lack of political will, inadequate governance, and inappropriate public policies and programmes (Asian Development Bank, ADB, 2003). Poverty is the result of an economic, political, environmental and social process that interacts with each other and frequently reinforces each other. Lesser assets, inaccessibility to markets, not accessible to common property resources and lesser job opportunities, jobs with low earnings, vulnerable to external and largely uncontrollable and unforeseen events-illness, violence, economic shocks, bad weather, natural disasters keep people in material poverty and weakens their bargaining power (WDR, 2000-01). The poor may be producers but can also be traders, workers, migrants, consumers and the managers of resources. Poverty is not a static concept and there is considerable upward and downward mobility around any poverty line. (Overseas Development Institute, ODI, 2002).

Global Urban Poverty

The global poverty has become an urban phenomenon during recent period (Ravallion, 2007). The incidence of urbanisation of poverty is a new experience in most of the developing nations, is caused by in-migration of poor from rural areas and natural growth of poor population. The global urban population will grow almost five billion by the year 2030. In 1950, less than 20 per cent of the population of poor countries lived in cities and towns, but by 2030 this will have risen to 60 per cent (World Bank, 2008). The absolute number of urban poor has increased in the last fifteen to twenty years at a rate faster than in rural areas (Halfani, 2007). Third world urbanisation is marked not only by its extremely rapid pace but is typically propelled by distress migration from collapsed agrarian economies (Davis, 2006). Severe destitution is growing in cities and towns and is being transferred from rural areas to urban areas via migration, leading to an overall urbanisation of poverty (ILO, 2013).

The pace of urban poverty reduction has been slower than the reduction in rural poverty, which is also one among the reasons for urbanisation of poverty. In cities across the globe, hundreds of millions of people exist in desperate poverty without access to adequate shelter, clean water, and basic sanitation. Most slum dwellers depend upon precarious employment in the informal sector, characterised by low pay and poor working conditions. The pace of urbanisation far exceeds the rate at which basic infrastructure and services can be provided, and the consequences for the urban poor have been dire (US Agency for International Development, 2007a).

Cities and towns are engines of economic growth. Indeed, cities have historically served poor people as platforms for upward mobility (ILO, 2013). During recent times the inability of cities to absorb the influx productively and generate enough jobs of decent quality has led to increasing levels of urban informality, poverty, and insecurity. The root of urban poverty lays the shortage of jobs and of the opportunity to earn an income through decent work (ILO, 2005). Cities and towns are emerging as sites of both hope and despair for millions of people (Karen Coelho and Anant Maringanti, 2012).

Urbanisation contributes to the sustained economic growth and provides opportunities for work. Many people benefitted via migration but people with low skills left behind. Globally one-third of the urban residents are poor ($2/day), which represents one-fourth of the world's total poor (Ravallian, Chen and Sangraula, 2007). Many though not all of the urban poor live in slums. The estimates are around one-third of the urban population in developing nations i.e.–nearly one billion people living in slums (UN-HABITAT, 2006).

The incidence of poverty is more in small cities and towns when compared to big cities. The pace of urban poverty reduction has been slower than the reduction in rural poverty is also one among the reasons for urbanisation of poverty. In cities across the globe, hundreds of millions of people exist in desperate poverty without access to adequate shelter, clean water, and basic sanitation. Most slum dwellers depend upon precarious employment in the informal sector, characterised by low pay and poor working conditions. The absolute number of urban poor has increased in the last fifteen to twenty years at a rate faster than in rural areas (US Agency for International Development, USAID, 2007b).

Poverty in India

About more than six and half decades of planning era the conceptualisation, measurement, incidence and reduction of poverty has been debated both politically and socially and still remains a central challenge. There is no uniform method and the formula has been developed by the economists and experts for poverty estimation as per time and situation of the country which is most suitable and generally acceptable. In India, both income-based and consumption-based poverty definitions are used. World Bank used the broader definition-to compare poverty among nations based on Purchasing Power Parity as well as the nominal relative basis. Each state in India has its own poverty threshold to determine the number of people living below poverty line and to reflect regional economic conditions. Determining poverty line is usually done by finding the total cost of all the essential resources that an average human adult consumes.

In India, the absolute poverty is more severe than relative poverty. The Lakdawala Committee recommended the poverty line approach, anchored in a calorie norm and associated with a fixed consumption basket. Tendulkar Committee made four major departures in estimating population living below poverty line (i) Consciously moved away from calorie anchor; (ii) Recommended to provide a uniform 'Poverty Line Basket' (PLB) to both the rural and urban population; (iii) Recommended a price adjustment procedure that is predominantly based on the same data set that underlies the poverty estimation, and (iv) incorporated an explicit provision in price indices for private expenditure on health and education (Govt of India, 2012).

Table 1.2 reveals that due to methodological differences there are variations in estimating the proportion of people living below poverty line and the number of poor people in India. Anyhow, rural poverty is more than urban poverty and the poverty level is decreasing according to both the methodologies. According to recent estimates by planning commission, in accordance with Tendulkar methodology, the rate of decline in poverty is much faster between 2004-05 to 2011-12 when compared to the period 1993-94 to 2004-05. Interestingly the decline in urban poverty is slower than the decline in rural poverty; this is due to the addition of migrated rural poor with the existing urban poor people. In the case of Rangarajan methodology both rural poverty and urban poverty and total poverty higher than what it is observed by Tendulkar committee.

The method of estimation of poverty line according to Tendulkar is based on per capita monthly consumption expenditure in place of calorie intake. Due to serious criticism of the planning commission and Tendulkar methodology of poverty estimation, the planning commission has constituted an expert group headed by Dr C. Rangarajan to review Tendulkar methodology. Dr Rangarajan recommended that, poverty line should be based on standard level criteria of expenditure on adequate nutrition, clothes, rent values of the house, conveyance and other non-food expenditure. He calculated average needs of calorie, protein, and fats as suggested by ICMR, with considering the diversity of age, gender, and occupation on all-India rural and urban basis separately, so that standard level of nutrition can be determined.

Table 1.2: Estimates of Rural and Urban Poverty in India from 1973-74 to 2011-12 (Lakdawala DT Committee, Tendulkar Committee and Rangarajan Committee Methodologies)

Years	*Percentage of People Below Poverty Line*			*Number of People Below Poverty Line (In Crores)*		
	Lakdawala DT, Committee Methodology					
	Rural	*Urban*	*Combined*	*Rural*	*Urban*	*Combined*
1973-74	56.44	49.01	54.88	26.13	6.00	32.13
1977-78	53.1	45.2	51.3	26.4	6.46	32.89
1983	45.65	40.79	44.48	25.20	7.09	32.29
1987-88	39.1	38.2	38.9	23.1	7.52	30.71
1993-94	37.27	32.36	35.97	24.40	7.63	32.04
2004-05	28.30	25.70	27.50	22.09	8.08	30.17
	Tendulkar Committee Methodology					
1993-94	50.1	31.8	45.3	32.8	7.4	40.37
2004-05	41.8	25.7	37.2	32.6	8.0	40.71
2009-10	33.8	20.9	29.8	NA	NA	NA
2011-12	25.7	13.7	21.9	21.6	5.2	26.93
Reduction in per cent points	8.1	7.2	7.9	61.5	23.4	84.9
	Expert Group Methodology (Rangarajan)					
2009-10	39.6	35.1	38.2	32.59	12.87	45.46
2011-12	30.9	26.4	29.5	26.05	10.25	36.30
Reduction in per cent points	8.7	8.7	8.7	65.4	26.2	91.6

Note:-NA- Not Available

Source: Planning Commission, Government of India 2012.

Urban Poverty in India

On the basis of the spread of poor people between rural and urban areas, poverty is of two kinds, i.e. rural poverty and urban poverty. There is more prevalence of rural poverty than urban poverty in developing countries. The maximum proportion of urban poverty in India is transmitted from rural areas by means of migration of poor people. The contribution of migrants to the total urban poverty cannot be lopsided. The interstate and even within the state migration from rural to urban areas though happens due to a plethora of reasons; however, the economic motives scores the highest. Since the rural people could not able to sustain their life in the rural areas partly because of the crisis in agriculture and failure of the rural poverty alleviation programmes.

Urban poverty manifests in the form of inadequate provision of housing and shelter, water, sanitation, health, education, social security and livelihoods along with special needs of vulnerable groups like women, children, differently-abled and aged people. Most of the poor are involved in informal sector activities where there is non-existent social security cover. The segments of the urban population face deprivation in terms of lack of access to sanitary living settlements comprising modest housing conditions, social exclusion, violence, insecurity of tenure, hazardous environmental conditions and lack of voice in governance (Govt of India, 2012).

Indian economy has witnessed a growth rate of eight per cent and more in recent years, but the number of people living below poverty line in urban areas has increased, even though the percentage of population living below poverty line has declined (India Urban Poverty Report, 2009). Though it was expected that higher economic growth will generate employment opportunities for growing labour force, it did not happen, but the informal sector has shown consistent growth of employment with low levels of earnings and productivity.

In India, urban poor live in officially recognised slum settlements where service provision is permitted, while illegal non-recognised squatter settlements, where it is not. In the former, service provision, if it exists at all, is patchy, poorly maintained, and severely under-resourced. Poor living in officially permitted areas will bring pressure on the political system, but this does not mean that their voices are heard. People in the non-recognised category, however, is invariably the most vulnerable among the poor. They live on the most precarious sites and in untenable conditions along polluted canal banks, on pavements, and along railway lines, in constant fear of eviction or relocation (Department for International Development, DFID, 2009).

The incidence of poverty in urban areas is more among the people working in the unorganised sector than in the organised sector and it is more among the informal workers than among the formal workers. Urban poverty poses the problems of housing and shelter, water, sanitation, health, education, social security and livelihoods along with special needs of vulnerable groups like women, children, and aged people. Poor people live in slums facing problems like over crowdedness, often polluted and lack basic civic amenities like clean drinking water, sanitation, health facilities, housing. Illiteracy, uselessness, indebtedness, indecent living, deviant behaviour, domestic violence, premature death, the vicious circle of poverty, incapacity to acquire skill, infant mortality, anemia, underweight, and often exposed to natural calamities also. Most of them are involved in informal sector activities where there is the constant threat of eviction, removal, confiscation of goods and almost non-existent social security cover.

Urban poverty in 2004-05 at the all-India level was (25.7 per cent), which is rather a high level. The rate at which poverty declined at the all-India level was (0.82 percentage) points per annum during the decade 1973-74 to 1983-84 and (0.84 percentage) points per annum during the decade 1983-84 to 1993-94, but declined to (0.61 percentage) points per annum during the period 1993-94 to 2004-05 (Table 1.3). Interestingly according to planning commission methodology, head count ratio has declined more sharply from 25.70 per cent to 13.7 per cent during the period between 2004-05 to 2011-12 (Govt of India, 2012).

Table 1.3: Number of People Living Below Poverty Line in Urban India (1973-74 to 2011-12)

Year	*Number of people (in Lakhs)*	*Head Count Ratio (Percentage)*
1973-74	600.47	49.01
1977-78	646.48	45.22
1983-84	709.39	40.79
1987-88	751.67	38.20
1993-94	763.36	32.36
2004-05	807.97	25.70
2011-12	528	13.7

Source: Planning Commission, Government of India, estimates of poverty (1997 and 2012).

Status of MPCE in Urban Areas

Monthly Per capita Consumption Expenditure (MPCE) is the index of standard of living. While analysing the NSSO data on poverty among type of households, socio-religious groups, Thorat, S.K., and Amaresh Dubey (2011), felt that among the household types in urban areas, during 1993/2010, the rate of growth of monthly per capita consumption expenditure in descending order it has been 3.5 per cent for other workers, 2.8 per cent for Regular Workers and Self Employed (RWSE), 2.2 per cent for Self Employed (SEMP) and the lowest for Casual Labour (CALA) at 1.8 per cent. During this period religious groups are concerned, Muslims had experienced lowest growth (2.1 per cent), Hindus and Other Religious Minorities (ORM) experienced similar growth (2.5 per cent), whereas social groups are concerned, SCs had experienced lowest growth (1.9 per cent), STs secured highest growth rate of 3.1 per cent (Table 1.4).

Table 1.4: Growth of MPCE at constant (1999-2000) prices by household type and socio-religious groups in urban areas during 1993-94 to 2009-10.

House hold type	*ST*	*SC*	*Others*	*Hindus*	*Muslims*	*ORM*	*Total*
SEMP	3.0	1.9	2.3	2.3	1.6	2.7	2.2
RWSE	3.8	2.0	2.9	2.8	2.9	2.5	2.8
CALA	1.1	1.3	2.0	1.7	2.3	1.6	1.8
OTHER	2.8	3.3	3.6	3.4	3.3	3.8	3.5
ALL	3.1	1.9	2.5	2.5	2.1	2.5	2.4

Source: Sukhadeo Thorat and Amaresh Dubey 'How inclusive growth has been during 1993/94 -2009/10 implications for 12th Plan Strategy', paper presented at the workshop organised by UNDP and planning commission during October 24-25, 2011 in New Delhi.

Women are poorer than men in both urban and rural areas because of gender discrimination in providing employment and paying wages and patriarchy. The severity of poverty is always higher for women, and they face greater hardship in lifting themselves and their children out of the poverty trap. Women generally have fewer employment opportunities, less occupational mobility, weaker skills and less access to training. Because of lower mobility, they face much sharper seasonal fluctuations in employment and earnings and have fewer chances of finding employment during slack seasons.

Rural-Urban Migration

Rural-urban migration from depressed areas to those with growing opportunities is caused by unequal distribution of population, resources, and opportunities. The persons with special qualifications and abilities move to the cities where their talents are needed, thereby increasing individual prosperity as well as that of the nation as a whole.

Migration is a socioeconomic phenomenon though non-economic factors also have some influence. "A large part of urban growth in the less developed countries has historically been linked to stagnation and volatility of agriculture and the lack of sectoral diversification within the agrarian economy, India is no exception to this phenomenon" (Government of India, 2009). Increasing transport, communication, industrialisation, urbanisation, availability of business, employment and educational opportunities in urban areas are the reasons for rural out-migration. Migration is a major force which shapes the urbanisation pattern in developing nations. Migrants are influenced by the description of urban life in media or by the success of relatives and known who have previously migrated to urban centres. Moreover, quality of life is good in cities and so is the possibility of economies of scale in the provisioning of various civic amenities and services by urban governments.

Rural-urban migration is the fastest growing type of migration in India. Migrants prefer to work relatively at higher wages in non-farm occupations in urban areas. Migrant labour makes enormous contributions to the urban economy by working in major sectors, such as construction, textiles, small industries, brick-making, stone quarries, street vending, domestic work, mines, fish and prawn processing and hospitality services (Deshingkar and J. Farrington, 2009).

Failure of agriculture to generate productive employment caused migration of labour to the secondary and tertiary sectors. When an agriculture labourer migrates to urban areas in search of work and finds employment, even if it may be casual work in unorganised services or industry, he does so because urban wage rates even in the unorganised sectors are better than those prevailing in agriculture.

Labour migration is a complex socioeconomic process. Among various streams of migration, poverty induced labour migration from rural to urban areas especially metropolitan cities has increased in the recent past. Streams of poor people, landless agricultural labourers, recently (during economic reforms) land lost small and marginal farmers migrate towards big cities, bypassing local small towns and cities, as they somehow know that the employment opportunities are more available in the cities of larger size, but these destinations fail to provide minimum level of employment and standards of living because of capital-intensive industrialisation and skills-oriented service sector on one hand and overcrowded informal sector on the other.

Migration helps to avoid starvation but fails to improve the standard of living, so it can be said that it is simply shifting of poverty from rural to urban. Migrant workers are the most vulnerable section and they are more likely to be found working at very low wages in hazardous physical conditions. Instances of various kinds of exploitation by employers and contractors are also widespread in the absence of any effective monitoring by the government agencies.

The enormous increase in growth of urban populations in developing countries during the last several decades is due to natural increase and in-migration of the population from rural areas. In most of the developing countries, the available number of jobs is lesser than the rapidly growing labour force. In the rural areas, both farm and non-farm sectors fail to absorb the growing labour force which caused to increase unemployment and under-employment. The capital intensity and labour-saving methods of agriculture displaced the larger number of workers from their jobs. The new industrial revolution which caused dismantling of the small scale and cottage industries led to the disappearance of traditional jobs. The size of land holdings has been decreasing due to population pressure and lack of alternative employment opportunities. Rural indebtedness, landlessness, and unemployment caused poverty and migration.

Urban Informal Employment

The grim situation in rural areas led to distress migration of poor within and outside the country for better earning opportunities. Eventually, during liberalisation, the availability of cheap capital caused an increase in capital intensity, leading to a reduction in labour cost of production, especially in the formal sector of the economy, hence, the urban informal sector became the major employment market for the migrants from the countryside. It is usually difficult for an unskilled rural migrant to readily find a well-paid job in the city. The World Bank papers observed that the high rate of rural-urban migration, however, has made the absorption of labour in low productivity services and manufacturing activities a highly visible feature in most cities of less developed countries and led to the concern that rural

Table 1.5: Employment (Millions) in Organised and Unorganised Sectors in India

(1999-2000 and 2009-10).

Year		*1999-00 (Workers)*		*2004-2005 (Workers)*			*2009-2010 (Workers)*		
Sector	***Informal***	***Formal***	***Total***	***Informal***	***Formal***	***Total***	***Informal***	***Formal***	***Total***
Informal	341.3 (99.6)	1.4 (0.4)	342.6 (100.0)	393.5 (99.6)	1.4 (0.4)	394.9 (100.0)	385.08 (99.4)	2.26 (0.6)	387.34 (100.0)
Formal	20.5 (37.8)	33.7 (62.2)	54.1 (100.0)	29.1 (46.6)	33.4 (53.4)	62.6 (100.0)	42.14 (57.8)	30.74 (42.2)	72.88 (100.0)
Total	361.7 (35.0)	35.0 (8.8)	396.8 (100.0)	422.6 (92.4)	34.9 (7.6)	457.5 (100.0)	427.22 (92.8)	33.00 (7.2)	460.22 (100.0)

Note: Figures in parenthesis are percentages of respective totals

Source: Cited by Santosh Mehrotra et al in (EPW).

underemployment is being exported to the urban informal sector. In urban areas, migrants without skills and capital can find jobs on the streets, hence the street economy is the source of livelihood for street vendors, cobblers, auto drivers, rickshaw pullers, etc.

Advances in technology and rapid increase in the labour force would tend to enlarge the size of the urban informal sector in future. "...advances in technology are progressively reducing the proportion of labour in the manufacturing process. Machinery are more efficient than they were and power is more readily available, when this is the situation, the tremendous growth of labour force and the increasing pressure on land will lead to swelling of the urban informal sector" (United Nations, 2007).

The Magnitude of Informal Employment

In India, the unorganised sector accounts for (92.8 per cent) of the total workforce of about 460.22 million (NSSO 66th round). Total employment in India has increased from 397 million to 457.5 in 2004-05 to 460 million 2009-10. Informal employment has increased from 341.3 million to 393.5 million in 2004-05 but declined to 385 million in 2009-10. Whereas formal employment has declined from 35 million to 34.9 million and further declined to 33 million during the same period (Table 1.5). The change in the organised or formal employment has been marginally negative. The entire increase in the employment in the organised sector over this period has been informal in nature, and the terms and conditions of employment are usually precarious.

Table 1.6 shows that in India the share of informal employment in unorganised sector are constant at (99.4 per cent), where there are hardly any social security benefits for workers in the unorganised sector. The entrepreneurs prefer to employ workers on a contract or daily wages. However, the worrysome trend is that the share of formal employment in the organised sector has also been falling continuously from (62 per cent) in 1999-2000 to (53 per cent) in 2004-05 and (42 per cent) in 2009-10, this is matched by corresponding increase in informal employment in the organised sector which is currently (58 per cent) compared to (38 per cent) in 1999-2000.Thus, while the organised sector's share in employment is increasing, it is only due to the increase in informal employment in that sector. This shows that vulnerable employment is increasing in the organised sector also as a result of market-oriented policies and globalisation.

Table 1.6: The Share of Informal and Formal Employment in Unorganised and Organised Sectors in India (1999-2000 to 2009-2010).

Sector	*Type of Employment*	*1999-2000*	*2004-05*	*2009-10*
Unorganised	Informal	99.6	99.6	99.4
	Formal	0.4	0.4	0.6
Total		**100**	**100**	**100**
Organised	Informal	37.8	46.6	57.8
	Formal	62.2	53.4	42.2
Total	-	**100**	**100**	**100**

Source: Computed from different rounds of NSSO and NCEUS (2007).

The majority of the workforce in the unorganised sector comprise those who failed, dropped out or did not have access to formal education. Only (five per cent) in the age group of 18-24 having vocational skills, so the remaining cannot get decent jobs. The planning commission (2001) noted that only (44 per cent) of all workers in 1999-2000 were illiterate and another (22.7 per cent) had to school only up to the primary level. The incidence of poverty is more among the employed than the unemployed, why because poor believe that some job is better than no job. Over 200 million working poor are in a vicious circle and live on ` 20 per day. The formal sector also adopting informal labour practices including contract work, outsourcing, and ancillarisation and so on. Formal sector workers becoming a minority, so trade unions are busy with defending their interests. At the same time, there is no common platform between the formal and informal sector workers for the well-being of informal workers (Thakur and Venkatratnam, 2007).

There is a significant increase in the self-employment category during the period 1999-2000 to 2004-05 in both rural and urban areas, but this kind of employment is not remunerative. Self-employment is also seen as an index of marketisation of the economy. Now the market is gaining importance over the state. The 61 round NSSO data reveals that nearly two-third of the jobs are in the category of self-employment in which there is no direct employer. This has led (Chandrasekhar and

Ghosh, 2007) to ask the question, "how one ensure decent work conditions when the absence of a direct employer?". The dangerous consequence of growing self-employment is the self-exploitation by workers in a competitive market.

During the reform period, there is a drastic increase in the unorganised component in the labour force employed in different sectors. In the agriculture sector, the share of unorganised workers accounts for (97.6 per cent) of the total workers. In the non-agriculture segment, unorganised workers account for (71.6 per cent) of the total workforce. (National Sample Survey Organisation, 61 round). The employment content of growth deteriorated as reflected in the substantial decline in employment elasticity from 0.41 during 1983-94 to 0.5 during 1999-2000. The organised employment growth at (1.20 per cent) per annum and fell to (0.53 per cent) per annum during the same period. The proportion of unorganised sector employment has considerably increased. Many believed that the inflexibility in labour market, high labour adjustment cost, job security, no relation between wages and productivity, sharp increase in real wages, government pricr permission to retrench workers or close down enterprise, faster growth of industrial wages relative to consumer goods prices are the reasons for decline in employment growth in the organised sector. This encouraged enterprises, irrespective of their size and organisational setup, to adopt a strategy of capital deepening (Ghose, 1994). The process of innovation and modernisation results in the substitution of capital for labour.

Table 1.7: Informal Sector Employment by gender (In Percentages) In India: 2004-05 to 2009-10

Area	*Gender*	*2004-05*	*2009-10*
Rural	Males	79.2	74.2
	Females	86.4	74.4
	Total	**81.6**	**74.2**
Urban	Males	73.9	68.5
	Females	64.4	61.6
	Total	**72.2**	**67.3**

Source: NSSO, Employment and Unemployment Survey, 61st and 66th rounds.

Table 1.7, reveals that informal sector employment has declined from (82 per cent) in 2004-05 to (74 per cent) in 2009-10 in rural areas. The corresponding figures are (74 per cent) and (67 per cent) in the case of the urban area. In both urban and rural areas, male workers have declined by five percentage points. But the decline is more pronounced in the case of rural female nearly (12 percentage) points during the period. No gender difference in informal sector employment in the rural areas observed in 2009-10.

The Vulnerable Employment

India has been going through this process of globalisation for the last two decades or so. The employment opportunities, no doubt have increased but the share of the informal sector in total employment has tremendously increased. Indeed, a significant part of the incremental employment generated during this period is in the unorganised sector. The declining trends in organised sector employment and the corresponding expansion of casualisation of employment point towards the worsening conditions of the workers (Kannan and Pillai, 2007).

Globalisation increased economic, social, and political insecurity, even for those who have benefited from globalisation. Increased insecurity has been more than compensated by the overall benefits of globalisation. The current growth patterns and an unbalanced globalisation process have produced uneven impacts and opportunities, widening income gaps within countries and development gaps across the globe and increasing the exposure of already vulnerable groups to greater economic volatility and insecurity. There is an alarming growing divide between the "haves" and the "have-nots", with increasing income inequality between the poorest and richest people and countries, United Nations Development Programme (UNDP, 2011).

During globalisation, wage inequalities are increased between formal and informal jobs because more skilled and highly educated workers are absorbed in formal sector. There are earnings differentials among informal jobs also i.e. casual, regular, home workers, contract workers, and self-employed workers. Liberalisation which made easier to import technological equipment and know-how by the manufacturing sector, further aggravated capital intensive techniques. Employment in informal sector is more flexible, such as casual, contract, and temporary forms, as a result, the decent work deficit has increased and coverage of social protection to workers has declined, which may endanger our aim to achieve inclusive growth if timely appropriate measures are not undertaken.

Globalisation affected labour market adversely, in terms of deteriorating the quality of employment. International Labour Organisation (ILO) has set the World Commission on Social Dimensions of Globalisation (WCSDG) to study the social aspects of globalisation. The world commission states in this context; "The current path of globalisation must change. Too few share in these benefits. Too many have no voice in its design and no influence on its course" (WCSDG, ILO, 2004).

The quality of employment is an important indicator of well-being in the present global scenario; it is very disturbing to note that quality of employment is declining. The majority of jobs are coming up in unorganised sector and are temporary, casual or contractual in nature, these types of jobs are called vulnerable employment. Vulnerable workers are always at high risk of dismissal and do not benefit from social safety net if they lose their jobs due to illness or disability.

Table 1.8, depicts the status of vulnerable employment across different regions of the world. The share of vulnerable employment is highest in South Asia followed by Sub-Saharan Africa. This shows that casualisation of the labour market, in these regions are highest. The vulnerable employment is lowest in developed economies and the European Union. South East Asia and the Pacific and East Asia regions also have more than 50 per cent share of vulnerable employment. The global employment trends report of ILO 2009, while making projections, states that the share of workers in vulnerable employment will be between 48.9 to 52.8 per cent of the total global workforce. Vulnerable employment has gender perspective also because women constitute major share in vulnerable employment as they are in a disadvantaged position in comparison to men in labour markets around the world.

Table 1.8: The Vulnerable Employment Shares per cent (World and Regions, 1998-2008)

Total	***1998***	***2002***	***2003***	***2004***	***2005***	***2006***	***2007***	***2008***
World	53.1	51.7	51.7	51.5	51.0	50.7	50.4	49.4
Developed economies and European union	11.2	10.2	10.3	10.6	10.5	10.3	10.1	10.1
Central and south eastern Europe (non-EU) and CIS	20.9	22.1	22.2	22.3	21.2	21.1	20.4	19.1
East Asia	61.6	57.0	56.6	56.7	56.5	56.0	56.0	53.4
South – East Asia and the pacific	63.5	64.9	64.8	63.2	62.7	.62.4	62.1	61.1
South Asia	80.3	78.9	79.1	78.9	78.9	78.7	78.0	77.1
Latin America and the Caribbean	34.0	34.4	34.6	34.1	32.6	31.5	31.0	31.2
Middle East	44.9	37.3	36.5	37.1	33.6	33.8	33.4	32.8
North Africa	45.5	41.3	41.4	42.8	41.2	39.4	37.6	36.8
Sub-Saharan Africa	79.8	77.9	77.4	76.2	74.8	74.3	73.4	72.9

Source: ILO, Trends Econometric Models, May 2009.

Casualisation of Employment

The growth of jobs without quality has become a specific feature of our economic reforms process. In this process, the rural poor, the weaker sections, the downtrodden, the illiterate persons and the scheduled castes and tribes are the worst sufferers. If educated persons in a large number are without jobs, the economy could not succeed to have the proper benefit of demographic dividends. Agriculture, with a rapidly declining share in GDP still, enjoys the top position with engaging about half of our working population, but this employment is distressed one with increasing casualisation and low paid job opportunities with unfavourable work conditions and without upward mobility. The manufacturing sector has not come to our expectation and the knowledge and the skill requirements in the manufacturing and services sector have not allowed us to have the appropriate benefits.

Deterioration of quality of employment is signified by the rising share of casual labor, decreasing the share of wage bill against rapidly rising profit share and worsening bargaining capacity of the working class, it is evident that the goal of inclusive growth remains a dream which has given way to quality jobless growth and in fact exclusive growth.

Poverty Reduction in India

Who Are the Poor?

People working in unorganised sector than in the organised sector, Informal workers than formal workers, Female headed households than male headed households, Rural residents than urban, Agricultural labour than industrial workers, Casual labour than self-employed and regular Workers, more in Hilly and rain fed, dry land areas than those of in the plain and irrigated areas, Landless labour than small and marginal farmers.

Why Poverty Should be Removed ?

Mahatma Gandhi stated that, poverty is the worst form of violence. Poverty is a form of exploitation and injustice, it is a misery people want to escape, so it calls to action.

- To avoid conflict and violence (increase social harmony)

- To increase political stability
- To maintain sustainable economic development
- To achieve inclusive growth
- To enhance reputation of the country among the other nations
- To enhance human happiness index
- To create meaning for human life
- To establish egalitarian society

Reducing poverty and inequalities should be a first priority of human kind. Inequalities and poverty are different forms of exploitation and injustice. If these two evils exist in any society over a period of time, results in conflict and violence. Existence of poverty and inequalities without conflict and physical violence is called as negative peace. If peace is to be positive for the establishment of harmonious society, poverty is to be removed. Poverty is a situation people want to escape, hence needed proper action. Wider gap between rich and poor is the source of political tension and a motive for new efforts to stimulate agriculture and rural development by the governments (World Development Report, 2008).

Indian planners believed (trickle-down theory) at increasing national and per capita income would eventually remove poverty and raise the standards of living of the masses. Our planners during Fourth Five Year Plan, realised that increase in national income is necessary to reduce poverty but not sufficient so that almost all further plans kept removal of poverty as one among the objectives. A large number of poverty alleviation programmes have been launched by central, state and local governments with a view to reducing poverty.

Anti-Poverty Strategies

To attack multidimensional nature of poverty, multiple instruments and strategies are required (Srinivasan, 2002). Reduction of poverty in India is treated as an international goal, so that poverty eradication is the long-term goal of Indian economic planning strategy. Public intervention is required particularly when there is a market failure. Public intervention for poverty alleviation, by formulating and implementing various programmes by the efficient policy means of (1) Access to community common resources like land, water, forests and the other flora and fauna for the poor, (2) Education, skills and asset development, (3) Access to adequate and timely institutional credit at liberal terms and low rate of interest, (4) Productive and qualitative employment at minimum living wages (5) Basic physical needs i.e. food, shelter, cloth and other requirements (6) Social safety and security measures.

For the eradication of poverty, two types of policies are required i.e. policies relating to augmenting general economic growth. General economic growth policies may side track some of the sections of the population from the main stream of the economy, in such case, for the achievement of constitutional objectives of the establishment of a socialistic pattern of society, special measures and programmes are required.

Anti-Poverty Measures

Anti-poverty measures should be multidimentional in nature to meet the needs of the heterogeneous population for the improvement of living standards. Anti-poverty programmes/ measures can be classified as (i) Wage employment programmes, (ii) Self-employment and skill development programmes, (iii) Food security programmes, (iv) Rural infrastructure programmes to made available – roads, markets, housing, sanitation, water and (v) Social security and safety nets and other welfare measures. The above programmes can be designed by solely by the government or non-government organisations or the joint ventures by the government and the private bodies. Poverty alleviation is not merely a redistributive function, it involves both capacity improving and safety net policies. Policies aimed at accelerating growth and directing the benefits of growth will help to reduce poverty in the long run. Direct redistribution such as providing basic education, health care, and employment policies provide safety nets to the poor.

Reservation System

Reserving access to seats in different legislatures, government jobs, and to enrollment in higher educational institutions. To address the historic oppression, inequality and discrimination faced by members of the dalit and other communities, created great social, economic and political disadvantage against them. Reservations for Scheduled Castes

15 per cent, Scheduled Tribes 7.5 per cent, Other Backward Classes 27 per cent, Differently-abled 3 per cent. Some of the state governments implementing reservation for women in elected bodies, jobs, education and welfare schemes to achieve gender equality thereby to reduce poverty.

Public Distribution System

Mere production of food grains does not ensure food security unless there is an efficient system of distribution in addition to inculcating purchasing power. Poor people spent more than 50 per cent of their income on food. Increase in food prices pushes them to the point of starvation. Increase in food prices can undermine the gains from poverty reduction and human development.

Indian Constitution Article 21 guaranteed right to life as fundamental right (without food this right has no meaning). Public Distribution System (PDS) in India as rationing was first introduced in 1939 during Second World War. Public Distribution System was so named because it is a scheme undertaken by the government to distribute food grains through fair price shops at subsidized prices. It is the largest food security system in the world, 100 per cent cost borne by the national government. State governments issued ration cards to the eligible BPL households. Monthly distribute rice, wheat, sugar, edible oil, and kerosene to the below poverty line families to meet at least half of the households basic requirements. To stop leakages and corruption, in 2015, in some regions government started direct benefit transfer (subsidy amount) in the bank accounts of the households in two regions on trial basis.

The National Food Security Act (NFSA), 2013, is enacted to protect all children, women, and men in India from hunger and food deprivation. There are compelling economic, social, political and ethical imperatives for such a legal guarantee of protection from hunger. NFSA aims to ensure public provisioning of food and related measures, to enable assured economic and social access to adequate food with dignity, for all persons in the country, at all times, in pursuance of their fundamental right to be free from hunger, malnutrition and other deprivations associated with the lack of food and related matters. Although the right to adequate nutrition connects with a wide range of provisions, the main focus of the NFSA should be on legal food entitlements that underscore the duty of central, state and local governments to provision of food to the people, through subsidised grain, direct feeding programmes and related interventions, ought to receive special attention especially because nutrition deficiencies at this stage lead to lifelong physical and cognitive deficiencies.

Anganwadi Scheme

Started by the national government in 1975 to combat child hunger, malnutrition, infant mortality and child mortality rate (children age below six years). It is a health and food security scheme. Each village and ward having one anganwadi centre managed by trained anganwadi worker (female). These centres provide supplementary nutritious food, non-formal pre-school education, nutrition and health education, immunisation, health check-up and referral services. These centres take care nursing and pregnant women (prenatal and post-natal immunisation), because of this system infant mortality and mal nutrition reduced drastically.

Mid-Day Meal Scheme

Healthy children are better able than sick or malnourished children to go to school and learn (World Bank, 2014). Children from low socio-economic category suffer from under nutrition, more often they drop out from schools at an early age lead to stagnation and wastage. The scheme aimed to increase enrollment, attendance, and attention towards studies. It lower the cost of schooling, by the means of providing an implicit subsidy to the parents (opportunity cost of sending school and cost benefit analysis). Started in 1995, to provides cooked mid-day meal (lunch) to the school going children studying class I to VIII in government and government aided schools.

It is the second largest food security programme in India, to support one-third of the daily nutrient requirement of the school children. National and state governments having shared financial liability for the implementation of the scheme. The scheme at school level is under the in-charge of school teacher/teachers. At local level gram panchayat/ municipality assign responsibility of the day-to-day management of the programme. W.e.f. 1-7-2016, government enhanced primary school children meal cost ₹ 4.13, upper primary children ₹ 6.18. During 2013-2014, about 10.45 crore children were covered under this scheme among 11.58 lakh schools across the nation (GoI, 2014). School drop-out rates dramatically reduced to 0 in India.

Mahatma Gandhi National Rural Employment Guarantee Scheme (MGNREGS)

Indian Constitution Article 21 guaranteed right to life as fundamental right (without work this right has no meaning). It is the largest social security guarantee scheme in the world, started in 2005 by the national government. State to provide a guarantee of wage employment for 100 days every year at least one member of rural household within 15 days that demands work. It is a step towards legal enforcement of the right to work under National Rural Employment Guarantee Act (NREGA), 2005. Unemployment compensation (equal to state minimum wage) to be paid by the government, in case the minimum employment could not be provided. It caused increase in rural wage rate and decrease in rural-urban distress migration due to unemployment and underemployment. In addition to that, this scheme caused to increase rural infrastructure building.

Rashtriya Swasthya Bima Yojna (Health Insurance)

It is the cashless and paperless scheme to provide health insurance to the BPL households from financial liabilities arising out of health shocks that involve hospitalisation. It is the Public Private Partnership model started in the year 2008, to provide inpatient health security to informal workers living below poverty line. Households can insure their health by just paying ₹ 30 per annum, entitled to hospitalisation coverage up to ₹ 30,000 per annum (for the whole family) anywhere in the country from the empanelled hospitals. Government pay premium to the insurance company on behalf of the smart card holders (registered households). A total of 3.75 crore card holders, providing coverage to a total of 11.25 crore beneficiaries at an average premium of approximately ₹ 400 per card (Goi, 2014). Premium will be borne by central and state government in the ratio of 75:25.

Right to Information Act, 2005

Any citizen of India may request information from a "public authority" executive, legislature and judiciary- Required to reply expeditiously or within thirty days. Application Fees: ₹ 10. Fees are kept to a minimum to made available information to the poor people. The objectives are - to ensure good governance, to stop misuse of power and public funds, to empower the citizens, to promote transparency and accountability in the working of the government, reduce corruption, and make democracy work for the people in real sense. The Act is a big step towards making the citizens informed about the activities of the government. The heads of the departments (officials) will be penalised, in case of not supplying/delayed in supplying/ wrong supplying of information.

Social Security

Social security is a human right, it is an important tool to prevent/ reduce poverty, inequality, social exclusion and social insecurity. Absence of social security arrangements poses problems not only for individual workers and their families but also to the economy and the society. It decreases workers earning capacity, productivity and reduces aggregate demand and increases social disharmony and political instability. Social security is an investment in people that empowers them to adjust to changes in the economy and in the labour market. To reduce poverty government implemented number of social security programmes viz. Indira Gandhi National Old Age Pension Scheme (IGNOAPS), Indira Gandhi National Widow Pension Scheme (IGNWPS), Indira Gandhi National Disability Pension Scheme (IGNDPS), National Family Benefit Scheme (NFBS), National Maternity Benefit Scheme (NMBS).

Financial Inclusion

Nationalisation of Banks and Priority Lending

Government nationalised 20 private sector banks for promoting social banking programme, thereby to made access formal credit to poor people. Banks were restricted to selecting unbanked locations for branch expansion from a list circulated by the central bank. Lending rates are lower in rural areas (rural poverty higher than urban). As on year 2017 directives from central bank, about 40 per cent of the credit from commercial banks should devolve to priority sector viz.

Agriculture, Micro Enterprises, advances to Weaker Sections (Education, Housing, Social Infrastructure, Renewable Energy and Micro Finance).

Credit market failure (financial exclusion) is considered as one among the major factors for the persistence of the incidence of poverty, hence provision of credit by the intervention of the government at remunerative terms is a main strategy to alleviate poverty. Generally, rich borrowers appropriate major pie of credit subsidies, which are meant for the poor, because they have resources and networks to manipulate. Hence, an innovative approach is brought into existence by number of countries, to reduce poverty, income and wealth inequalities through financial inclusion, because financial inclusion will not happen on its own. A few developing economies like Bangladesh, South Africa, Bolivia etc have achieved financial inclusion through rigorous exercises.

Rangarajan's committee on financial inclusion defines it as: "Financial inclusion is the process of ensuring access to financial services and timely and adequate credit where needed by vulnerable groups such as weaker sections and low-income groups at an affordable cost" (Rangarajan, 2008, 26).The financial services include - savings, loans, insurance, credit, payments etc. The financial system has to provide its function of transferring resources from surplus to deficit areas and surplus units to deficit units where the marginal utility and productivity is more, aiming to help people come out of poverty.

Financial inclusion is necessary to achieve inclusive growth. The 'inclusive growth' as a strategy of economic development received attention owing to a rising concern that the benefits of economic growth have not been equitably shared. Growth is inclusive when it creates economic opportunities along with ensuring equal access to them. Apart from addressing the issue of inequality, the inclusive growth may also make the poverty reduction efforts more effective by explicitly creating productive economic opportunities for the poor and vulnerable sections of the society. The inclusive growth meant for trickle down benefits to the hitherto excluded population. The concept "Inclusion" should be seen as a process of including the excluded as agents whose participation is essential in the very design of the development process, and not simply as welfare targets of development programmes (Planning Commission, 2007).

The Eleventh and 12th Five Year Plans mentioned inclusive growth as a key objective. Inclusive growth is possible along with other factors, by achieving financial inclusion through micro finance. Beginning with the nationalisation of banks in 1969: efforts have been made to take the banking system closer to the people. Expansion of banking network, the introduction of lead bank scheme and setting up of regional rural banks are in progress.

Microfinance is a major employment-generating instrument for reducing the vulnerability of the poor to shocks (economic crises, natural or man-made calamities, sickness or death in the family) by building up household assets. Microfinance allows the poor to develop an important form of self-insurance against crisis. Micro finance is a broader concept whereas micro credit is narrow concept. Micro credit caters the needs of financially excluded people by providing small loans. Micro finance includes support services along with loan component. In micro credit, more emphasis is placed on loans. Micro finance, thereby, opens up channels for thrift, market assistance, technical assistance, capacity building, insurance, social and cultural programmes. Micro finance has an element of credit plus while micro credit is only credit. Microfinance institutions in many parts of the world have reported improved food expenditures and employment opportunities among their clients.

Devolving credit through various means in ever-increasing doses alone can lead to poverty alleviation in a sustainable manner. One time availability of the huge amount of credit tends to mismanagement and visualisation. Poverty alleviation is possible only if serious issues like livelihoods, entitlements, agro-processing, land /water rights, underemployment issues, supplementary income sources, etc are given priority. Only then, can a serious assault on poverty be possible? These issues need to be tackled with a constructive approach. Credit helpful to diversify and protect their sources of income hence increases social security. Access to credit can lead to an increase in the standards of living of the struggling masses, especially those who are chronically being deceived by money lenders.

A number of small and marginal farmers became landless labour because once upon a time they borrowed money at the high rate of interest from non-institutional credit sources. Failure to repay caused indebtedness, serfdom and subdivision of land holdings. Access to microfinance has also been found to promote increased expenditures on education and related improvements in health among poor clients. In this respect, it can enhance the human capital formation and in turn, enhances productive capacity in the long run.

Poor needed finance to meet the needs such as education, purchase of livestock, land development, working capital needs in agriculture and other family ventures, business, jewellery, medical expenses, purchase of land, house repairs, house construction, LPG connection, etc. Poverty could also be the result of high cost of living and high cost of production. Professor C. K. Prahalad pointed out in his celebrated book 'Fortune at the Bottom of the Pyramid', that the poor live in the costly environment and often pay relatively higher price for comparable services. The most prohibitive price they often pay is to the financial services.

The Other Programmes

Prime Minister's Rozgar Yojana (PMRY) 1993, Rural Employment Generation Programme (REGP) 1995, National Social Assistance Programme (NSAP): 1995-96, Swarna Jayanti Shahri Rozgar Yojana (SJSRY): 1999, Indira Awaas Yojana (IAY): 1999-2000, Antyodaya Anna Yojana (AAY): 2000, Pradhan Mantri Gram Sadak Yojana (PMGSY):2000, Annapurna Yojana 2000, Pradhan Mantri Gramodaya Yojana (PMGY): 2000-01, Valmiki Ambedkar Awas Yojana (VAMBAY), National Food For Work Programme:2004, Drought Prone Areas Programme (DPAP), Desert Development Programme, (DDP) And Integrated Wastelands Development Programme (IWDP): 2004-05, Small and Cottage Industries, National Rural Employment Guarantee Scheme (NREGS): 2006, Prime Minister Employment Generation Programme (PMEGP):2008, Integrated Child Development Scheme (ICDS) etc.

The Recent Anti-Poverty Measures

Pradhan Mantri Jan-Dhan Yojana (PMJDY)

Pradhan Mantri Jan-Dhan Yojana (PMJDY) is initiated in 2014 to made available financial services viz banking/Savings and Deposit Accounts, Remittance, Credit, Insurance, Pension in an affordable manner to the excluded sections i.e. weaker sections and low-income groups. The plan intends to access to banking facilities with at least one basic banking account for every household. The account can be opened in any bank branch or Business Correspondent (Bank Mitra) outlet. PMJDY accounts are being opened with zero balance. However, if the account-holder wishes to get a cheque book, he/she will have to fulfil minimum balance criteria.

Special Benefits under PMJDY Scheme: Interest on deposit, accidental insurance cover of ₹ 1.00 lakhs, no minimum balance required, life insurance cover of ₹ 30,000, easy transfer of money across India, beneficiaries of government schemes will get direct benefit transfer in these accounts. Access to pension, accidental insurance cover, RuPay debit card, Overdraft facility up to ₹ 5000 is available per account household, preferably lady of the household, after satisfactory operation of the account for six months.

Atal Pension Yojana (APY)

To address the longevity risks and encourage workers working in the unorganised sector to voluntarily save for their retirement. People who work in the private sector or employed in occupations that do not give them the benefit of pension can apply for the scheme. The scheme intends to bring pension benefits to allow people of the unorganised sector to enjoy social security with minimum contribution per month. The new scheme is launched on 1st June 2015, the scheme is designed to convert the pension less society into pensioned society.

Under the APY, subscribers would receive a fixed monthly pension of ₹ 1000, ₹ 2000, ₹ 3000, ₹ 4000, ₹ 5000 at the age of 60 years, depending on their contributions, which itself would vary according to the age of joining the scheme. The minimum age of joining APY is 18 years and maximum age is 40 years. The minimum period of contribution by any subscriber under APY would be 20 years or more.

The APY will be applicable to all persons in the unorganised sector, who are not a part of any statutory social security schemes, and who are not income tax payers, subject to the condition that the benefit of central government co-contribution of 50 per cent of the subscriber contribution or ₹ 1000 per annum, whichever is less, would be available to the subscribers for a period of five years, i.e. from 2015-16 to 2019-20, who joins the NPS before 31st December, 2015. However, the scheme will continue after this date but government co-contribution will not be available.

For joining the scheme, the prospective applicant should have a bank account or open an account. The bank account is to have the facility of auto debit for enabling standing instructions to transfer the contributions on a periodical basis. The amount collected under the scheme is to be managed by pension funds as per the investment pattern specified by the government. Individual applicants will have no choice of pension funds or investment. The pension would also be available to the spouse on the death of the subscriber and thereafter, the pension corpus would be returned to the nominee.

Pradhan Mantri Suraksha Bima Yojana (PMSBY)

The scheme will be a one year cover, renewable from year to year. Accident insurance scheme offering accidental death and disability cover for death or disability on account of an accident. The scope of coverage: All savings bank account holders in the age 18 to 70 years in participating banks will be entitled to join. In the case of multiple saving bank accounts held by an individual in one or different banks, the person would be eligible to join the scheme through one savings bank account only. Aadhar would be the primary Know Your Customer (KYC) for opening the bank account.

Enrollment Modality / Period : The cover shall be for the one year period stretching from 1st June to 31st May for which option to join / pay by auto-debit from the designated savings bank account on the prescribed forms will be required to be given by 31st May of every year. Benefits: death ₹ 2 Lakhs, total and irrecoverable loss of both eyes or loss of use of both hands or feet or loss of sight of one eye and loss of use of hand or foot ₹ 2 Lakhs, total and irrecoverable loss of sight of one eye or loss of use of one hand or foot ₹ 1 Lakhs. Premium:

₹ 12 per annum per member. The premium will be deducted from the account holder's savings bank account through 'auto debit' facility in one instalment on or before 1st June of each annual coverage period under the scheme.

Pradhan Mantri Jeevan Jyoti Bima Yojana (PMJJBY)

The scheme will be a one year cover, renewable from year to year, insurance scheme offering life insurance cover for death due to any reason. The scope of coverage: All savings bank account holders in the age 18 to 50 years in participating banks will be entitled to join. In the case of multiple saving bank accounts held by an individual in one or different banks, the person would be eligible to join the scheme through one savings bank account only. Aadhar would be the primary KYC for the bank account. Enrollment period: Initially on launch for the cover period 1st June 2015 to 31st May 2016. Subscribers will be required to enrol and give their auto-debit consent by 31st May 2015.

Benefits: ₹ 2 lakhs is payable on member's death due to any reason. Premium: ₹ 330 per annum per member. The premium will be deducted from the account holder's savings bank account through 'auto debit' facility in one instalment, as per the option was given.

Skill India, 2015

The new programme aims at providing training and skill development to 500 million youth of our country by 2020. The emphasis is to skill the youths in such a way so that they get employment and also improve entrepreneurship. Paucity of jobs combined with oversupply of new entrants to the job, kept the skilled and semi-skilled wages low. This programme provides training, support and guidance for all occupations that were of traditional type like carpenters, cobblers, welders, blacksmiths, masons, nurses, tailors, weavers etc. Tailor-made, need-based programmes would be initiated for specific age groups which can be like language and communication skills, life and positive thinking skills, personality development skills, management skills, behavioural skills, including job and employability skills. Improved productivity through skill development, increase capabilities for more earnings, thereby inclusive growth will be possible. Skills development is the shared responsibility of government, employers and individual workers, with NGOs, community-based organisations.

Pradhan Mantri Awas Yojana, 2015

This scheme aimed at housing for all by 2022. One of the biggest challenges faced by the country will be providing affordable housing, sanitation and development, and a safe environment to the fast increasing city dwellers. Real estate prices have also skyrocketed over the past couple of decades leaving the common man with only dreams of owning a house. This scheme will ensure every urban poor will be enabled to own a house. Each house provided under the scheme will involve a central government grant of about INR 1 lakh which may go up to INR 2.3 lakhs. Benefits of the scheme are availed by women, economically backward groups and the Scheduled Castes and Scheduled Tribes.

Problems in Removing Poverty

- Defining poverty
- Defining poverty line
- Identifying poor
- Formulation of suitable programmes
- Measuring the impact of each programme (evaluation)
- Lack of awareness and participation
- Inclusion and exclusion errors
- Low budgeting
- Governance

Problems in Implementing Anti-Poverty Measures

Anti-poverty programmes in India have weak organisational base, weak linkage between different programmes, inappropriateness of choice of projects, use of contractors, higher material costs, wage rate is less than minimum level, delayed labour payments, unauthorised deductions, lack of involvement of beneficiaries in designing and implementing programmes and defective executing agencies. The attitudes of the public servants are indifferent, not accountable and failed to generate necessary awareness among the people for the success of these programmes. Most of the programmes comprehensively not covered the whole nation. Most of the target group approaches and area oriented approaches could not come to expectations. Many of the programmes were not well integrated, subsidy giving programmes lack any planned approach to increase incomes of the poor.

States are facing resources crunch, hence the larger amount of funds allocated for anti-poverty programmes are being diverted to other needs by the state and local level governments. In some of the cases funds either unutilised or underutilised from the available pie. There is no linkage between the wages paid under various programmes and the inflation rate. Food grains supplied under various schemes are either inadequate to meet the needs or low qualitative in nature, hence failed to increase the nutritional levels of the poor. Anti-poverty programmes did not bring needed results due to many reasons such as inadequate funding, inappropriate policy framework and lack of effective delivery mechanism (Bandhopadhyaya, 2007).

The major criticism against government initiated anti-poverty programmes are, the approach adopted is more technocratic and the top down in implementing these programmes. Major limitations of the existing poverty alleviation strategies are that the higher proportion of non-poor and non-eligible persons are among the beneficiaries. Leakages due to inappropriate works, inefficient implementation and high level of corruption. Qualities of assets provided under these programmes are poor. There is considerable overlap among the schemes that are implemented by centre and state governments.

Efforts made by the government and other agencies to bring awareness to the poor about the extent and nature of poverty alleviation programmes are inadequate. The specific benefits entitled under each programme and procedure for availing them has not been effective. Leakages, corruption, lack of sectoral integration are major drawbacks. Policies are guided by the ideologies of the convenience of politicians and administrators rather than by the compulsions of ground realities and requirements of the poor people. Some of the programmes are carried in a piecemeal fashion and even closed away after some time.

World Bank (2008), made the following observations regarding efforts to remove poverty in India viz (1) Well-to-do classes rather than the poor got the lion's share of the benefits, (2) In terms of the resources spent, anti-poverty programmes yielded less significant results in raising the living standards of the poor, (3) To reach one rupee by way of benefit to the poor the government had to spend rupees fourteen, (4) Defective planning, disjoint programmes, defective resource allocation formula and bad administration, (5) Failure to understand the real nature and root cause of poverty, (6) Unsatisfactory supporting institutions like credit, marketing infrastructure and (7) Lack of people's participation etc.

Conclusion

Poverty is not simply having a very low income: it is about multidimensional deprivations facing hunger, malnutrition, illiteracy, unsafe drinking water, lack of access to basic health services, social discrimination, physical insecurity and political exclusion. Living in poverty increases the likelihood of poor health, illiteracy, reduced functioning/disability and dying from easily preventable causes. Poverty eradication happens through a combination of large-scale social and economic change, policy actions and specific interventions.

2

Problems of the Urban Poor

Introduction

Socio-economic features of any given population will reveal the variety of problems poor are facing. The socio-economic features of the households have considerable influence on social status and living standards of the people. The level of literacy and education, occupational pattern, work status, assets, income and consumption pattern of the people reveal the magnitude and dimensions of deprivations of different groups of people. To know the problems of urban poor, the following methodology is adopted.

Methodology

This study is based on both primary and secondary data sources. Primary data is collected from 500 sample respondents (Males 478, Females 22), through household survey during 2014-2015, in slums and shanties of all the three administrative regions (East, Central and South) with the help of structured questionnaire by following clustered systematic Random Sampling method. Chandigarh city is selected for the study because it occupies the third rank in per capita income among the Indian cities; hence it attracts a large number of migrant poor people from different parts of India. The paradox of poverty amidst plenty (existence of slums and poverty in the planned and wealthy city), motivated to undertake this study, for suggesting policy measures for further improvement.

Theoretical Base

Kuznets, 'process of urbanisation' is the theoretical base of this study i.e. "Urbanisation as an integral part of economic growth and distributional change (including poverty reduction) in poor countries. In this process, it will open new economic opportunities in urban areas and attract rural workers. Urbanisation entails gains to the poor; both directly as migrants and indirectly via remittances, but the gains are not large enough for all poor to escape poverty" (Kuznets, 1955).

Discussion

Geographical Distribution of the Sample Respondents

After dismantling of labour colony number 5, Kashmir Colony and Bapu Dham Colony, the larger proportion of poor people were accommodated in new flats constructed by Chandigarh housing board in Dhanas. There were more than 8000 families (economically poor) living in these flats, hence relatively larger proportion of the respondents (43.4 per cent) were selected from this area for the study. In descending order 118 (23.6 per cent) of the respondents were considered from 4 number colony, while 66 (13.2 per cent) of the respondents were selected from Janata Colony sector 25, about 42 (8.4 per cent) of the respondents were selected from New Indira Colony (Mani Majra), and the remaining respondents were selected from Sanjay Labour Colony (Industrial area), Bhatt Colony at Mauli Jagra, Kalyan Colony at Khudda Jassu (Table 2.1).

Table 2.1: Selection of Sample Respondents from Different Clusters in Chandigarh

Name of The Cluster	*Number of Respondents*	*Percentage*
EWS Colony (Dhanas)	217	43.4
4 Number Colony (Industrial area P-I)	118	23.6
Jananta Colony (Sector 25)	66	13.2
New Indira Colony (Mani Majra)	42	8.4
Sanjay Labour Colony (Industrial area P-I)	34	6.8
Bhatt Colony (Mauli Jagra)	13	2.6
Kalyan Colony (Khudda Jassu)	10	2.0
Total	**500**	**100.0**

Source: Field Survey Data.

Figure 2.1, reveals that the larger proportion (43.4 per cent) of the respondents were selected from EWS colony Dhanas, because about 8000 households living in this colony, other than this all the study areas are slums in the beautiful planned city Chandigarh. Colony no. 4 is the biggest slum in Chandigarh, from this colony (23.6 per cent) of the respondents, while a lesser number of respondents (2.0 per cent) were selected from Kalyan colony (Kudda Jassu).

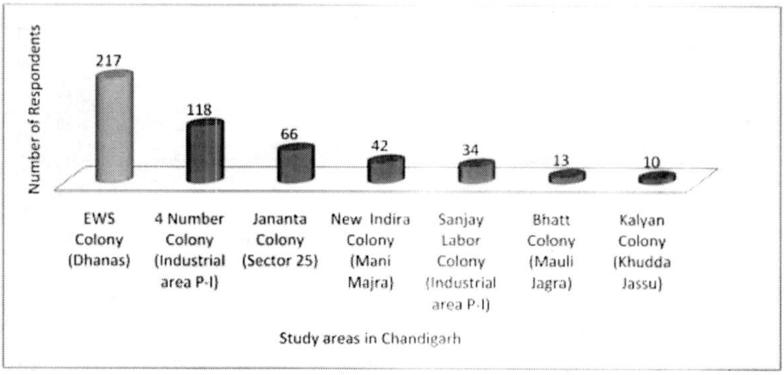

Source: Field Survey Data.

Fig. 2.1: Geographical Distribution of the Sample Respondents.

Literacy and the Level of Education

Education is an important route for social mobility and it helps to break the vicious circle of poverty. Literacy and level of education were basic indicators of the level of development achieved by a society. Education is an important instrument for human capital formation and empowerment. It enhances rational behavior and earning capacity of individuals. A Higher level of education and literacy lead to a greater awareness and also contributes to the improvement of economic and social conditions. A person who can both read and write a simple message with understanding at least one language was considered as literate for the purpose of the survey. Table 2.2, contains information about educational qualifications of the heads of the households. Among the sample 500 households, that the higher majority (45.8 per cent) of the respondents were illiterates. Higher education is access to the only lower proportion of respondents is the matter of concern, this could be due to lack of affordability and awareness. Precariously literacy rate is lesser than India's literacy level (74.04 per cent) as well as Chandigarh (86.43 per cent), is the reason for the lower level of skills and earning capacity. Maximum number of respondents were literate up to some level and were somewhat aware of the schemes meant for them.

Table 2.2: Levels of Educational Attainment

Level of Education	*Number of Respondents*	*Percentage*	Literacy Rate in Chandigarh (86 Per cent) (Census 2011)
Illiterates	229	45.8	
Primary Education	88	17.6	
Secondary Education	162	32.4	
Senior Secondary	17	3.4	
Graduation and above	4	0.8	
Total	**500**	**100.0**	

Source: Field Survey Data.

Figure 2.2, demonstrates that more than half of the respondent households are illiterates or semi-literates. A number of schooling years of education are very less among the workers. The increase in a number of workers who have dropped secondary education is the recent phenomenon. The very negligible proportion of the respondents having senior secondary and higher education.

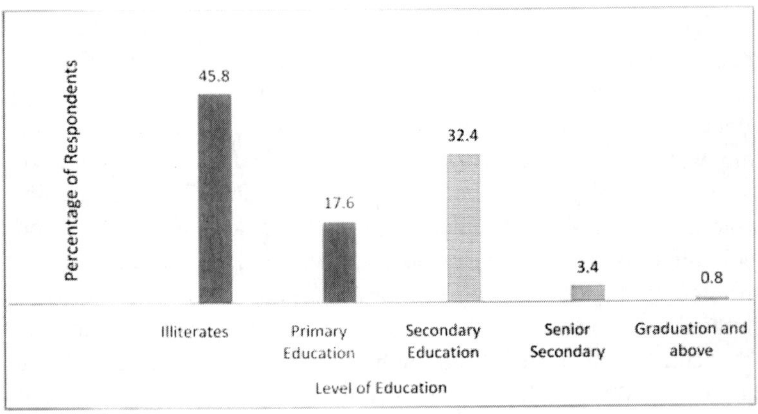

Source: Field Survey Data.

Fig. 2.2: Education Level of the Sample Respondent Households.

Social Groups

Caste and class were closely related and these two were different indicators of position in the social and economic hierarchy, but this relationship is changing over time due to shift in production relations and various other reasons. Overall, we can say both continuity and change in these relations. In this study, there were in all three social groups, namely, Scheduled Castes (SCs), Other Backward Classes (OBCs), and Other Categories (OCs). Table 2.3, reflects that the caste composition of the sample respondents recorded strictly according to the notifications issued by Chandigarh administration from time to time. The survey data suggest that the majority (42.8 per cent) of the respondents were SCs, followed by (16.2 per cent) were OBCs and the remaining belonged to other categories. Though the PDS is targeted poorer sections of all social categories, but a high percentage of scheduled caste people were benefitted from these schemes.

Table 2.3: Social Groups (According to Chandigarh Administration Notifications)

Name of the Social Group	*Number of Respondents*	*Percentage*	SC Population in Chandigarh (18.9 Per cent) (Census 2011)
SCs	214	42.8	
OBC's	81	16.2	
Others	205	41.0	
Total	**500**	**100.0**	

Source: Field Survey Data.

It is very clear from Figure 2.3, among total respondents, the higher proportion of them are Scheduled Castes and Other Backward Classes. The relatively lesser proportion of the workers belongs to general category. Though poverty is concentrated among SCs and OBCs, the other category of people also not free from the clutches of poverty.

Religious Affiliation

Distribution of the sample respondents according to religion, indicates the social composition perse. The finding of the household survey shows that, the overwhelming majority of households (90.4 per cent) belonged to Hindu religion, followed by (9.0 per cent) were

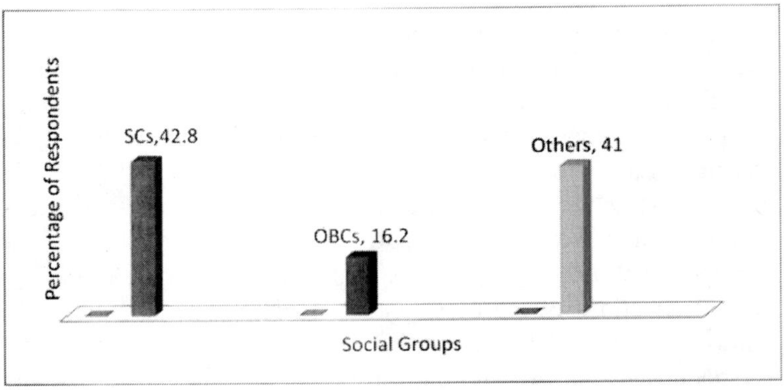

Source: Field Survey Data.

Fig. 2.3: Social Categories of the Households(Percentage).

Muslims, while the insignificant proportions were Christians and Sikhs (see Table 2.4). There is no communal violence in Chandigarh, hence social harmony among different religious groups is also one among the reasons for in-migration of poor belongs to different religions.

Table 2.4: Distribution of Respondents by Religious Groups

Religious Group	*Number of Respondents*	*Percentage*
Hindus	452	90.4
Muslims	45	9.0
Christians	2	0.4
Sikhs	1	0.2
Total	**500**	**100.0**

Source: Field Survey Data.

Figure 2.4, demonstrates that the larger proportion of the respondents are Hindus, followed by Muslims, Christians, and Sikhs. Respondents belong to Sikh religion are in very less proportion.

Nationality /State of Origin

Almost all the respondents were permanent in migrants. Chandigarh city is the hub of rich people so that purchasing power among the residents is high; hence migrants felt this city is a safer

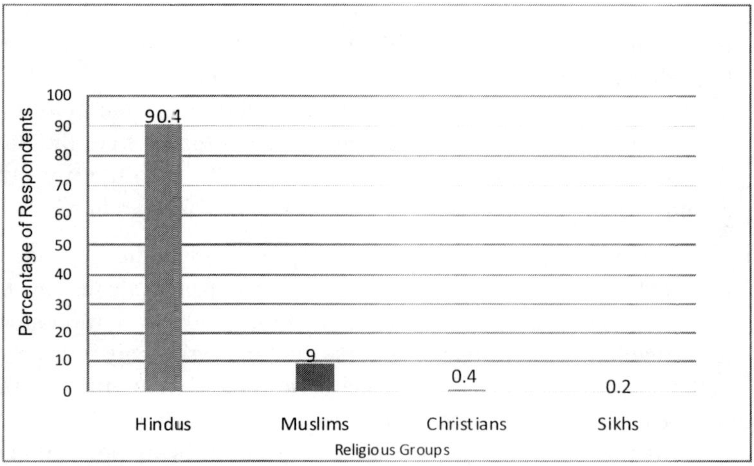

Figure 2.4: Religious Groups of the Respondents.

place to make their earnings by marketing their goods and services. It is a planned city having connectivity by road and rail from all parts of the nation. The survey reports that the significant proportion (68.4 per cent) of the respondents were migrated from Uttar Pradesh, followed by (16.8 per cent) from Bihar, and (10.6 per cent) from Haryana state.

Table 2.5: Nationality /State of origin

State/ Country of origin	*Number of Respondents*	*Percentage*
Uttar Pradesh	342	68.4
Bihar	84	16.8
Haryana	53	10.6
Punjab	8	1.6
HP	4	0.8
Orissa	2	0.4
Gujarat, Maharashtra, MP, Rajasthan, WB	5	1.0
Nepal	2	0.4
Total	**500**	**100.0**

Source: Field Survey Data.

the remaining from Punjab, HP, Odisha, Gujarat, Maharashtra, MP, Rajasthan and WB, while only two were from Nepal (Table 2.5). Lack of employment opportunities, lesser wages, failure of monsoons, loss of land holdings i.e. landlessness at the native place were the push factors, while social networks, availability of education and employment opportunities were the pull factors for migration.

Figure 2.5, illustrates that the larger proportion of the respondents migrated from Uttar Pradesh. Both push and pull factors are responsible for migration. In addition to poverty and indebtedness in rural areas, they established good social networks with the earlier migrants living in the city are the reason for a larger proportion of migrants from this state. Bihar occupies the second position in sending unskilled poor to Chandigarh. Other than Haryana, the very insignificant proportion of the poor migrated from the other states.

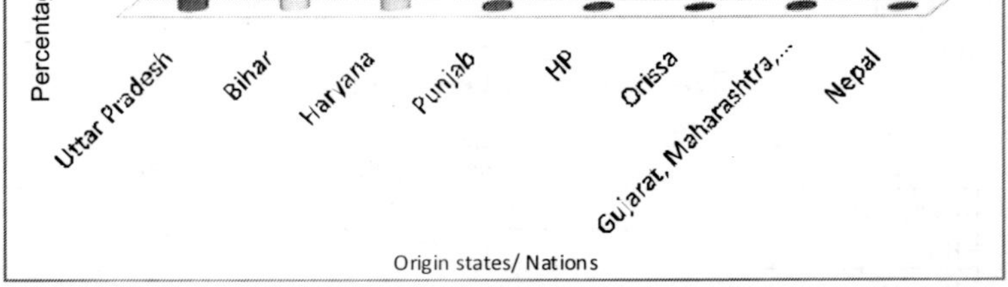

Source: Field Survey Data.

Fig. 2.5: Respondents Nationality/ State of origin.

Size of the Household

The size of the family determines the number of dependents and per capita income of the family members. As referred in Table 2.6, that the significant proportion (37 per cent) of the respondents were having five members in their family including self, while (20.4 per cent) of the respondents were having six members each in their families, whereas only (0.6 per cent) of the respondents were having 10 members in their family. The mean family size of the respondents is 5.13 members, which is lesser than the mean family size of India 5.30, but higher than Chandigarh 4.3, is the index of high dependency load.

Table 2.6: Size of the Households

Household Size (1)	*Number of Respondents (2)*	*Percentage (3)*	*Total Members of the Households (Column 1×2)(4)*	Size of the households in Chandigarh (Mean Household size 4.3) (Census 2011)
1	5	1.0	5	
2	13	2.6	26	
3	35	7.0	105	
4	87	17.4	348	
5	185	37.0	925	
6	102	20.4	612	
7	50	10.0	350	
8	14	2.8	112	
9	6	1.2	54	
10	3	0.6	30	
Grand Total	**500**	**100.0**	**2567**	
Mean Household Size 5.13				

Source: Field Survey Data.

Owning of Cultivable Lands

Ownership of land holdings determines social status in rural areas. According to literature, there is a strong correlation between class and caste. Most of the respondents were belongs to scheduled castes and backward classes, hence they were landless labour. The large numbers of respondents at their native place were attached labour, casual labour, sharecroppers or unemployed. Table 2.7, reflect that the predominant majority (89.6 per cent) of the respondents were landless labour, while the remaining were landed labour owned less than one hectare of land. These lands have remained as combined property of the whole family members and being cultivated by the parents. Crops if any out of these lands were consumed in maximum cases by the parents only, hence income from lands were not considered/ added with other income of the respondents.

Table 2.7: Owning of Cultivable Lands

Size of Land holdings		*Number of Respondents*	*Percentage*
Units in Local usage in UP and Bihar	*Hectares*		
1-3 Bighas	0.252-0.758	21	4.2
1-10 Kanals	0.0505-0.505	9	1.8
1-15 Biswas	0.0126-0.189	17	3.4
1-10 Kattas	0.0126-0.126	5	1.0
No Lands	0	448	89.6
Total		**500**	**100.0**

Source: Field Survey Data.

Household type

The household type was decided based on the sources of the household's income during the 365 days preceding the date of survey.The unorganised urban labour markets may be viewed as extension of rural labour markets. New entrants to urban areas seek jobs through relatives and friends, having chances of getting jobs in the unorganised sectors where labour laws either do not operate or which were wholly outside the purview of laws. Wages differ by age, sex, health, and experience and on similar considerations. The unorganised sector, which is characterised by the temporary, seasonal and changing nature of employment often resulting in long periods of unemployment, absence of a fixed employer and employee relationship, wages were lesser than the minimum and not fixed on the basis of collective bargaining or backed by law (Papola, 2004).

During globalisation casualisation of employment is taking place to a greater extent. Structural changes lead to the transfer of jobs from formal to the informal sector. The maximum number of jobs created during globalisation lacks quality is a big problem to enhance living standards. The survey find that larger proportion (37.4 per cent) of the workers were casual labour, followed by self-employed (29.0 per cent), regular workers were (25.8 per cent). There were a number of respondents found unemployed during the survey period due to different reasons. The maximum proportion of the respondents were employed, but their employment is uncertain and availability of work is confined to a limited number of hours, is the reason for meager earnings (Table 2.8).

Apart from the problem of unemployment and under-employment, casual employment dominates the scene (Table 2.8). Out of the total workforce, the majority of the (37.4 per cent) respondents were working as casual labour. Their work and earnings were very much uncertain. A considerable proportion of the respondents (29 per cent) were self-employed as rickshaw pullers, auto drivers, street vendors etc. About one-quarter of the respondents (25.8 per cent) were regular workers, their availability of work and earnings were stable when compared to the other two categories of workers. Precariously about (37.8 per cent) of the respondents were unemployed due to sickness, incapacity, non-availability of work etc. Employment patterns reveal the trend that a large percentage of the respondents have no job security, hence ensuring social security and employment security would be of priority of the government.

Table 2.8: Distribution of Respondents by Household Type

Categories of households	*Number of respondents*	*Percentage*
Casual Labour	187	37.4
Self Employed	145	29.0
Regular Workers	129	25.8
Non Workers (others)	39	7.8
Total	**500**	**100.0**
Males 478, Females 22		

Source: Field Survey Data.

Figure 2.6, demonstrates that almost all the migrant poor respondents are informal labour, working as casual labour, self-employed and regular workers in descending order. Other than regular workers, the other categories of workers earnings are very much uncertain. A significant proportion of the workers were unemployed due to sickness, non-availability of work etc.

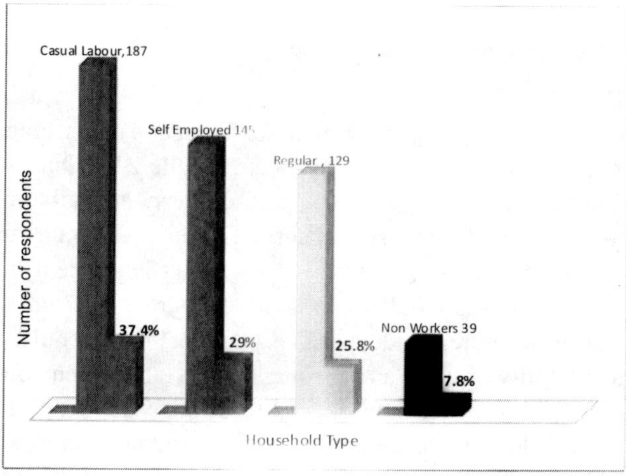

Source: Field Survey Data.

Fig. 2.6: Distribution of the Respondents by Households Type.

Occupation Pattern of the Respondents

Workers working in different occupations according to their belongingness to a social group, social network, availability of capital, skills, qualifications, and experience. Better the occupation better will be the earnings. Table (2.9) presents that the relatively greater majority of the respondents (34.2 per cent) were engaged as construction workers

Table 2.9: Occupation Pattern of Sample Respondents

Nature of occupation	*Number of Respondents*	*Percentage*
Construction Workers and Unspecified Casual Workers	171	34.2
Factory Workers	44	8.8
Street Vendors	42	8.4
Drivers (Auto, Truck)	32	6.4
Rickshaw Pullers	23	4.6
Workers in Offices and Shops	22	4.4
Cart Pushers	17	3.4
Sweepers	15	3.0
Rag Pickers	14	2.8
Painters	11	2.2

(Contd...)

Domestic Workers	8	1.6
Other Informal Workers	62	12.4
Non Workers	39	7.8
Total	**500**	**100.0**

Source: Field Survey Data.

and work as unspecified casual workers, followed by (8.8 per cent) regular workers (factory workers) and a sizeable proportion of the workforce (8.4 per cent) were street vendors. The remaining respondents other than unemployed were working as drivers (Auto, Truck), Rickshaw pullers, workers in offices and shops, Cart Pushers, Sweepers, Rag pickers, Painters, Domestic workers etc.

Monthly Income

Monthly income determines the standard of living. Though the maximum proportion of the workers working a larger number of hours, their earnings were very low because they are working as informal labour. Table 2.10, indicates that the predominant majority (47 per cent) of the worker's monthly earnings were in the range of ₹ 4000-5999, only meager proportion (0.4 per cent) of the worker's monthly earnings were in the range of ₹ 14000-17999. Household mean monthly income is just ₹ 5223.6, which is very much inadequate to maintain a minimum standard of living in the city.

Table 2.10: Monthly Income from all the Sources (₹)

Income Range	*Number of Respondents*	*Percentage*
₹ 1-2000	9	1.8
2001-4000	72	14.4
4001-6000	235	47.0
6001-8000	135	27.0
8001-10000	34	6.8
10001-12000	11	2.2
12001-14000	2	0.4
14001-18000	2	0.4
HH Mean Monthly Income ₹ 5223.6		
Total	**500**	**100.0**

Source: Field Survey Data.

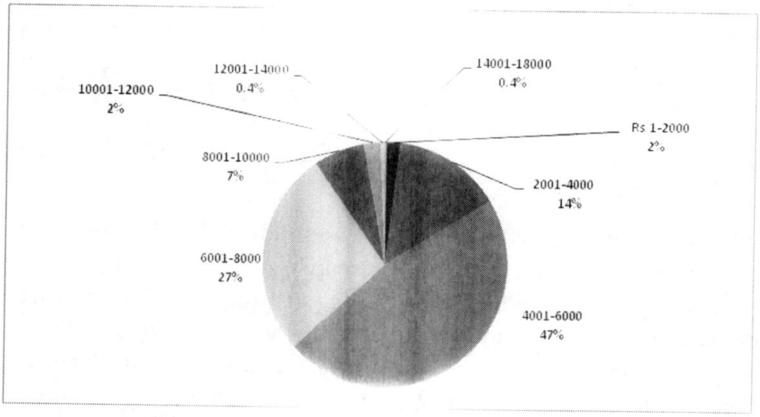

Source: Field Survey Data.

Fig. 2.7: Monthly Earnings of the Respondents (₹).

Figure 2.7, demonstrates that precariously about 14 per cent of the respondent's monthly earnings are in the range of ₹ 2001 to 4000, they are the extreme poor respondents moreover they are casual labour facing underemployment and unemployment. The larger proportion of the respondent's monthly earnings are in the range of ₹ 4001-6000, moreover these earnings also uncertain. The very negligible proportion of the respondent's monthly earnings are in the range of ₹ 8000 to 18000.

Annual Income from all the Sources

Annual income which determines consumption expenditure and savings. If other things being constant more the income more will be the standard of living. Annual income includes pension, wages/earnings of self-employed (self and other family members). Table 2.11, reflects that the larger proportion (60 per cent) of the respondent's annual income is in the range of ₹ 51,000-1,00,000, while (34 per cent) of the respondent's annual income is in the range of ₹ 1-50,000. Annual mean Income of the respondents households is ₹ 63,966.4, annual per capita income of the members of household is ₹ 12,469.08, Monthly per capita income of the members of household ₹ 1039.09, Daily per capita income of the members of household is ₹ 34.63, all of them are living below poverty line income of daily $1 is the matter of discourse.

Table 2.11: Annual Income from All the Sources (₹)

Annual Income	*Number of Respondents*	*Percentage*
1-50,000	170	34.0
50,001-1,00,000	300	60.0
1,00,001-1,50,000	27	5.4
1,50,001-2,00,000	1	0.2
2,00,001-2,50,000	1	0.2
6,00,001- 6,50,000 (6,12,000)	1	0.2
HH Mean Annual Income ₹ 63,966.4		
Total	**500**	**100.0**

Source: Field Survey Data.

Note: Income from lands was not included because, lands are combined property, being cultivated and crops are availed by the parents only.

Annual mean Income of the Respondents households	₹ 63,966.4
Annual mean per capita income of the members of HH	₹ 12,469.08
Monthly mean per capita income of the members of HH	₹ 1039.09
Daily mean per capita Income of the members of HH	₹ 34.63
Note: Almost all the households living below poverty line income of daily $1	

Incidence of Poverty among the Respondents

Identification of urban poor households is necessary to know the nature and dimension of deprivation that the poor were subjected and also necessary for effectively targeting the beneficiaries under various poverty alleviation programmes. Poverty threshold or poverty line is the minimum level of income deemed adequate in a given country to meet minimum needs. Determining the poverty line is usually done by finding the total cost of all the essential resources that an average human adult consumes. According to world bank estimates in 2010, about 400 million (32.7 per cent) of the total Indian population fall below the international poverty line of US $1.25 per day (PPP), while 68.7 per cent live on less than US $2 per day. In Chandigarh, on an average 7.1 per cent of the population is living below poverty line of income $1.25 (PPP).

The incidence of poverty among the respondents in Chandigarh (Tendulkar Methodology)

According to Tendulkar committee methodology, in rural areas national poverty line ₹ 816 per capita per month and ₹ 1,000 per capita per month in urban areas. Whereas daily per capita consumption expenditure in rural areas ₹ 27.2, in urban areas ₹ 33.33. Thus, for a family of five members, all-India poverty line in terms of consumption expenditure would amount to about ₹ 4,080 per month in rural areas and ₹ 5,000 per month in urban areas, whereas in rural areas 216.5 million (25.7 per cent), in urban areas 52.8 million (13.7 per cent), in total 269.3 million (21.9 per cent) of Indian population living below poverty line. It is further estimated that for Chandigarh rural monthly income ₹ 1054, for urban ₹ 1155 is considered for the estimation of people living below poverty line. Accordingly in Chandigarh rural 1.64 per cent, in urban 22.31 per cent, both rural and urban combined 2.35 lakhs (21.81 per cent) of the population living below poverty line.

According to the criteria, (Tendulkar Committee) adopted by planning commission in 2013, (₹ 33.33 daily expenditure) almost all the family members of the respondents on an average were living above the poverty line because their household per capita income is ₹ 34.63. According to World Bank, criteria of $ 1.25 PPP ($1=₹ 68.75), almost all respondent households were living below poverty line. Before declaring respondents were living above poverty line based on new criteria, it is noteworthy to see the Human Development Indicators such as literacy, education level, health, housing and availability other amenities also.

In Chandigarh in 2012, the rural monthly per capita expenditure is ₹ 2543.57 in urban ₹ 3000.27, daily consumption expenditure of rural ₹ 84.78 whereas for urban ₹ 100.09 (Chandigarh statistical abstract, 2013).While respondents monthly per capita income in the study area is ₹ 1039.09 and daily income is ₹ 34.63 only. It can be said that these respondents' incomes were worse than mean income of Chandigarians.

Monthly Savings

Monthly savings depends on income and consumption expenditure, where S=Y-C. In case of informal employment increment of income is not linked with price index. The growing cost of living and uncertain earnings are the reasons for lesser savings or no savings. Lesser the savings more the hardships to be faced to meet unexpected contingencies. Table 2.12, reveals that the predominant segment (70.2 per cent) of the respondents annual savings were zero, while (13.6 per cent) of the respondents monthly savings were in the range of ₹ 500-1000. The mean monthly savings of household is ₹ 278.4, while the mean monthly per capita savings were ₹ 54.22 only, it is less than all India average.

Table 2.12: Monthly Savings (₹)

Savings Range	*Number of Respondents*	*Percentage*
Zero Savings 351 (70.2 per cent)		
0-500	351	70.2
500-1000	68	13.6
1000-1500	58	11.6
1500-2000	4	0.8
2000-2500	17	3.4
2500-3000	0	0.0
3000-3500	1	0.2
3500-4000	0	0.0
4000-4500	1	0.2
HH Mean monthly savings 278.4		
Total	**500**	**100.0**

Source: Field Survey Data.

Figure 2.8, indicates that the maximum number of sample respondents' monthly savings are in the range of ₹ 0-500, the only negligible proportion of the respondents able to save monthly more than ₹ 500; it is less than India's mean monthly savings. Uncertainty of work, meager uncertain earnings and increasing prices of essential commodities are the reasons for no savings or low savings.

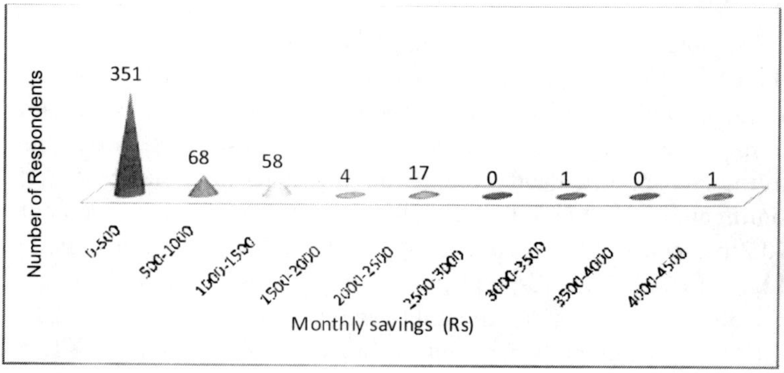

Source: Field Survey Data.

Fig. 2.8: Monthly Savings of Respondent Households.

Level of Indebtedness

Non-availability of credit from formal sources is the axe for financial inclusion. Availability credit from informal sources is uncertain and involves a high rate of interest burden. Moreover, respondents felt that "if we borrow how we can repay, because of no certainty of earnings, hence we survive with whatever we have". Table 2.13, confirmed that the predominant majority (84.2 per cent) of the respondents were non-borrowers from any source, while among the debtors the larger proportion of the respondents borrowed the amount ranges between ₹ 1000-50,000, while (1.4 per cent) of the respondents borrowed ₹ 50,000 - 1,00,000. As on the date of survey, mean household indebtedness is ₹ 5976; per capita indebtedness of the members of the household is ₹ 1164.

Table 2.13: Level of Indebtedness (₹)

Range of Indebtedness (₹)	*Number of Respondents*	*Percentage*
0	421	84.2
1000-50,000	68	13.6
50,000-1,00,000	7	1.4
1,00,000-1,50,000	2	0.4
1,50,000-2,00,000	1	0.2

(Contd...)

2,00,000-2,50,000	0	0.0
2,50,000-3,00,000	1	0.2
Mean HH Indebtedness ₹ 5976 Per capita indebtedness of members of HH ₹ 1164		
Total	**500**	**100.0**

Source: Field Survey Data.

Source of Borrowing

The predominant proportion (84.2 per cent) of the respondents borrowed from no source due to non-availability and fear of repayment problem, followed by (13.8 per cent) of the respondents borrowed from friends and relatives, (1.2 per cent) respondents borrowed from financier, only the negligible proportion (0.8 per cent) managed to borrow from banks (Table 2.14). It is revealed that informal sources of finance playing a major role in meeting credit needs of some of the respondents.

Table 2.14: Sources of Borrowing

Source of Borrowing	*Number of Respondents*	*Percentage*
Have no source to borrow	421	84.2
Banks	4	0.8
Financier	6	1.2
Friends and relatives	69	13.8
Total	**500**	**100.0**

Source: Field Survey Data.

Figure 2.9, illustrates that the larger proportion of the sample households find difficult to borrow even from private sources due to different reasons like lack of creditworthiness, no guarantee of future repayment, non-availability due to lack of social networks etc. Only (14 per cent) respondents managed to get loans from friends and relatives. Number of documents to be submitted cumbersome procedures and illiteracy are the reasons for not getting loans from banks.

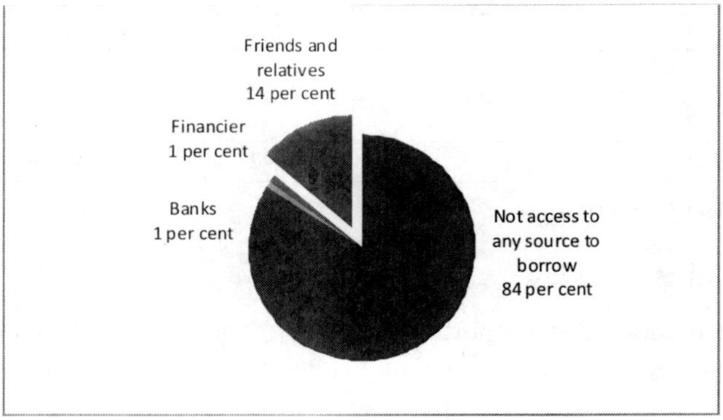

Source: Field Survey Data.

Fig. 2.9: Source of Borrowings.

Reasons for Borrowing

The purpose for which credit is borrowed determines repayment capacity. If credit is borrowed for productive purposes, relatively more will be the repayment capacity due to further income generation. Precariously among the borrowed, the major segment (7.8 per cent) of the respondents spent on ill health is a matter of great concern. Table 2.15, reflects that about (3.0 per cent) of the respondents spent for the marriage of daughter, while (2.4 per cent) respondents to meet the household expenditure, while (2.0 per cent) respondents spent for construction or renovation of the house.

Table 2.15: Reasons for Borrowing

Reason	*Number of Respondents*	*Percentage*
Not Borrowed loan / Not available	421	84.2
Income Generating Assets	2	0.4
Court Civil Case	1	0.2
House Construction	10	2.0
Maintain Family	12	2.4
Ill Health	39	7.8
Marriage of Daughter	15	3.0
Total	**500**	**100.0**

Source: Field Survey Data.

Figure 2.10, illustrates that the major proportion of the respondents have no debt, is not a positive indication, because they failed to get credit from any source. Among the borrowed the larger proportion of the respondents borrowed to meet out of pocket expenditure on health, followed by to meet marriage expenses of their daughters.

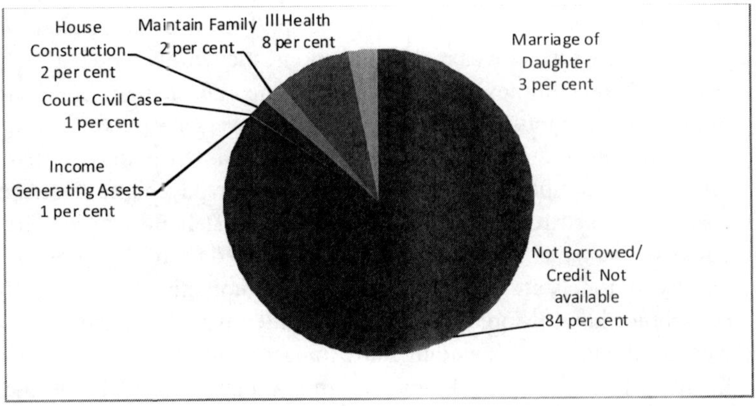

Source: Field Survey Data.

Fig. 2.10: Reasons for Borrowing.

INFRASTRUCTURE AND AMENITIES

Quality of Dwelling Units

The overall condition of housing in the survey areas was poor; more than half of the survey households live in low-quality dwellings. Conditions of dwellings are most precarious in slum areas. Soon after dismantling colony number 5 and Kashmir Colony, Chandigarh administration constructed about 8000 one room set of all-weather dwellings with all the facilities for economically weaker sections in Dhanas, which is five kilometers away from the heart of the city. These dwellings were given to permanent residents after fulfilling some of the conditions on charging monthly rent of ₹ 800 from each household.

It is interesting to note that the significant proportion of the respondents (43.4 per cent) were living in pucca dwellings, constructed by the government, given to long-term migrant permanent residents on rent basis is a positive index. Still, a considerable proportion (27.6 per cent) of the respondents were living in public places in kutcha dwellings, while (25 per cent) live in huts and the remaining are in semi-pucca dwellings is a matter of great concern (Table 2.16).

The slum dwellers long run problem of housing has solved, but some of the new problems were cropped up are the reasons for economically further weaken. Female domestic worker who hails from these housing complexes were worked in the houses in different parts of the city, their jobs were insecure and their wages were very meager on an average not more than ₹ 1500 per month. Now they forced to remain as unemployed by staying at home or pay higher transport charges, caused reduction of their net earnings. If they absent from doing work, will increase the burden of work on working women in the city for timely attending their duties after completing their respective household chores. Moreover, medical facilities available at the premises were minimal, lead to spending more transport charges to avail medical facilities from the city. The maximum numbers of residents in these complexes were working as informal labour (casual, regular and self-employed), have to travel a long distance to do insecure and thinly paid jobs by paying more transport charges or if they go by bicycle or by the walk will further increase the number of hours of work already overburdened. Sometimes even by facing all the hurdles, at the end there is no guarantee of availability of work, hence forced to come back with empty hands.

Table 2.16: Possession of Quality of Dwelling Units

Quality of Dwelling	*Number of Dwellings (Respondents)*	*Percentage Pucca*	Houses in Chandigarh (83.2 Per cent) (Census 2011)
Pucca	217	43.4	
Semi Pucca	20	4.0	
Kutcha	138	27.6	
Hut	125	25.0	
Total	**500**	**100.0**	

Source: Field Survey Data.

Figure 2.11, indicates that the minor proportion of the respondents are residing in pucca dwellings, while the larger proportion of the

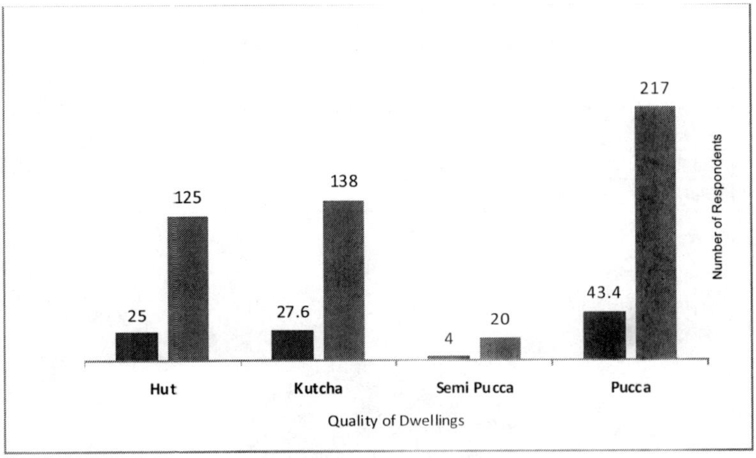

Source: Field Survey Data.

Fig. 2.11: Possession of Quality of Dwelling Units.

respondents are residing in semi-pucca, Kutcha, and huts. It indicates the low level of standard of living and unhygienic housing conditions.

Number of Dwelling Rooms

Availability of a number of square meters space per head is the index of comfortable living. Per head availability of space is very limited due to higher rent bills. More the space, more will be rent burden in case of rent payers. The household survey indicates that a very higher segment (72.4 per cent) of the respondents living in one room is the index of poor quality of life. Normally in each family, there were minimum four or five members. Parents and children, newly wedded couple were living in the same room indicates there is no privacy for anybody, the remaining (27.6 per cent) reside in two room set (see Table 2.17).

Figure 2.12, focuses that the larger proportion of the respondents even with families residing in one room dwellings indicates the alarming situation of square meters of space available for living. Only the minor proportions of the respondents are living in two-room dwellings.

Table 2.17: Number of Dwelling Rooms.

Number of Rooms	*Number of Respondents*	*Percentage*	Households by one dwelling room in Chandigarh (39.3 Per cent) (Census 2011)
One Room	362	72.4	
Two Rooms	138	27.6	
Total	**500**	**100.0**	

Source: Field Survey Data.

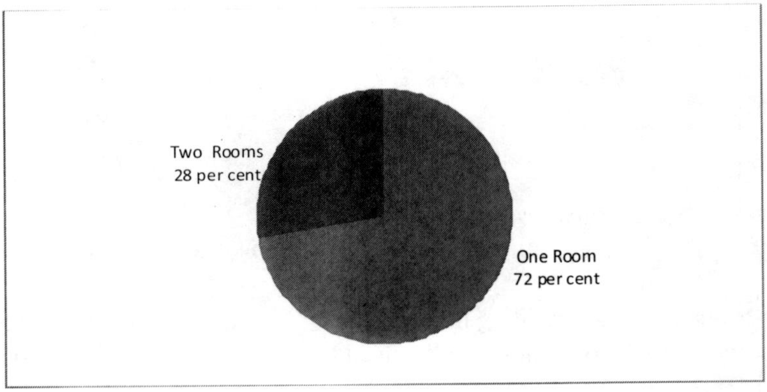

Source: Field Survey Data.

Fig. 2.12: Number of Dwelling Rooms.

Ownership Status of Dwellings

Information on ownership of dwellings is the index of distribution of housing wealth and standard of living of the people. Housing is a major problem in urban areas due to limited space and higher real-estate prices. It is very difficult for migrant informal workers with their limited income to buy and owning house/room/or staying in comfortable rented accommodation. Table 2.18, reflects that the majority of the households (55.6 per cent) reside in unofficial huts built on public space. The remaining (44.4 per cent) living in rented dwellings. House rents eat away the major portion of their hard earnings. Most of the huts were on government lands, dwellers in these huts are very much insecure because these dwellings can be destroyed and they can be evicted at any time without prior intimation. These respondents have long experience of shifting their residence from one public open space to another space due to forced evictions by the government.

They have to lose their belongings at the time of eviction and forego a number of man-days to gather material and construct new huts elsewhere.

Table 2.18: Ownership Status of Dwelling Units

Status	*Number of Respondents*	*Percentage*	Rented households in Chandigarh (47.0 Per cent) (Census 2011)
Hut Built on Public Space	278	55.6	
Rented	222	44.4	
Total	500	100.0	

Source: Field Survey Data.

Figure 2.13, demonstrates that the larger proportion of the respondents precariously living in insecure and unsafe dwellings i.e. huts built on public space. They can be evacuated at any time without prior notice is the index of insecurity. Only the minor proportions of the respondents are living in rented accommodation.

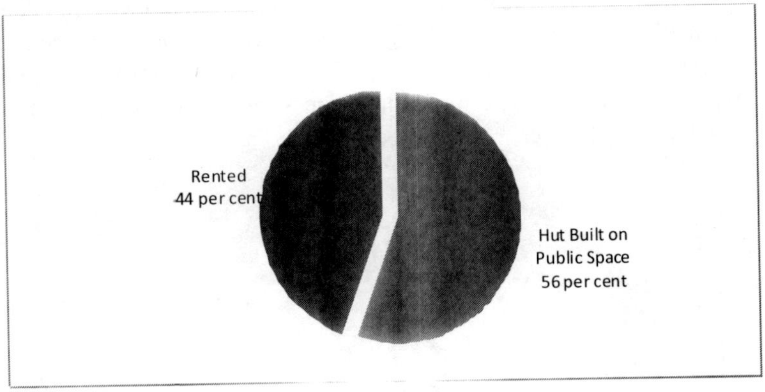

Source: Field Survey Data.

Fig. 2.13 : Ownership Status of Dwelling Units.

Source of Drinking Water

Contaminated water is the reason for a number of water-borne diseases. Table 2.19, presents that, more than half of the proportion of the respondents (52.4 per cent) were access to community tap water at free of cost nearer to their dwellings, about (45.2 per cent) have pipe water connection inside the house, while the remaining negligible proportion depends on community bore well. There are huge rush and queue for filling water because water supply confined to a limited number of hours. In Dhanas, reasonably a large number of dwellings having tap water connection inside the room, but this is the unpurified underground water causing a number of water-borne diseases. Moreover other than the ground floor, respondents living in the remaining floors were facing the problem of water shortage due to low pressure.

Table 2.19: Main Source of Drinking Water.

<table>
<tr><th>Source</th><th>Number of Respondents</th><th>Percentage</th><td rowspan="5">Main Source of Drinking Water in Chandigarh (96.7 Per cent) (Census 2011)</td></tr>
<tr><td>Tap in the House</td><td>226</td><td>45.2</td></tr>
<tr><td>Community Tap</td><td>262</td><td>52.4</td></tr>
<tr><td>Community Bore Well</td><td>12</td><td>2.4</td></tr>
<tr><td>Total</td><td>500</td><td>100.0</td></tr>
</table>

Source: Field Survey Data.

Figure 2.14, indicates that the lesser proportion of the respondents are having a tap in their dwellings, while larger proportion depends on community bore well and community tap. At community bore well / tap they have to waste more time and sometimes no guarantee of availability of water.

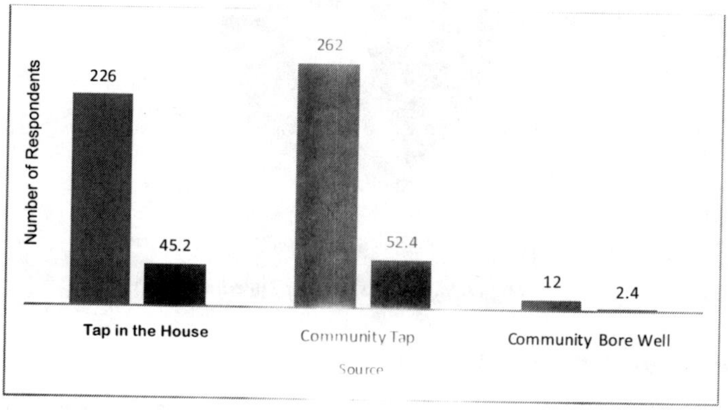

Source: Field Survey Data.

Fig. 2.14: Main Source of Drinking Water.

Access to Household Assets

Let us now look at ownership of domestic assets, which throws some light on the living conditions of sample households. Use of automobiles and electronic goods were increasing due to increase in income levels in both rural and urban areas in India. Consumption of these goods is an index of comfortable living. The maximum proportion of the respondents were having very meager assets. Table 2.20 indicates that about (21.4 per cent) of the respondents were having fan only in their dwelling. About (5.2 per cent) of the respondents were having TV only. The maximum numbers of households were having both Fan and TV. Precariously (10.4 per cent) households having nothing is the index of destitution. It is interesting to note that the ownership of mobile phones was widespread; the majority of the households owned at least one mobile phone.

Table 2.20: Access to Household Assets

Household Assets	***Number of Respondents***	***Per cent***	None of the assets possessed by the households in Chandigarh (2.3 Per cent) (Census 2011)
Fan only	107	21.4	
TV only (Black and White 5, color 21)	26	5.2	
TV and Fan	183	36.6	
Fan, TV and Refrigerator	42	8.4	
Fan, TV, Refrigerator and Motor Vehicle,	17	3.4	
Fan, TV, Refrigerator Motor Vehicle and Computer	2	0.4	
Other Than Computers Having Two or More Than Two of The Above Household Assets	71	14.2	
None of the assets possessed by the sample households (even no mobile phone)	52	10.4	
Total	**500**	**100.0**	

Source: Field Survey Data.

Type of Sanitation in Use

Sanitation is an important requirement for better health of the people. Poor sanitation is closely related to various health ailments.

In the context of the high density of population, the problem becomes more severe. Availability of improved sanitation facility is very scarce for poor people because they live in peripheries of the city (slums) where the environment is unhygienic and dirty. Dwellings constructed by the government for poor people were having improved sanitation facility. The larger proportion of the households depends on community paid sanitation or open defecation. For a single use of community paid sanitation contractor charge ₹ 2 to 3 from the residents. The maintenance of toilets is worse and away from some of the dwellings. A maximum number of females than males use community paid sanitation. Table 2.21, confirmed that about (48.2 per cent) of the dwellings having improved sanitation within the house, about (20.0 per cent) of the respondents access to community paid sanitation, about (23.4 per cent) of the respondents depends on open defecation. I hope Pradhan Mantri Swasthya Bharat Abhiyan will make a ray of hope to solve the problem.

Table 2.21: Type of Sanitation in Use

Sanitation facility	*Number of Dwellings (Respondents)*	*Percentage*	Households having latrine water closet in Chandigarh (87.1 Per cent) (Census 2011)
Improved Sanitation Within The Premises of the Dwelling	241	48.2	
Community Paid Sanitation	100	20.0	
Open Defecation	117	23.4	
Community Paid Sanitation/ open Sanitation	37	7.4	
Septic Toilet /open Defecation	5	1.0	
Total	**500**	**100.0**	

Source: Field Survey Data.

Figure 2.15, illustrates that more than half proportion of the respondents are not accessible to improved sanitation in the beautiful and planned city Chandigarh, is the index of destitution and vulnerability. The minor proportions are accessible to improved sanitation. Lack of improved sanitation causes a number of diseases and financial burden if they want to use community paid sanitation.

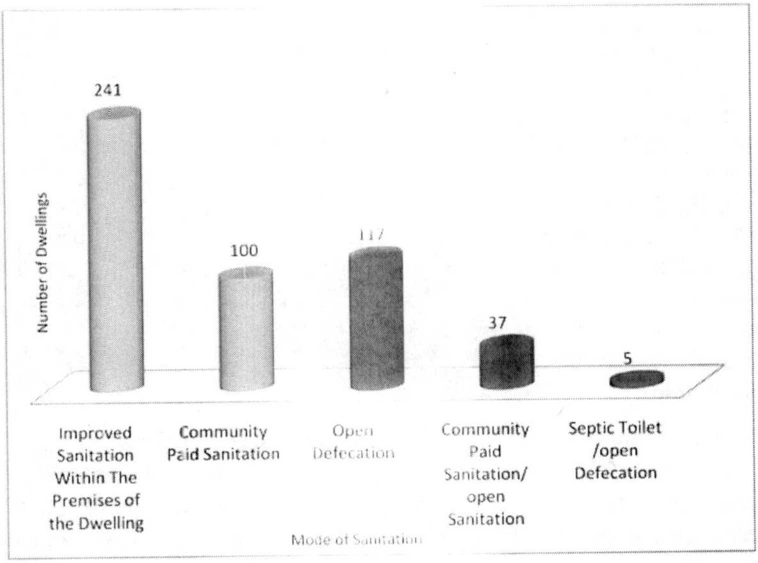

Source: Field Survey Data.

Fig. 2.15: Type of Sanitation in Use.

Source of Cooking Fuel

Non-availability of safe cooking energy is one among the major problems that the poor people are facing in the cities. Either inadequacy or the high price of some of the energy sources are the reasons for dependency on multiple sources of cooking fuel. About (37 per cent) of households use Kerosene oil and Fire Wood for cooking energy, (25.8 per cent) of the respondents uses both Kerosene oil and LPG (see Table 2.22), while the minor proportion of the respondents depends on only LPG. Kerosene oil available from ration depots is inadequate, hence numbers of respondents buy kerosene oil and diesel at a high market price from the open market and black market also reasons for high cost of living. Some of the female counterparts and children were busy with gathering firewood; instead of doing more productive activity are the reasons for the persistence of poverty.

Table 2.22: Source of Cooking Fuel

Type of Cooking Fuel	*Number of Respondents*	*Percentage*	
LPG only	14	2.8	Households use LPG for cooking in Chandigarh (71.6 per cent) (Census 2011)
Kerosene oil only	99	19.8	
Kerosene oil, Fire Wood	185	37.0	
Kerosene oil, LPG	129	25.8	
Kerosene oil, LPG, Fire Wood	61	12.2	
Fire Wood only	12	2.4	
Total	**500**	**100.0**	

Source: Field Survey Data.

Conclusion

The economic status of the respondents are relatively better than at their native place still, larger proportion of them are living below income poverty and consumption poverty lines. They are living at the peripheries of the city where civic amenities are scarce or not available. Other than regular workers, casual workers facing the problem of unemployment and under employment.

3

Public Distribution System

Introduction

Food occupies the first rank in Maslow hierarchy of human needs. Food security is a global concern in general and developing nations in particular. Mere production of food grains does not ensure food security unless there is an efficient system of distribution in addition to inculcating purchasing power. The presence of food in the economy (in the market), does not entitle a person to consume it (Dreze and Sen, 1989, p. 9)

The very existence of human race is under threat without food. Globally, food prices are increasing rapidly since 2007. In India, the maximum proportion of people spent more than 50 per cent of their income on food items, an increase in food prices hit them very hard and pushes them to the point of starvation. The per capita annual food grain available in India in 2006 was 179 kg, against 552 kg in Europe, and 909 kg in America (Murthy, 2008).

Among the number of causes, inflation is a major cause of food insecurity in India. Deregulation of fuel prices and reduction of fuel subsidies are the reasons for the rise in the general price index. The rise in food prices will affect mostly the vulnerable sections, those who are working as informal labour in both formal and informal sectors of the economy. Workers who settled in the informal sector belong to socially backward groups, they are prone to food insecurity.

Rising food prices may lead to income gains for net producers of food grains, but adversely affect the poor in rural and urban areas, because poor are the net buyers of food grains. Increases in food prices can undermine the gains from poverty reduction and human development.

Poor people vulnerable to hunger, even small shocks push them into starvation which ultimately affects productivity and social harmony. Moreover right to adequate food is the human right under international law; hence ensuring food security totally should not be left to the market forces. Keeping in view the existence of market imperfections (price fluctuations, scarcity, low quality, black marketing, exclusion) government took initiatives to distribute certain quantities of essential commodities (mainly food grains) such as rice, wheat, pulses, and non food item, kerosene oil etc at subsidised prices at regular intervals to the vulnerable sections through public distribution system by the means of fair price shops to ensure food security at household level. Public Distribution System was so named because it is a scheme undertaken by the government or any public authorities. The price at which commodities under Public Distribution System, made available is called the issue price, the difference between the market price and issue price forms the basis for the operation of Public Distribution System in India.

Public Distribution System concerns with biological approach to redress the problem of poverty. Public Distribution System (PDS) in India as rationing was first introduced in 1939 in Bombay during Second World War by the British government as a measure to ensure equitable distribution of food grains to the urban consumers on the eve of rising prices. In 1942, government laid down the basic principles of Public Distribution System for India, by setting up the food department to deal with basic issues such as procurement, contracts for purchasing agents, public distribution, inspection and storage to stabilise prices. Midst high food inflation and Bengal famine, government appointed Food Grains Policy Committee in 1943, which recommended the introduction of rationing in urban centres with a population of more than 100,000. By the year 1947, about 54 million people in urban areas were covered by statutory rationing and another 19 million by other forms of public distribution (Dantwala, 1993, p. 182).

Partition of India and Pakistan worsened India's food situation which lead to confusion between price control and decontrol exercises. In 1957, government appointed Food Grains Enquiry Committee under the chairmanship of Ashok Mehta which recommended controls of a flexible indirect nature, opening of more Fair Price Shops (FPSs) and continuing the zonal policy of bringing together surplus and deficit areas within zones, controlling prices within each zone.

On the eve of green revolution, for procurement and price setting, to meet the interests of farmers and consumers, Food Corporation of India (FCI) and the Agricultural Prices Commission (now Commission for Agricultural Costs and Prices) respectively came into existence in 1965. By the 1970s; Public Distribution System had emerged into a universal scheme for the distribution of subsidized food. The outreach of Public Distribution System, it was extended to tribal blocks and areas of high incidence of poverty in the 1970s and 1980s. Until 1992, Public Distribution System was a general entitlement scheme for all consumers without any specific targeting. Revamped Public Distribution System (RPDS) was launched in June 1992, in 1775 blocks throughout the country, with a view to strengthen and streamline the Public Distribution System as well as to improve its reach in the far-flung, hilly, remote and inaccessible areas where a substantial section of the poor live. To increase the coverage that the number of FPSs, has increased among these two-third FPS located in rural areas.

The universal public distribution system suffered from number of loopholes such as leakages, non-poor benefitted more than really poor, losses in transport and storage, urban bias, limited coverage in those states where poor people are more, hence to remove the deficiencies in universal Public Distribution System, the new system i.e. the Targeted Public Distribution System came into operation from June 1997. Under this two-tier system, Below Poverty Line (BPL) families receive food grains at heavily subsidized prices i.e. half the economic cost, while APL receives at an economic cost. The state governments were assigned the task to streamline the PDS by identifying BPL and APL families on the basis of experts committee (Lakdawala) methodology and percentage of BPL households were determined based on the state-wise poverty estimates of the Planning Commission for 1993-94 and population projections of the Registrar General of India for 1995.

Targeted Public Distribution System also suffered with inefficiencies and leakages. Margin given to FPS owners is very less; moreover they have to bear transport and handling charges which resulted in black marketing of Public Distribution System commodities. Planning Commission (2004-05), felt that the consumption of food grains from FPS shops was only (46 per cent) of the grains supplied to them in 2004-05, while it is (72 per cent) during last decade, leakages from the Public Distribution System doubled after targeting (Planning Commission, 2008).

Svedberg (2012), study indicates that each rupee transferred to poor households through the Targeted Public Distribution System (TPDS), the Government of India (GOI) had a budget expenditure of ₹ 9, and the said figure is ₹ 3.65 given by Planning Commission (2008). There is problem of mistargeting like unfair exclusion, unjustified inclusion, failed to deliver subsidy to the targeted population, caused enactment of National Food Security Act in 2013, this act aimed to provide food and nutritional security in human life cycle approach, by ensuring access to adequate quantity of qualitative food at affordable prices to people to live a life with dignity and for matters connected therewith or incidental thereto.

Public Distribution System in Chandigarh

The Department of Food Supplies and Consumer Affairs, Union Territory, Chandigarh functioning to ensure supply of the essential PDS commodities at subsidized prices to the residents of Chandigarh who are registered with the Fair Price Shops. The PDS commodities presently being supplied through the FPSs are: Wheat, Rice, Sugar and Kerosene Oil. The citizens who want to avail the benefits under TPDS will have to get ration cards under the Above Poverty Line (APL), Below Poverty Line (BPL), and Antyodaya Anna Yojna (AAY) categories and the same has to be registered with the nearest FPS. The Inspectors of the department conduct a household survey to verify the credentials/ statements, given in the application form for ration card, to identify the APL, BPL and AAY families. The criteria for categorisation of a family into BPL and AAY are fixed by the Government of India.

Every family will have one ration card with the name and coloured photograph of all the family members on the ration card, including head of the family with address, names and age of all other family members. The names of the family members can be edited (inclusion and deletion) as per the requirement. In case a family wants to change its address or wants to surrender the ration card, the same can be done through procedure. Specified commodities namely, Wheat, Rice, Sugar and Kerosene Oil are distributed under TPDS at the approved government rates. These commodities are distributed through Fair Price Shops outlets to registered ration card holders. A manual ration card/ smart ration card is issued to any Indian who is permanent resident of Chandigarh. The biometric impression is taken at the time of receiving the application.

The Targeted Public Distribution System function through a network of 61 fair price shops (FPSs) and 11 Kerosene stores across the city including rural Chandigarh. The beneficiaries holding cards would get their monthly quota of ration from these FPSs. The procedure for issue of licenses or authorisation to the FPS for distribution of essential commodities under the TPDS is clearly laid down in Chandigarh Public Distribution System (Licensing and Control) Order, 2002. The license clearly indicates the period for which the license is valid.

Direct Benefit Transfer System

Chandigarh became the first union territory/state to implement DBT scheme for food grains as a whole. Direct benefit transfer system has started from September 2015 by linking ration card with Aadhar card and Bank account of the beneficiaries to reduce transaction costs and to avoid delay and leakages in imparting benefits under Public Distribution System. Direct Benefit Transfer scheme for food grains under which cash subsidy amount will be credited to the bank account, equivalent to entitlement of food grains under NFSA, 2013.

Under NFSA, 2013 priority households entitled for 5 Kgs of food grains in 3: 2 kgs ratio of wheat and rice @ ₹ 2 and 3 per kg respectively.

In case of AAY, 35 Kgs of food grains per households in 3:2 ratio of wheat and rice @ ₹ 2 and 3 per kg respectively. Under NFSA 2013, the department enrolled/digitized 56,689 households. About 41,563 priority households (1,79,962 units) and AAY households 56 (288 units) total of 41,619 eligible households got an amount of ₹ 1,70,65,996 as subsidy in the month of September 2015 and the same amount in the month of October also. Whereas the number of eligible households has increased to 42,004 (priority households 41,948 and AAY households 56), in the month of November and December due to submission of proper documents and linking JAM technology. The amount of subsidy also increased to ₹ 1,72,33,862. Under this scheme priority households (PH) will get ₹ 95 per month (round off), Antyodaya Anna Yojna (AAY) households will get ₹ 663 per household/card/family (round off). Government transfer @ ₹ 16.125 per kg for wheat and @ ₹ 23.125 kg for rice as subsidy. This amount per kg fixed on the basis of Minimum Support Price of the respective crop which will be multiplied with ₹ 1.25 (retailer's commission). Procedural delays in crediting subsidy amount causing more inconvenience to the poor people.

DISCUSSION

Methodology

Evaluation of this programme is based on both primary and secondary data sources. After mapping the respondents in different clusters of the city, pilot survey is carried out and final field survey is conducted by using integrated questionnaire by personal visit at the place of residence of the beneficiaries as well as non-beneficiaries during 2014-15. A total of 500 sample respondents (beneficiaries) and 80 non-beneficiaries were selected from different slums and shanties based on clustered stratified systematic random sampling method. This study targeted both the gender, (beneficiaries as well as non-beneficiaries) who are residing in the city for more than one year. Both migrants and local people are taken into consideration for the study. Administrative staff of the concerned departments also interviewed to know the difficulties in implementation of Public Distribution System in Chandigarh.

Geographical Coverage

Like other major cities in India, in Chandigarh also poor people are mainly concentrated in peripheries of the city slums and shanties. After dismantle of colony number 5 and Kashmir Colony and Bapudham Colony, more than 8000 families were accommodated in new flats constructed by Chandigarh housing board in Dhanas, hence relatively larger proportion of the respondents (43.4 per cent) were selected from this area for the study. In descending order 118 (23.6 per cent) of the respondents were considered from 4 number colony, while 66 (13.2 per cent) of the respondents are selected from Janata Colony sector 25, about 42 (8.4 per cent) of the respondents are selected from New Indira Colony (Mani Majra), and the remaining respondents are selected from Sanjay Labour Colony (Industrial Area), Bhatt Colony (Mauli Jagra), Kalyan Colony (Khudda Jassu) (Table 3.1).

Table 3.1: Selection of Sample Respondents from Different Clusters in Chandigarh

Name of the Cluster	*Number of Respondents*	*Percentage*
EWS Colony (Dhanas)	217	43.4
4 Number Colony (Industrial Area)	118	23.6
Janata Colony (Sector 25)	66	13.2
New Indira Colony (Mani Majra)	42	8.4
Sanjay Labour Colony (Industrial Area)	34	6.8
Bhatt Colony (Mauli Jagra)	13	2.6
Kalyan Colony (Khudda Jassu)	10	2.0
Total	**500**	**100.0**

Source: Field Survey Data.

Work Status of Sample Respondents (Head of the Household)

Table 3.2, indicates that the greater majority (37.4 per cent) of the respondents are working as casual labour, followed by (29 per cent) are self-employed as rickshaw pullers, auto drivers, street vendors, about one-quarter of the respondents (25.8 per cent) are regular workers. The availability of work and earnings are stable when compared to the other two categories of workers. Precariously about (7.8 per cent) of the respondents are unemployed due to sickness, incapacity, non-availability of work etc.

Table 3.2: Work status of Sample Respondents (Head of the Household)

Categories of workers	*Number of Respondents*	*Percentage*
Casual Labour	187	37.4
Self-Employed	145	29.0
Regular Workers	129	25.8
Unemployed	39	7.8
Total	**500**	**100.0**

Source: Field Survey Data.

Economic Classification of Sample Respondents (PDS)

On the basis of income and other socio-economic indicators, total population of the city is classified by the Chandigarh administration into three different economic categories, viz. BPL, PH, APL. This type of classification is useful for effectively targeting anti-poverty programmes by making positive discrimination. The larger majority (43 per cent) of the respondents were selected from (BPL) Below Poverty Line category, followed by (28.4 per cent) Priority Households (PH), and the remaining (28.6 per cent) are from Above Poverty Line (APL) category (Table 3.3).

Table 3.3: Economic Classification of Sample Respondents (PDS)

Category of Respondents	*Number of Respondents*	*Percentage*
BPL	215	43.0
Priority Households	142	28.4
APL	143	28.6
Total	**500**	**100.0**

Source: Field Survey Data.

Type of Ration Cards and Entitlements of PDS Items

Chandigarh administration, by implementing National Food Security Act, NFSA (2013), decided monthly entitlements of different quantities of PDS items at highly subsidised prices to different types of ration card holders (households). Table 4.4 demonstrates that for BPL household each member of the family is entitle to get 3 Kgs of

Table 3.4: Type of Ration Cards and Entitlements of PDS Items

Category of PDS beneficiary	Price (Rs/Kgs) and Quantity Entitlement (Kgs/Member)								Number of Respondents	Percentage
	Wheat		Rice		Sugar		Kerosene oil (Rs /Ltr)			
	Price	Quantity	Price	Quantity	Price	Quantity	Price	Quantity/ members		
BPL	2	3	3	2	13.50	1	15.07	3 for up to 3, 4 for 4 to 5, 6 for 6 and above.	215	43.0
BPL (PH)	2	3	3	2	NA	NA	do		142	28.4
APL/TO	7	35 (per family)	NA	NA	NA	NA	do		143	28.6
Total									**500**	**100.0**

Source: Source: Field Survey Data.

Note: At the time of conducting survey in 2014, PDS in Chandigarh is in transition stage from the Targeted Public Distribution System to implementation of National Food Security Act 2013. Hence there are three categories of beneficiaries were taken into consideration of this study i.e. BPL, BPL (PH), APL (TO). While at the time of finalisation of this report again PDS is in transition stage from NFSA to Direct Benefit Transfer system.

wheat @ ₹ 2 per kg, the same is for members of PH households, while in case of APL/TO households, irrespective of number of family members each household is entitled to get 35 Kgs of wheat @ ₹ 7 per kg. Entitlement of Additional wheat is concerned up to five members 10 kgs, for 6 members 5 Kgs, @ ₹ 7 per kg. If the household is having more than six members he/ she is not entitled to additional wheat. This provision is not taken into account for this study because of improper and irregular implementation.

In the case of rice, each member from BPL household, monthly entitle to get 2 Kgs @ ₹ 3 per kg, the same is the case with PH households, whereas APL households are not entitled to Rice. While in the case of sugar, each member of BPL household is entitled to get 1 kg @ ₹ 13.50, PH households and APL/TO households are not entitled to get sugar. In the case of entitlement of Kerosene oil all the card holding families if they have no LPG connection are entitled to get 3 liters up to 3 members, 4 liters for 4 to 5 members, 6 liters for 6 and above members @ ₹ 15.07 per liter (Table 3.4).

Monthly off-take of Wheat

Off-take of wheat is concerned, that the maximum proportion (40 per cent) of the respondents monthly off-take 11 to 15 Kgs of wheat, while (14.0 per cent) respondents off-take 16 to 20 Kgs of wheat.

Table 3.5: Monthly off-take of Wheat (Kgs) by the Beneficiaries

Wheat (Kgs)	*Number of Respondents*	*Percentage*
1-5	2	0.4
6-10	29	5.8
11-15	200	40.0
16-20	70	14.0
21-25	51	10.2
26-30	5	1.0
31-35	143	28.6
Total	**500**	**100.0**

Source: Field Survey Data.

If the households receive timely information and not out of station, are the potential buyers of the items. The mean monthly availability of wheat per household is 21.12 Kgs, while the per capita mean monthly availability to members of the household is 4.11 Kgs. The available quantity is enough to meet the need of 10 days only, for the remaining days they have to buy from the open market at an exorbitant price (Table 3.5).

Monthly off-take of Rice

Table 3.6, indicates that the larger proportion (44.2 per cent) of the beneficiaries monthly off-take is 6 to 10 kgs of rice. The mean monthly availability of Rice per household is 7.43 kgs, while the mean monthly per capita availability of rice to the members of the household is 1.44 kgs is hardly enough to meet the requirement for four days only, for the remaining days they have to buy low quality of rice from open market or suffer from hunger

Table 3.6: Monthly off-take of Rice (Kgs) by the Beneficiaries

Rice (Kgs)	*Number of Respondents*	*Percentage*
0	43	8.6
1-5	9	1.8
6-10	221	44.2
11-15	112	22.4
16-20	15	3.0
Total	**500**	**100.0**

Source: Field Survey Data.

Monthly off-take of Sugar

Table 3.7, presents that the larger proportion (57 per cent) of the respondents not getting sugar, hence they forced to buy from higher market price which imposes more burden. About (25.2 per cent) of the respondents monthly getting 1 to 5 Kgs of sugar and the remaining (17.8 per cent) are getting 6 to 10 Kgs of sugar. Monthly availability of sugar per household is 2.3 Kgs; monthly per capita availability of sugar to the members of the households is 450 grams. Almost all the eligible beneficiaries said that, the availability of sugar is very much irregular due to reasons unknown to them is a matter of great concern.

Table 3.7: Monthly off-take of Sugar (Kgs)

Sugar (Kgs)	*Number of Respondents*	*Percentage*
0	285	57.0
1-5	126	25.2
6-10	89	17.8
Total	**500**	**100.0**

Source: Field Survey Data.

Monthly off-take of Kerosene Oil

Acquiring material for cooking energy is a big problem in cities due to non-availability of natural resources. The quantity of kerosene oil made available by the government through fair price shops is very much limited and inadequate to meet the cooking needs. The government neither directly selling in the open market nor permitted sale and purchase in the open market, hence it gave big scope for black marketing of kerosene oil. People buy kerosene at price range between ₹ 60 to ₹ 70 per liter and also buy diesel from the petrol pumps. Beneficiaries those who are having LPG connection are not entitle to get kerosene oil. The findings of the household survey showed that about (7.6 per cent) respondents are not getting kerosene oil because they have LPG connection. The larger majority (57.2 per cent) of the respondents monthly getting 5 to 6 liters of kerosene oil. Monthly mean availability of Kerosene oil per household is 4.74 liters, while the monthly per capita availability of Kerosene oil to the members of the household is 0.923 liters only (Table 3.8).

Table 3.8: Monthly Purchase of Kerosene Oil (Liters)

Kerosene Oil (Liters)	*Number of Respondents*	*Percentage*
0	38	7.6
1-2	0	0.0
3-4	176	35.2
5-6	286	57.2
Total	**500**	**100.0**

Source: Field Survey Data.

Monthly Waiting Time at FPS

The precarious scene one can see at fair price shops, that the larger number of people of all age groups stand in queues for a number of hours by facing all types of weather conditions to buy PDS items. Sometimes they have to stand in queue for more than one day also due to stock exhaust or dispute with the fair price shop owner, closing of depot at the end of the day, bad weather conditions, distribution of different items on different days etc. School going children forced to become absent to the schools and workers have to forego wages in the lure of getting PDS items. Sometimes they have to stay in line from 4 am even during the winter season, because fair price shop owner don't distribute more than one day and nobody knows at what time he/ she start and close selling. If they don't stand in a queue, will forego ration for that month. The survey reports that the significant majority (24.8 per cent) of people have to stand in queue for 5 to 6 hours. The mean waiting time in queue for buying ration and kerosene oil 6.19 hours. Some of the FPS owners distribute rice and wheat on different days, hence monthly waiting time for the consumers covered under these FPS are more than 10 hours (Table 3.9).

Table 3.9: Monthly Waiting Time at Fair Price Shops

Waiting Time (Hours)	*Number of Respondents*	*Percentage*
1-2	52	10.4
3-4	114	22.8
5-6	124	24.8
7-8	98	19.6
9-10	65	13.0
11-12	33	6.6
13-14	9	1.8
15-16	4	0.8
17-18	1	0.2
Total	**500**	**100.0**

Source: Field Survey Data.

Figure 3.1, indicates that, the larger proportion of the respondents have to wait monthly 5 to 6 hours at fair price shops. Precariously the monthly waiting time ranges between 1 to 18 hours.

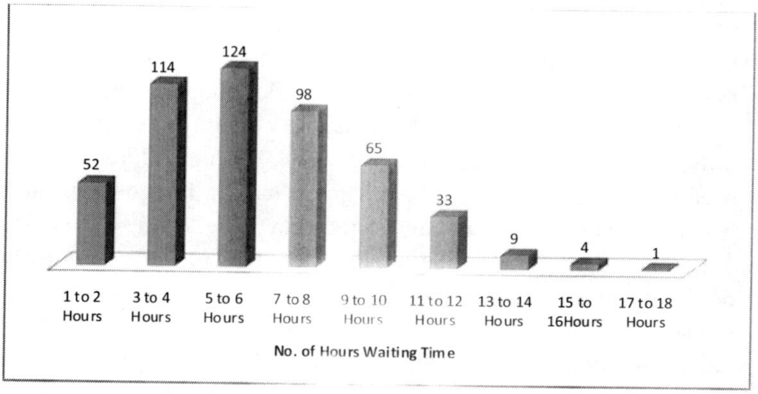

Source: Field Survey Data.

Fig. 3.1: Monthly Waiting Time at Fair Price Shops.

Monthly Time Spent (Waiting and Travel)

Respondents / family members spend a large number of hours not only waiting in queues but also for travel and transport. Table 3.10, demonstrates that for travel and waiting that a great majority (21.4 per cent) of the respondents monthly spend 7 to 8 hours, while monthly mean time spent 7.19 hours. It implies monthly they spent about one day, hence implied earnings of one day is to be deducted to get a net benefit from availing benefits under PDS.

Table: 3.10: Monthly Time Spent (Waiting and Travel) by Respondents/ Family Members for Buying PDS Items

Time (Hours) Spent Including Travel	*Number of Respondents*	*Percentage*
1-2	9	1.8
3-4	96	19.2
5-6	106	21.2
7-8	107	21.4

(*Contd...*)

9-10	102	20.4
11-12	43	8.6
13-14	15	3.0
15-16	10	2.0
17-18	2	0.4
Total	**500**	**100.0**

Source: Field Survey Data.

Monthly Number of Kms Travel

Respondents/family members have to travel a number of kilometers from residence to the place of distribution and back home by buying PDS items. They have to go by walk/ bicycle/ rickshaw/ auto/ scooter as a mode of conveyance for this purpose. People residing at Dhanas Colony have to travel more distance to buy kerosene oil, also people residing in Sanjay Labour Colony have to travel more distance to buy all the PDS items. Table 3.11, reflects that the greater majority (41.4 per cent) of respondents/ family members have to travel 7 to 8 Kms both the sides. About (7.6 per cent) of the respondents do not entitle for kerosene oil but food grains available nearer to their residence. Time taken to travel will depend on the mode of conveyance they use. The monthly mean distance they have to travel 4.81 Km. Location of fair price shops at a distant place from residence is the reason for travelling longer distance and wastage of money and time.

Table 3.11: Monthly Number of Kms Travel (to and fro) by Respondents/ Family Members to Buy PDS Items

Number of KMs	*Number of Respondents*	*Percentage*
NA	38	7.6
1-2	161	32.2
3-4	53	10.6
5-6	41	8.2
7-8	207	41.4
Total	**500**	**100.0**

Source: Field Survey Data.

Figure 3.2, indicates that the larger number of respondents/ family members forced to travel 7 to 8 km per month to buy PDS items from

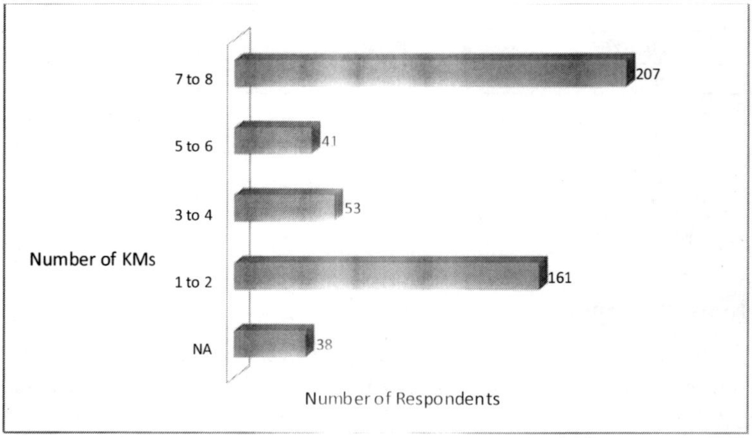

Source: Field Survey Data.

Fig. 3.2: Monthly Number of Kms Travel (to and fro) by Respondents/ Family Members to Buy PDS Items.

the fair price shops, while 161 respondents said that they have to travel 1 to 2 km on both sides to avail benefits. About 38 respondents do not entitle for kerosene oil but food grains available nearer to their residence.

Number of Days Distribution of Ration

As per rule, fair price shops have to open during all the working days in the month. Except paying commission amount on sale, the government not paying salary for the owners to keep open during all the days. The commission amount whatever receiving is inadequate as well as uncertain and irregular, it is giving chance for leakage of PDS items. These owners have to do side business or forced to do some work elsewhere for survival. Table 3.12, shows that the larger majority (26.6 per cent) of the respondents felt that fair price shops kept open one to two days per month, followed by (23.6 per cent) respondents felt these shops open monthly not more than five to six days. The mean number of days that the FPS owners distribute ration about 5.06 days, while (2.6 per cent) of the respondents from Mauli Jagra Colony revealed that it is uncertain when the owner distribute nobody knows. Information asymmetry is a big problem, FPS owners don't know the exact dates of arrival of stock for distribution and respondents don't know exact dates of distribution of PDS items. After fulfilling the formalities of completion of paperwork and payment of the amount by the FPS owner, the stock may reach the shop at any time. Soon after the arrival of stock, the owner starts distribution. Hence every day respondents/family members have to in touch with the FPS owner/ staff, otherwise, owner says "it is your mistake, you did not turn up while I am selling, distribution is over, come next month for next months quota."

Table 3.12: Perception of Respondents on Number of Days Distribution of Ration by FPS Owners

Number of Days of Distribution	*Number of Respondents*	*Percentage*
Uncertain	13	2.6
1-2	133	26.6
3-4	88	17.6
5-6	118	23.6
7-8	68	13.6
9-10	69	13.8
11-12	5	1.0
15-16	6	1.2
Total	**500**	**100.0**

Source: Field Survey Data.

Fair/Unfair Trade Practices

There are mixed opinions regarding fair and unfair trade practices adopted by FPS owners with regarding weights and measures. The considerable number (39.2 per cent) of the respondents felt that weights and measures are fair, while an equal number of respondents felt unfair and indifferent. Some of the respondents felt that FPS owners use electronic weighing machines, hence they don't know its genuineness, moreover, there is no facility for cross-checking of the weighed items at home (Table 3.13).

Figure 3.3, focuses Fair /Unfair Trade Practices (Weights and Measures) adopted by FPS Owners. About 39 per cent of the respondents said that FPS owners are fair, while 31 per cent of the respondents said that they are not certain.

Table 3.13: Perceptions of Respondents on Fair/Unfair Trade Practices (Weights and Measures) Adopted by FPS Owners

Fair/Unfair Trade Practices	*Number of Respondents*	*Percentage*
Fair	196	39.2
Unfair	151	30.2
Indifferent	153	30.6
Total	**500**	**100.0**

Source: Field Survey Data.

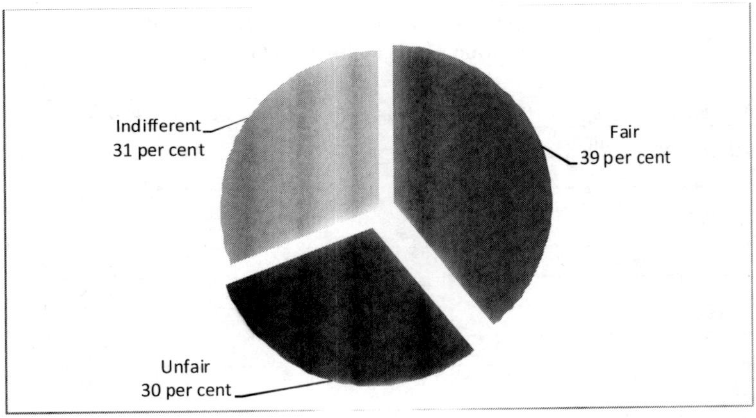

Source: Field Survey Data.

Fig. 3.3: Perceptions of the Respondents on Fair /Unfair Trade Practices (Weights and Measures) Adopted by FPS Owners.

Cash Transfers Vs Distribution of PDS Items

Direct Benefit Transfers (DBT) in Public Distribution System is the transfer of subsidy amount directly into the beneficiary bank accounts to reduce transaction cost and corruption if any, is an alternative to the existing physical distribution of commodities at a subsidized price through fair price shops by the government. There are some instances of revelation of dissatisfaction in implementation of the present system in many states. Chandigarh is not exception i.e.

leakages, corruption, poor quality, wrong weights and measures, inclusion and exclusion errors in identification of poor, information asymmetry, fear of uncertainty of availability of commodities, uncertainty in distribution of number of days, irregular and untimely distribution, wrong timings etc.

Cash transfer scheme is not free from defects. (1) There is an uncertainty prevailing in the availability of work ((unemployment and underemployment) and earnings of informal migrant workers (casual, self-employed and regular temporary workers) are meager, hence at the end of the day no capability to buy food grains from the open market, (2) Money received in lump sum will be spent on unmet number of needs, but once ration is available through PDS, can be consumed during the whole month which will ensure food security at some extent, (3) Some of the male counterparts are having habit of spending money on drinking alcohol and gambling without bothering their family sufferings, (4) Though cash will be transferred to the bank accounts of female counterparts, in the patriarchal society there is possibility of snatching away money by some of the irresponsible male counterparts, may further cause domestic violence, (5) Most of the customers are illiterates have no habit of properly preserving pass books/ ATM cards/ secret pin code etc, (6) Poor households marginal propensity of consuming is more than one, they have number of unmet needs, transferred amount may spend for different purposes, may reduce the consumption of adequate quantities of reasonable quality of food grains may further strain on nutrition levels and health of women and children (7) There will be general rise in demand for essential commodities in the open market, as a result hoarding and black marketing will be a possibility which will further spurt in prices, may impose burden on almost all the consumers in general and poor in particular.

The household survey indicates that a higher majority (87 per cent) of the respondents felt that cash transfer is not beneficial, while (12.2 per cent) of the respondents revealed that cash transfer is beneficial, whereas the negligible proportion (0.8 per cent) are indifferent between the two (Table 3.14).

Table 3.14: Opinion of PDS Consumers on Cash Transfers vs. Distribution of PDS Commodities

Opinion on cash transfer	*Number of Respondents*	*Percentage*
Beneficial	61	12.2
Not Beneficial	435	87.0
Indifferent	4	0.8
Total	**500**	**100.0**

Source: Field Survey Data.

Quality of PDS Commodities

In addition to the stock of food grains for a number of months at FCI godowns, sometimes kept these items at PDS godowns in the open air causes a change of colour and taste. Respondents complained that FPS owners mix both good quality and bad quality of food grains. Sometimes they sell blacken wheat even not good for animal consumption. An FPS owner mercilessly says "If you want you to take, otherwise go and complaint, what can we do, we got this type of quality of items". Table 3.15, reflects that a majority of the respondents (68.6 per cent) felt that FPS owners sell sometimes the normal and sometimes poor quality of items, while (25.8 per cent) of the respondents said items are normal quality, whereas the lesser fraction (5.6 per cent) felt that items are poor in quality.

Table 3.15: Perceptions Regarding Quality of PDS Commodities

Quality of PDS Commodities	*Number of Respondents*	*Percentage*
Sometimes Normal and Sometimes poor	343	68.6
Normal	129	25.8
Poor	28	5.6
Total	**500**	**100.0**

Source: Field Survey Data.

Figure 3.4, indicates that the larger proportion of the respondents stated that, the quality of PDS items sometimes normal and sometimes poor, while (26 per cent) of the respondents said that the quality is normal, about (6 per cent) said that the quality is poor.

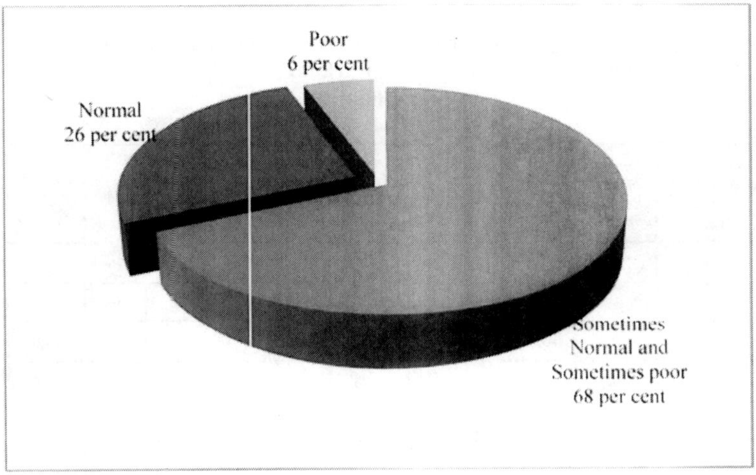

Source: Field Survey Data.

Fig. 3.4: Perceptions Regarding Quality of PDS Commodities.

Measuring Gross and Net Impact

The derivation of gross subsidy is based on certain assumptions

1. The market prices of different PDS items in different residential localities are taken into account and mean price is derived.
2. Kerosene oil price in black markets of different localities are taken into account and mean price is derived, reason by neither government selling kerosene oil in the open market nor permitted private trade.
3. The price of the wheat flour in different residential localities is taken into account and milling price is deducted, then mean price of wheat is derived.
4. All the PDS items available monthly as per the entitlement.
5. If FPS or kerosene oil depot is located within one km of the residential locality, time for travel and expenditure involved for travel is not taken into consideration.
6. Gross subsidy = Market price × quantity of entitled PDS items– PDS price × quantity of entitled PDS items.

Table 3.16: Monthly Gross Benefit Accrued to Respondent Households (₹) (Gross Benefit = Market Price × Quantity-PDS Price × Quantity)

Amount of gross benefit Range (₹)	*Number of BPL Respondents*	*Percentage*	*Number of Priority Respondents*	*Percentage*	*Number of APL Respondents*	*Percentage*	*Total*	*Percentage*
1-400	0	0.0	16	11.25	0	0.0	16	3.2
401-500	1	0.46	18	12.67	17	11.88	36	7.2
501-600	8	3.72	27	19.01	59	41.25	94	18.8
601-700	30	13.95	14	9.85	64	44.75	108	21.6
701-800	13	6.04	34	23.94	0	0.0	47	9.4
801-900	75	34.88	21	14.78	3	2.09	99	19.8
901- 1000	49	22.79	9	6.33	0	0.0	58	11.6
1001-1100	3	1.39	3	2.11	0	0.0	6	1.2
1101- 1200	27	12.55	0	0.0	0	0.0	27	5.4
1201 – 1500	9	4.18	0	0.0	0	0.0	9	1.8
Total	**215**	**100.0**	**142**	**100.0**	**143**	**100.0**	**500**	**100.0**

Source: Field Survey Data.

Note: BPL households Mean Monthly gross benefit ₹ 898.85, member households per capita gross benefit ₹ 159.37

Priority households Mean Monthly gross benefit ₹ 665.11, member households per capita gross benefit ₹ 139.72

APL households Mean Monthly gross benefit ₹ 598.91, member households per capita gross benefit ₹ 126.35

Mean (sample as a whole) monthly household gross benefit ₹ 747.03

Mean (sample as whole) Monthly member households per capita gross benefit= ₹ 145.44

Mean (sample as a whole) member households daily gross benefit = ₹ 4.84

member households Mean per capita daily income ₹ 34.63 + daily gross benefit ₹ 4.84= ₹ 39.47

Number of BPL Households 215, Total Family Members 1213, mean 5.64 (mean family size)

Number of priority Households 142, Total Family Members 676, mean 4.76 (mean family size)

Number of APL Households 143, Total Family Members 678, mean 4.74 (mean family size)

Sample of 500 respondents, Total family members are 2567, mean family size 5.13

Table 3.16. confirmed that the larger majority (34.88 per cent) of the BPL beneficiaries enjoyed monthly gross subsidy in the range of ₹ 801-900, while (23.94 per cent) of the priority card holders enjoyed monthly gross benefit in the range of ₹ 701 to 800, whereas (44.75 per cent) of the APL card holders enjoyed monthly gross benefit in the range of ₹ 601 to 700. In total (21.6 per cent) of the respondents procured monthly gross subsidy in the range of ₹ 601 to 700. In the case of the mean monthly subsidy enjoyed by different types of card holder's are ₹ 898.85, ₹ 665.11, ₹ 598.91, BPL, Priority, and APL card holders respectively. Sample as a whole monthly per household gross benefit is ₹ 747.03, mean monthly per capita gross benefit is ₹ 145.439, and mean daily gross benefit is ₹ 4.84. Per capita daily income of the households in the study area is ₹ 34.63 and by adding the gross subsidy, the per capita income will be increased to ₹ 39.47 (irrespective of implicit and explicit expenses involved in buying PDS items).

Benefit Net of Opportunity Cost

The derivation of net subsidy from gross benefit is based on certain assumptions

1. Opportunity cost of daily earnings (not receipts) are taken into consideration.
2. Sample as a whole daily mean earnings are ₹ 166.02.
3. Those who are unemployed, fellow workers mean earnings are considered as their earnings, after verifying that they are skilled/ semi-skilled/ unskilled/ type of occupation they had before unemployed.
4. Daily earnings are calculated separately for different type of ration card holders, hence earnings are different.

Net of opportunity cost derived after deducting the one day mean earnings from the gross subsidy. The larger majority (38.13 per cent) of BPL respondents captured monthly net benefit in the range of ₹ 601-700 (per capita net benefit ₹ 128.77), while among the Priority households the significant majority (26.05 per cent) got monthly net benefit in the range of ₹ 501-600 (per capita net benefit ₹ 106.10), and the rest APL households got monthly net benefit in the range of

₹ 401-500 (per capita net benefit ₹ 92.40). Sample as a whole the major proportion of the respondents derived monthly net benefit in the range of ₹ 401-500. Sample as a whole the per households monthly net benefits ₹ 581.01 and per capita monthly net benefit is ₹ 113.170. By adding daily per capita net subsidy of ₹ 3.77 to the per capita daily income of ₹ 34.63, daily per capita income has increased to ₹ 38.4, still, all of them living below poverty line (Table 3.17).

Table 3.17: Monthly Benefit Net of Opportunity Cost (Gross Benefit-Opportunity Cost of Waiting and Travel Time) Accrued to Respondent Households (₹)

Amount of Net Benefit Range (₹)	*Number of BPL Respondents*	*Percentage*	*Number of Priority Respondents*	*Percentage*	*Number of APL Respondents*	*Percentage*	*Total*	*Percentage*
1-100	0	0.0	1	0.70	0	0.0	1	0.2
101-200	0	0.0	5	3.52	0	0.0	5	1
201-300	0	0.0	6	4.22	0	0.0	6	1.2
301-400	8	3.72	21	14.78	42	29.37	71	14.2
401-500	30	13.95	36	25.35	98	68.53	164	32.8
501-600	4	1.86	37	26.05	0	0.0	41	8.2
601-700	82	38.13	23	16.19	2	1.39	107	21.4
701-800	4	1.86	10	7.04	1	0.69	15	3
801-900	50	23.25	3	2.11	0	0.0	53	10.6
901- 1000	28	13.02	0	0.0	0	0.0	28	5.6
1001-1100	4	1.86	0	0.0	0	0.0	4	0.8
1101- 1200	3	1.39	0	0.0	0	0.0	3	0.6
1201-1300	2	0.93	0	0.0	0	0.0	2	0.4
Total	**215**	**100.0**	**142**	**100.0**	**143**	**100.0**	**500**	**100.0**

Source: Field Survey Data.

Note: Mean monthly net benefit to BPL households is ₹ 726.28, per capita net benefit ₹ 128.77

Mean monthly net benefit to Priority HH ₹ 505.07, per capita net benefit ₹ 106.10

Mean monthly net benefit to APL HH ₹ 438.00, per capita net benefit ₹ 92.40

Per household monthly net benefit, sample as a whole ₹ 581.01

member households Per capita monthly net benefit sample as a whole = ₹ 113.17

Sample as a whole member households Per capita daily income ₹ 34.63 + daily net benefit ₹ 3.77= ₹ 38.4

Opportunity cost of one day mean earnings are deducted from the gross benefit, because monthly mean time spent for getting food grains and oil (including time taken for travel) is 7.19 Hours.

Travel and Transport Charges

Transaction costs make PDS items more expensive. Non-availability of PDS items at the proximity of residences is a big problem. Moreover, no decentralisation of fair price shops is also the reason for wastage of time, man days, and incurring travel and transport charges. Respondents/family members generally use bicycles, scooters, autos and rickshaws for travel and transport in connection with bringing PDS items. People residing in Dhanas have to travel to bring kerosene oil, while people residing in Sanjay Labour Colony have to spend more money and time to get all the items. Table 3.18 reveals that the larger majority (46.8 per cent) of the beneficiaries not making any expenses in this connection, while (25.4 per cent) respondents spent ₹ 20 to travel both the sides (17.6 per cent) spent ₹ 30. Mean travel expenses per month per household ₹ 10.69; to be added to the price of PDS items to know the net benefit from PDS.

Table 3.18: Monthly Travel and Transport Charges Incurred to buy PDS items (₹)

Amount (₹)	*Number of Respondents*	*Percentage*
0 (Bring by Walk, Bicycle, Own Vehicle on the way from work)	234	46.8
NA (Kerosene Not Available)	38	7.6
10	6	1.2
15	7	1.4
20	127	25.4
30	88	17.6
Total	**500**	**100.0**

Source: Field Survey Data.

Note: Mean monthly Travel and transport costs incurred by BPL HH ₹ 10.84

Mean monthly Travel and transport costs incurred by Priority HH ₹ 11.93

Mean monthly Travel and transport costs incurred by APL HH ₹ 11.75.

Mean monthly Travel and transport costs incurred by sample whole HH ₹ 11.56

Table 3.19: Monthly Benefit Net of Travel and Transport Costs (Gross Benefit- Travel and Transport Costs) Accrued to Respondent Households (₹)

Amount of benefit Range (₹)	*Number of BPL Respondents*	*Per-centage*	*Number of Priority Respon-dents*	*Percen -tage*	*Number of APL Respondents*	*Percent-age*	*Total*	*Percent-age*
1-300	0	0.0	7	4.92	0	0.0	7	1.4
301-400	0	0.0	10	7.04	17	11.88	27	5.4
401-500	1	0.46	17	11.97	0	0.0	18	3.6
501-600	8	3.72	27	19.01	59	41.25	94	18.8
601-700	30	13.95	14	9.85	64	44.75	108	21.6
701-800	16	7.44	34	23.94	0	0.0	50	10.0
801-900	72	33.48	21	14.78	3	2.09	96	19.2
. 901- 1000	49	22.79	9	6.33	0	0.0	58	11.6
1001-1100	16	7.44	3	2.11	0	0.0	19	3.8
1101-1200	14	6.51	0	0.0	0	0.0	14	2.8
1201-1500	9	4.18	0	0.0	0	0.0	9	1.8
Total	**215**	**100.0**	**142**	**100.0**	**143**	**100.0**	**500**	**100.0**

Source: Field Survey Data.

Note: Monthly mean net benefit BPL per HH ₹ 887.27, member householdspercapita monthly net benefit = ₹ 157.31
Monthly mean net benefit per Priority HH ₹ 647.61, member households per capita monthly net benefit = ₹ 136.05
Monthly mean net benefit per APL HH ₹ 579.57, member households per capita monthly net benefit = ₹ 122.27
Sample as a Whole Monthly mean net benefit per HH ₹ 731.21, member households per capita monthly net benefit = ₹ 142.53

Benefit Net of Travel and Transport Charges

If the opportunity cost of waiting and travel time not deducted, but only by deducting travel expenses really made to buy PDS items from gross benefit, the net benefit as follows. Table 3.19, indicates that, among different income categories, the larger majority (33.48 per cent of the BPL respondents monthly benefitting ₹ 801-900 (per capita net benefit ₹ 157.31), among the priority households the major proportion 34 (23.94 per cent) got benefit in the range of ₹ 701-800 (per capita net benefit ₹ 136.05), among APL households (44.75 per cent) of the respondents secured net benefit in the range of ₹ 601-700 (per capita net benefit ₹ 122.27), while sample as a whole about (21.6 per cent) of the respondents monthly got net benefit of ₹ 601-700 (per capita net benefit ₹ 142.53 only).

Net Benefit, Net of Opportunity Cost of Time for Travel and Transport and Expenditure on Travel and Transport

From gross benefit by deducting opportunity cost of waiting and travel as well as transport expenses, net subsidy accrued to different categories of card holders can be derived. Table 3.20, confirmed that, among BPL beneficiaries the larger majority (37 per cent) derived monthly net benefit range of ₹ 601-700 (per capita Monthly ₹ 126.71), Among PH beneficiaries a great majority (23.23 per cent) derived monthly net benefit range of 501-600 (Per capita Monthly ₹ 102.43), Among APL beneficiaries (54.54 per cent) derived monthly net benefit range of 401-500 (Per capita Monthly ₹ 88.32), whereas sample as a whole the maximum proportion (26.6 per cent) of the respondents derived monthly net benefit ranges ₹ 401-500. Sample as a whole Per capita Monthly net subsidy of ₹ 110.23 only.

Monthly Subsidy Loss and Gain Trade-off

It can be compared and contrasted the benefits derived by different income categories (a type of ration card holders) and loss of subsidy and the final net benefit accrues to the respondents in question. BPL beneficiaries derived higher net benefit than that of the other two categories because they are entitled to all the PDS items. Loss of subsidy due to travel and transport is higher for APL than the other two categories because they use personal motor transport instead of mass

Table 3.20: Net Benefit, Net of Opportunity Cost of Waiting Time, Travel and Transport Expenses (Gross – Opportunity Cost of Waiting Time, Travel and Transport Expenses)

Amount net benefit Range (₹)	*Number of BPL Respondents*	*Percentage*	*Number of Priority Respondents*	*Percentage*	*Number of APL Respondents*	*Percentage*	*Total*	*Percentage*
1-300	0	0.0	20	14.07	17	11.88	37	7.4
301-400	8	3.72	30	21.12	45	31.46	83	16.6
401-500	31	14.41	24	16.90	78	54.54	133	26.6
501-600	6	2.79	33	23.23	0	0.0	39	7.8
601-700	80	37.0	23	16.19	2	1.39	105	21
701-800	26	12.09	9	6.33	1	0.69	36	6.2
801-900	27	12.55	3	2.11	0	0.0	30	6.0
901- 1000	28	13.02	0	0.0	0	0.0	28	5.6
1001-1300	9	4.18	0	0.0	0	0.0	9	1.8
Total	**215**	**100.0**	**142**	**100.0**	**143**	**100.0**	**500**	**100.0**

Source: Field Survey Data.

Note: Monthly Net Benefit Per BPL HH 714.70, member households Per capita Monthly ₹ 126.71
Monthly Net Benefit per Priority HH 487.58 member households Per capita Monthly ₹ 102.43
Monthly Net Benefit per APL HH 418.66 member households Per capita Monthly ₹ 88.32
Sample Whole Monthly Net Benefit per HH 565.53 member households Per capita Monthly ₹ 110.23
Member households Per capita daily net benefit is ₹ 3.67, by adding per capita income to it, that the total daily per capita income will increase to ₹ 34.63 + ₹ 3.67= ₹ 38.30

Table 3.21: Monthly Mean Subsidy Gain and Loss Trade-off

Sl. No.	Nature of Benefit (₹)	Accrued (₹) to Households				Accrued (₹) to Members of HH			
		BPL	PH	APL	All	BPL	PH	APL	All
1.	Gross Benefit= (Market price ×quantity –PDS price × quantity)	898.85	665.11	598.91	747.03	159.37	139.72	126.35	145.43
2.	Net benefit of Travel and Transport Costs =Gross benefit-travel and transport costs	887.27	647.61	579.57	731.21	157.31	136.05	122.27	142.53
3.	Net benefit of waiting and travel time =Gross benefit- opportunity cost of waiting and travel time	726.28	505.07	438.00	581.01	128.77	106.10	92.40	113.17
4.	Net benefit= Gross benefit- opportunity cost of waiting, travel time and travel and transport costs)	714.70	487.58	418.66	565.53	126.71	102.43	88.32	110.23
5.	Lose of subsidy due to travel and transport costs	11.58	17.5	19.34	15.52	2.06	3.67	4.08	2.9
6.	Lose of subsidy due to waiting and travel time	172.57	160.04	160.91	166.02	30.6	33.62	33.95	32.26
7.	Total loss of subsidy (Difference between gross and final net)	184.15	177.53	180.25	181.54	32.66	37.29	38,03	35.16

Source: Field Survey Data.

transport. On the other hand loss of subsidy is more in case of BPL households because they have to wait in queue more than the others by virtue of that they are entitled to almost all the PDS items, moreover they have to wait more time for paid conveyance than that of using personal conveyance (Table 3.21).

Fair Price Shops

More than 100 fair price shops (the number is not stable due to closures and mergers) were located in different parts of the city. About 10 Fair Price Shop owners interviewed randomly. Shop owners are both males and females, local and migrants having qualifications between classes 8th to graduation. They run their business in rented and own accommodation. Government don't pay rent, pay only commission on the quantity of goods sold. Labour cost will be borne by selling empty gunny bags. To economise expenses some of them maintain grocery shops as a side business. Due to inadequate earnings some of them working as informal labour elsewhere, hence shops kept open only a few hours during few days only. As on the date of the interview, they are getting a commission of ₹ 49.16 per quintal on other than NFSA grains sold. Only a few owners felt that, if bad quality goods received, they sent back to godown but maximum owners don't send back but sell by mixing good quality of grains with bad quality of goods. Every month there is the uncertainty of dates for receipt and sale of grains, because even after paying money for the entitled quantity by the FPS owners, it depends on delivery of goods by FCI to the concerned warehouses, is the reason for communication gap and dispute between ration card holders and FPS owners.

FPS owners felt that government-issued ration cards for about 20 years back, hence all the pages in these ration cards have filled and no space to make entries. Filled bags weighed at FCI warehouse but not at the point of delivery at the warehouse, causes sometimes underweight about 2 to 3 Kgs per bag is the reason for the loss. Every year due to the cancellation of bogus cards and mergers, the number of ration cards attached with different shops has declined, hence the viability of Fair Price Shops are under threat.

The Problem of Ration Cardlessness

Number of poor people in the city, are not having ration cards, among them about 80 households were interviewed. The maximum proportions of them are residing in city slums with their families for more than 10 years. The mean number of years stay in the city are 13.28 years. Maximum percentage of them has no residence proof in the city. The applicant households have to fulfill some of the conditions while submitting the application form for new ration card viz... (1) annual income limit of the household from all the sources should not be more than ₹ 1.5 lakhs, (2) For residence proof they have to submit household survey number which is allotted by the estate office of UT administration or Aadhar card with address proof in the city or voter card and (3) Certificate of having no ration card at native place / last place of residence or proof of family members names are not in the parents ration card at native place.

The maximum proportion of the migrants are illiterates and migrated long back, hence they have no contact with the village officials and revenue authorities, hence not in a position to get such certificates. Due to non-submission of address proof in the city, they failed to get Aadhar card or voter card. Some of them are residing in rented accommodation, but house owners reluctant to give residence certificate. Only two respondents stated that they paid money to the agents for getting ration card. Some of the respondents felt that there is a long gap between submission of application forms and spot verification by the food supply department officials.

Conclusion

The public distribution system is functioning to achieve food security at household level. There is wastage of time by standing queue and travel causes reduction of the net benefit goes to beneficiaries. There should be transparency in implementing the programme by using information and communication technology. By creating awareness among the beneficiaries about their rights and duties will give fruitful results. Beneficiaries associations, good governance, and political commitment are the backbone for the success of the scheme. In the light of drawbacks in physical distribution of PDS commodities, Direct

Benefit Transfer will be the better solution. For the successful implementation of Direct Benefit Transfer system, ensure price stability, time to time enhance the cash benefit by linking with price index, decentralize bank branches and due respect should be given to the voice of the female counterparts in respect of spending the direct benefit amount.

4

Mid-day Meal Scheme

Introduction

Education is thought to play major role for capital formation and economic development leading to higher living standards. Not only does education provide better job market opportunities, leading to higher wages and an improved standard of living, but evidence also suggests that improved schooling inputs can lead to a greater sense of political awareness reduced acceptance of traditional authority and increased gender equality, Friedman *et al* (2011). Education is a powerful instrument for social transformation and economic development through the human capital formation.

Primary education is thought to be associated with especially high returns, Psacharopoulos, Patrinos (2002). Investment in elementary education amplifies the productivity in all the sectors of the economy much more than other levels of education, and that economic returns to investment in primary education are greater than those arising from other levels of schooling, Christopher (1980). State Governments are spending a considerable portion of their limited resources to provide educational facilities. In spite of these efforts, the goal of a cent per cent universalisation of elementary education appears to be far and elusive due to inherent socio-economic factors present in the society.

Healthy children are better able than sick or malnourished children to go to school and learn (World Bank, 2014). The decision to send a child to school, like other household investment decisions, can be made by a cost-benefit framework (Dreze and Kingdon, 2001). Most of the children from low socio-economic society suffer from undernutrition, more often they drop out from schools at an early age, which directly affects their personality development and human capital formation of the nation. Poor enrollment and high school dropout rate are attributed to the poor nutritional status of the children compounded by poor socio-economic conditions, child labour and lack of motivation. (Ayeni and Adelabu, 2012).

There are many school meal or feeding programmes introduced in different countries according to their need. By recognising the importance of healthy human resources for faster economic growth, advanced nations introduced school meal programmes much earlier than the developing nations. The Great Britain introduced in 1945, United States America and Switzerland in 1946, Japan and Australia in 1947 and 1950 respectively. Among the developing nations – China in 1964, Indonesia in 1967, Thailand and Singapore in 1970 and 1975 respectively (Parikh and Yasmeen, 2004).

MDM is one among the wide range of policies aimed at encouraging school enrollment thereby to achieve universalisation of primary education to achieve MDMs. MDMS thought to increase enrollment through two main channels. First, they lower the cost of schooling, thereby providing an implicit subsidy to parents. Second, by improving child nutrition school lunches are thought to faster learning, thereby increasing the returns to education. School feeding programmes are popular in the developing world and beyond, not only because of their educational but also for their nutritional benefits. Moreover, MDM scheme could have been to give direct income support to eligible disadvantaged households. Consider the choice a household makes between spending money on food for the children and spending money on other goods.

Next to Public Distribution System, Cooked Mid-Day Meal Scheme is the second largest food security programme in India, envisaged to support one-third of the daily nutrient requirement of school going children. Mid-Day Meal in schools has had a long history in India. Prior to independence in 1925 (uncooked mid-day meal) was introduced for disadvantaged children in Madras Municipal Corporation.

By mid-1980s three states viz. Gujarat, Kerala, Tamil Nadu and the UT Pondicherry had universalised cooked Mid-Day Meal Programme with their own resources for children studying at the primary stage. By 1990-91 number of states started implementation with their own resources or with international assistance from agencies like UNICEF, FAO, CARE, WHO, etc.

A study in Birbhum district of West Bengal found in its evaluation of MDMS, that the scheme had led to a significant increase in enrollment and attendance of children, the increase being particularly marked in the case of girls and children from the scheduled castes and scheduled tribes. It also found that the MDMS had averted severe undernourishment, reduced social distances and curbed teacher absenteeism (Pratichi Trust, 2005).

In Rajasthan more than two-thirds of parents found the quality of the mid-day meals to be satisfactory and 85 per cent wanted the scheme to continue (Mathur *et al.*, 2005). A survey in seventy 'most backward' villages of Madhya Pradesh reported that (90 per cent) of teachers and cooks said the meal was being regularly provided, and that (96 per cent) of parents wanted the scheme to continue. Also, (63 per cent) of parents and (74 per cent) of teachers felt that the meal has helped improve the children's learning abilities. There was a (15 per cent) increase in overall enrollment, the increase was much higher in the case of SC and ST children (43 per cent), girls (38 per cent), SC and ST girls (41 per cent) (Jain and Shah, 2005).

Afridi (2005), reports improved functioning of MDMS in Madhya Pradesh while noting that there is room for further improvement. Rama Naik (2005), reports that the MDMS had led to a considerable increase in student enrollment and a decrease in teacher absenteeism in Karnataka, she also found that mid-day meals were being served regularly and that there was a high degree of satisfaction with the scheme on the part of both parents and students.

A study in Chittorgarh district Rajasthan found that, "overall implementation of MDM scheme is good and has had some impact on enrollment, retention, and attendance of students in primary schools". The quality of education, nutrition and health has also improved to some extent, but the schools are still lacking infrastructure facilities like kitchens, storerooms, latrines, sufficient classrooms and water facility (CART, 2006).

Studies says that, there is a positive relationship between nutritional status and educational development. Right to life under Article 21 of the Indian Constitution supports children right to food. With a view to enhancing enrollment, retention and attendance and simultaneously improving nutritional levels among children from class I to V, the National Programme of Nutritional Support to Primary Education (NP-NSPE) was launched as a Centrally Sponsored Scheme on 15th August 1995 in 2408 blocks in the country to provide hot fresh cooked meal, by the year 1997-98 it was extended to all blocks of the country.

Responding to writ petition filed in 2001 by People's Union for Civil Liberties (PUCL), Rajasthan, Supreme Court pointing out that "while on the one hand, the stocks of food grains in the country are more than the capacity of storage facilities, on the other there are reports from various states alleging starvation deaths." The court instructed the government to release public food stocks, arguing that the right to life under Article 21 of the Indian Constitution included the right to food. Supreme Court issued an interim order directing states to introduce cooked mid-day meals, i.e. a warm school lunch, in all public schools.

In consequence of pressure from civil society organisations coupled with the intervention of Supreme Court in 2001 and 2004, implementation of MDMS has accelerated and a number of reforms has taken. In 2007, the scheme has been further revised to cover children in upper primary classes from VI to VIII. Central and state governments having shared financial liability for the implementation of the scheme. The coverage of the scheme among the number of schools and number of beneficiaries has increased considerably. During 2013-2014, about 10.45 crore children were covered under this scheme among 11.58 lakh schools across the nation (GoI, 2014).

In September 2004, the scheme was revised to provide cooked mid-day meal with 300 calories and 8-12 grams of protein to all children studying in classes I – V in government and aided schools and EGS/ AIE centres. In addition to the free supply of food grains, the revised scheme provided Central Assistance for (a) Cooking cost @

₹ 1 per child per school day, (b) Transport subsidy was raised from the earlier maximum of ₹ 50 per quintal to ₹ 100 per quintal for special category states, and ₹ 75 per quintal for other states, (c) Management, monitoring and evaluation costs @ 2 per cent of the cost of food grains, transport subsidy, and cooking assistance, (d) Provision of a mid-day meal during summer vacation in drought affected areas.

In 2006, the scheme was further revised to provide assistance for cooking cost at the rate of (a) ₹ 1.80 per child/school day for states in the North Eastern Region, provided the NER states contribute ₹ 0.20 per child/school day, and (b) ₹ 1.50 per child/ school day for other states and UTs, provided that, these states and UTs contribute ₹ 0.50 per child/school day. In 2007, the scheme has been further revised to cover children in upper primary (classes VI to VIII) initially in 3479 Educationally Backwards Blocks (EBBs). Around 1.7 crore upper primary children were included by this expansion of the scheme. From 1st April 2008, the programme covers all children studying in government, local body, and government-aided primary and upper primary schools and the EGS/AIE centres including Madarsa and Maqtabs supported under SSA of all areas across the country. The calorific value of a mid-day meal at upper primary stage has been fixed at a minimum of 700 calories and 20 grams of protein by providing 150 grams of food grains (rice/wheat) per child/school day.

From the year 2009 onwards the following changes have been made to improve the implementation of the scheme (a) Food norms have been revised to ensure balanced and nutritious diet to children of the upper primary group by increasing the quantity of pulses from 25 to 30 grams, vegetables from 65 to 75 grams and by decreasing the quantity of oil and fat from 10 grams to 7.5 grams. (b) Cooking cost (excluding the labour and administrative charges) has been revised from ₹ 1.68 to ₹ 2.50 for primary and from ₹ 2.20 to ₹ 3.75 for upper primary children from 1.12.2009 to facilitate serving meal to eligible children in prescribed quantity and of good quality. The cooking cost for the primary is ₹ 2.69 per child per day and ₹ 4.03 for upper primary children from 1.4.2010.

It can be said a silver line in implementing MDMS in India. About 8.41 crore in Primary and 3.36 crore Upper Primary children i.e. a total of 11.77 crore children were estimated to be benefited from

MDM Scheme during 2009-10. About 11.04 Crore children were covered under MDM Scheme during 2009-10. During 2010-11, about 11.36 crore children (i.e. 7.97 Cr. children in primary and 3.39 Crore children in upper primary) had been covered in 12.63 lakhs institutions. During 2011-12 total coverage of children against enrollment was 10.52 Crore (i.e. Primary-7.71 crore and Upper Primary 3.36 crore children). During 2012-13, 10.68 Cr. children (Elementary level) had been covered in 12.12 lakh Schools. About 10.45 Cr. children were covered in 11.58 lakh Schools during 2013-14.

To achieve the objectives, since its inception, the scheme has been revised from time to time- the present provisions of the scheme as on December 2015 are as follows- The nutritional content in the mid-day meal which made available daily at free of cost so as to supplement 450 calories worth of food for primary class studying children and 700 calories worth of food for upper primary class studying children, while in case of daily protein supplementation it is 12 grams and 20 grams for primary and upper primary respectively. In addition to that adequate quantities of micronutrients like Iron, Folic Acid, and Vitamin-A etc also made available according to the requirements. Cooked Mid-Day Meal contains the following quantities of rice, wheat, vegetables, pulses, oil, fat, salt and condiments (Table 4.1).

Table 4.1: Food Norm With Effect From 1-12-2009

Sl. No.	*Items*	*Quantity per child per school day*	
		Primary	*Upper Primary*
1.	Food Grains	100 gms	150 gms
2.	Pulses	20 gms	30 gms
3.	Vegetables (including green leafy)	50 gms	75 gms
4.	Oil and fat	5 gms	7.5 gms
5.	Salt and condiments	As per need	As per need

Source: Government of India (2015).

In addition to food grains MDM involves two other major inputs viz...The cost of cooking and provision of essential infrastructure. Cooking cost per child is not static; it goes on revised by the government in accordance with a price index. The cooking cost will be borne by central and state governments/North Eastern states /UTs in different proportions (Centre and the NER states on 90:10 basis and with other States/UTs on 75:25 basis). The cooking cost for upper primary classes kept more than primary classes due to the requirement of larger quantities per child (Table 4.2).

The Revised Cooking Cost Rates w.e.f. 1-7-2016

Government of India increased the cooking cost by 7 per cent w.e.f. 1-7-2016 for 2016-17 over and above cooking cost for the year 2015-16. The cooking cost will be shared between central and states in the ratio of 60:40 for non- the NER States, 100 per cent for UTs and 90:10 for the NER States and three Himalayan states viz. Himachal Pradesh, Jammu and Kashmir, and Uttarakhand. The rates of cooking costs for primary and upper primary schools as follows.

Table 4.2: The Revised cooking cost rates w.e.f. 1-7-2016

Stage	*Cooking cost child per day*	*60:40 for non-NER States*		*90:10 for NER States and three Himalayan state*		*100 per cent for UTs*
Primary	₹ 4.13	2.48	1.65	3.72	0.41	4.13
Upper Primary	₹ 6.18	3.71	2.47	5.56	0.62	6.18

Source: Ministry of school education, Government of India, 2016.

The above cooking cost rates indicate the minimum mandatory contribution of centre and states, however, states and UTs may contribute more.

A separate provision for payment of honorarium to cook-cum-helper @ ₹ 1000 per month has been made. One cook-cum-helper may be engaged in a school having up to 25 students, two cooks-cum-helpers for schools having 26 to 100 students and one additional cook-cum-helper for every addition of up to 100 students. The expenditure towards the honorarium of cook-cum-helper is shared between the centre and the NER States on 90:10 basis and with other States/UTs on 75:25 basis. To provide assistance to States/UTs for Management, Monitoring and Evaluation (MME) at the rate of 1.8 per cent of total assistance on (a) free food grains, (b) transport cost, (c) cooking cost and (d) Honorarium to cook-cum-helpers. Another 0.2 per cent of the above amount will be utilised at the Central Government for management, monitoring, and evaluation (MHRD, 2015).

The management system of the scheme implementation is the backbone for its success; it required close co-operation and coordination among different agencies. Though central governments shoulder much of the financial burden, it is the responsibility of the state governments to provide facilities for preparation and distribution of cooked food. At the national level department of school education and literacy has set up steering-cum-monitoring committee. Every state government/ UT administration, district/block level designated one of its departments as a nodal department which will take responsibility for implementation. At local level gram panchayat/municipality assign responsibility of the day-to-day management of the programme, at the school level, the village education committee/school management and development committee or parent-teachers association will take care of implementation.

To ensure transparency in implementation and to avoid corruption, MDM brought under RTI Act 2005. All the implementing schools and centres have to display information with regarding the quality of food grains received, date of receipt, the quantity of food grains utilised, other ingredients purchased, utilised, the number of children given meal, daily menu, the roster of community members involved in the programme etc.

MDMS Infrastructure in India

The level of infrastructure would affect the efficacy of MDM, but the schools are still lacking infrastructure facilities like kitchens, storerooms, latrines, potable/drinking water. Cooking devices and containers for storage of food grains and other ingredients, utensils for cooking, serving and dining halls, is the backbone for the success of Mid Day Meals Scheme. The cost of cooking and provision of essential infrastructures are the responsibility of the state government. Most of the literature on MDMS stated that the cost of infrastructure is a contentious issue in MDMS implementation and for which the state governments are not willing to provide, due to financial constraints and other petty reasons. Karnataka, Kerala, Tamil Nadu and Gujarat have made comparatively good progress in building a sound infrastructure for the MDMS, however, the states like Bihar, Uttar Pradesh, West Bengal, the case is just opposite.

Kitchen-cum-Stores: States/UTs have been given central assistance for construction of 10.06 lakh Kitchen-cum-Stores since 2006-07 till 2013-14, against which 6.82 lakh kitchen-cum-stores have been constructed so far. A common unit cost of construction of kitchen shed @ ₹ 60,000 for the whole country was impractical and also inadequate. Now the cost of construction of kitchen-cum-store will be determined on the basis of plinth area norm and State Schedule of Rates. The Department of School Education and Literacy vide letter No.1-1/2009-Desk (MDM) dated 31.12.2009 had prescribed 20 sq.mt. Plinth area for schools having up to 100 children. For every additional up to 100 children, additional 4 sq.mt plinth areas will be added. States/UTs have the flexibility to modify the slab of 100 children depending upon the local condition. The cost of construction of Kitchen-cum-store is shared between the centre and the NER States on 90:10 and with other states /UTs on 75:25 basis.

Table 4.3, reveals that among the states Arunachal Pradesh performed well (by achieving 99 per cent of construction out of the sanctioned) when compared to the other states, whereas Pondicherry performed well when compared to the other UTs. Among the poor performers A&N Islands, Chandigarh and Dadra Nagar Haveli is at bottom with 0 per cent construction. Progress in the construction of the above infrastructure further facilitates better implementation of MDMS.

Table 4.3: The Physical Progress on Construction of Kitchen-Cum-Stores (Primary + Upper Primary as on 31-3-2012

States/UTs	No. of Kitchen-cum-stores sanctioned during 2006-07 to 2011-12	Physical Progress of Kitchen-cum-stores	
The best performed 10 States and UTs		*Constructed*	*Percentage*
Pondicherry	92	92	100
Arunachal Pradesh	4131	4085	99
Sikkim	859	763	89
Uttar Pradesh	122572	103966	85
Punjab	18969	16015	84
Tripura	4614	3846	83
Gujarat	19868	16025	81
Nagaland	2223	1777	80
Madhya Pradesh	97099	77396	80

(Contd...)

Rajasthan	77298	59415	77
Daman and Diu	26	20	77
The Poor Performed 10 States and UTs			
A and N Islands	34	0	0
Chandigarh	10	0	0
D and N Haveli	50	0	0
Andhra Pradesh	75283	3077	4
Kerala	2470	318	13
Mizoram	2396	632	26
Maharashtra	65783	18064	27
Tamil Nadu	14340	4275	30
Jharkhand	39001	12546	32
All India	**9,55,473**	**5,60,546**	**59**

Source: Ministry of Human Resources Development, Government of India.

Availing Cooking Gas: Use of cooking gas will make possible to prepare even in extreme weather conditions. Moreover, it reduces time spent for cooking. Making availability of other resources like firewood, Kerosene oil, coal and other waste material create health implications on students as well as cooking staff. Table 4.4, indicates that Daman and Diu made 100 per cent success in providing cooking gas for the preparation of MDM, while Assam, Gujarat, Meghalaya, Orissa, Delhi, Lakshadweep precariously even no single institution having the facility. At all-India level, the situation is not more optimistic because only 22 per cent of the institutions are using gas for cooking MDM. (Table 4.4).

Table 4.4: Gas Based Cooking of MDM in India as on 31-11-2011.

States and UTs	*Number of Institutions cook MDM by using gas*	*Percentage*
The best performed states and UTs		
Daman and Diu	126	100
Punjab	18969	84
Himachal Pradesh	12709	84
Karnataka	46414	84
D and N Haveli	278	77
Uttar Pradesh	107058	67
Nagaland	1789	65
Haryana	8799	59

(*Contd...*)

Tripura	3470	53
Sikkim	447	51
The poor performed States and UTs		
Assam	0	0
Gujarat	0	0
Meghalaya	0	0
Orissa	0	0
Delhi	0	0
Lakshadweep	0	0
Pondicherry	3	1
Chandigarh	4	1
Arunachal Pradesh	41	1
Kerala	108	1
All India	**2,72,976**	**22**

Source: Ministry of Human Resources Development, Government of India.

Kitchen Devices: Availability of an adequate number of Kitchen devices (utensils) and other machinery are essential for timely completion of the cooking process. Most of the states procured kitchen devices, remaining states also moving in positive direction. At the national level, 91 per cent of the institutions procured the sanctioned devices for preparation of MDM. Institutions in Assam and Manipur and the other states showed less progress in procuring devices are a mark of negligence on essential infrastructure (Table 4.5). Central government provides assistance for provisioning and replacement of kitchen devices at an average cost of ₹ 5,000 per school.

Table 4.5: Physical Progress towards Procurement of Kitchen-Devices as on 31-3-2012

States and UTs *The best performed 10 states and UTs*	*Target (Units Sanctioned during 2006-07 to 2011-12)*	*Procured*	*Percentage*
Andhra Pradesh	78457	78453	100
Arunachal Pradesh	4431	4431	100
Chhattisgarh	59210	59210	100
Haryana	15305	15305	100
Himachal Pradesh	15096	15096	100
Karnataka	42588	42588	100

(*Contd...*)

Meghalaya	9374	9374	100
Mizoram	2428	2428	100
Nagaland	2751	2751	100
Punjab	18969	18969	100
The poor performed 10 states and UTs			
Assam	62267	17666	28
Manipur	3107	1457	47
Kerala	4079	3102	76
Maharashtra	121343	94787	78
Bihar	86428	70122	81
Jharkhand	37132	31125	84
Tripura	6510	5629	86
Jammu and Kashmir	21504	18818	88
Sikkim	879	782	89
Gujarat	33540	29868	89
All India	**11,85,479**	**10,74,309**	**91**

Source: Ministry of Human Resources Development, Government of India.

Status of the Scheme in Chandigarh

The National Programme of Nutritional Support to Primary Education (NP-NSPE) popularly known as Mid-Day Meal (MDM) scheme aimed to cover all students in classes (I-VIII) in Government/ Government-aided schools and Madrasas. The MDM scheme began in 1995 with dry Meal in the form of fruit bread, baked porridge, raw wheat, rice and sweet/salted Mathis. In January 2006, the scheme was converted to provide cooked meal on a trial basis. Subsequently, this scheme was extended to all Government/Government-aided schools and Madrasas. The objective of the programme is to give a boost to Universalisation of Elementary Education (UEE) by increasing enrollment, attendance, retention and simultaneously improving the nutritional status of children in elementary classes. It can be appreciated that in some of the schools during 2015 this scheme is extended to nursery school children also, however, the expenditure involved for this will be borne by UT Chandigarh administration only.

Process of Scheme Implementation

Cooked and wholesome meal is being served to eligible students. In order to ensure the supply of good quality and hygienic food, three reputed cooking institutes have been engaged to prepare and provide cooked meal viz. (1) Dr Ambedkar Institute of Hotel Management, Sector-42, Chandigarh, (2) Chandigarh Institute of Hotel Management, Sector-42, Chandigarh, (3) Hotel Shivalikview (CITCO), Sector-17, Chandigarh. Besides above, 7 school based kitchens are also being maintained in Government Model Sr. Sec. Schools in sector-10, 15, 26, 44, 47, 38 and 42. In all 119 institutes (109 Government Schools, 6 Government-aided schools and 4 Madarsas) have been covered under the Mid-Day Meal Scheme (Table 4.6).

Table 4.6: Total Enrollment of children for Mid-Day Meal (as on 30.09.2014)

Status of classes	*(Number of children)*		
	Government/Government Aided Schools)	*Madarsas*	*Total*
Primary	60,596	587	61,183
Upper Primary	43,887	192	44,079
Total	**1,04,483**	**779**	**1,05,262**

Source: District Education Office, UT Chandigarh.

Note: Mid-Day Meal Scheme is being implementing in Chandigarh among 109 government schools, 6 Government aided schools. 4 Madrasa.

Coverage of Children/Working Days

In UT Chandigarh, total strength of eligible students of class 1st to 8th in respect of government/government-aided schools and Madarsas are 1,05,262. Approximately 54,000 Meal are prepared and supplied daily in schools, for the consumption of about 72,000 students, this number might be low because substantial number of the student are from economically sound families. Some of the students bring their own Tiffin's from their home as well as takes a small quantity of MDM in the school. Thus, the Meal supplied by the cooking agencies is sufficient for more number of students as compared to the number of Meal supplied by the cooking agencies. The quantity of food is supplied as per time to time requirement of schools (expected number of children attend school) to avoid any wastage of food. In this regard, a study has also been got conducted from the Centre for Research in Rural and Industrial Development (CRRID). In the report, CRRID has also stated that students of UT, Chandigarh take less MDM but improvement in overall enrollment, retention rates, enhancing the overall nutrition of the children and social equality has been found. Thus, the coverage of children under MDMS in UT, Chandigarh is about 48-50 per cent. However, efforts are being made by the department to improve the coverage of children by revising the MDM menu according to the tastes of the children.

Funds Allocation and Expenditure

Expenditure under the scheme is shared between centre and state on 75:25 ratio. Interestingly UT contribution is more than the central government contribution. The funds allotted and expenditure incurred during 2014-2016 is shown in (Table 4.7).

Table 4.7: Funds Allocation and Expenditure (₹ lakhs)

Year	*Centre Contribution*	*UT Contribution*	*Total*	*Expenditure*		
				GOI	*State*	*Total*
2014-15	587.09	686.00	1273.09	486.57	686.00	1172.57
2015-16	111.62	530.00	641.62	134.81	107.55	242.36 (Up to 31.8.2015)

Source: District Education Office, UT Chandigarh.

Type of Food Served

Preparation and supply of food are entrusted to three hotels being managed by UT administration. Wheat flour and rice will be supplied by UT government at free of cost to these hotels based on the requirement. Transport cost will be borne by UT government; the remaining expenditure will be borne by these hotels. On a mutual consensus, basis rates were decided. The number of schools equally divided among these hotels for supplying food every day based on the requirement given by Mid-Day Meal in-charges of the schools. Preference will be given to females and SC, SC teachers while entrusting duty of MDM in-charges, they have to perform this duty in addition to their workload in the respective schools without any remuneration. Ayas (MDM workers) appointed on a temporary basis by paying monthly ₹ 2226, to serve food and clean utensils in the schools.

Table 4.8, indicates, parantha-based menu is entrusted to Dr Ambedkar Institute of Hotel Management, Sector-42 Chandigarh, to distribute food to all the schools on a rotation basis.

Table 4.8: Prantha Based Menu

Day	Menu
Monday	Prantha + Rajmah
Tuesday	Prantha + Karhi Pakora
Wednesday	Prantha + Dal Chana + Vegetable
Thursday	Prantha + Rajma
Friday	Prantha + Karhi Pakora
Saturday	Prantha + Mix Dal

Source: District Education Office, UT Chandigarh.

Table 4.9, indicates that rice-based menu is entrusted to Hotel Shivalik View (CITCO) Sector-17 Chandigarh, to distribute food to all the schools on rotation basis.

Table 4.9: Rice Based Menu

Day	Menu
Monday	Rice + Dal Chana with vegetables
Tuesday	Rice + Karhi pakora
Wednesday	Rice + Dal Chana with vegetables
Thursday	Rice + Rajmah
Friday	Rice + Karhi pakora
Saturday	Rice + Rajmah

Source: District Education Office, UT Chandigarh.

Table 4.10: Veg. Pulao Based Menu

Day	Menu
Monday	Veg. Pulao + Arhar Dal
Tuesday	Veg. Pulao + Karhi nutri
Wednesday	Veg. Pulao + Mix Dal
Thursday	Veg. Pulao + Rajmah
Friday	Veg. Pulao + Karhi pakora
Saturday	Veg. Pulao + Nutri, Potato, Peas

Source: District Education Office, UT Chandigarh.

Table 4.10, indicates that Veg Pulao Based Menu is entrusted to Chandigarh Institute of Hotel Management, Sector-42 Chandigarh, to distribute food to all the schools on rotation basis.

Inspectors of MDM have been engaged at the cooking institutes to ensure that the cooked food is prepared by the respective cooking institutes as per the above mentioned weekly menu, besides monitoring the cooking process. Principals/heads of the schools are deputed daily on rotation, to supervise the cooking of MDM at the cooking institutes. They check the quantity, quality of MDM and cleanliness/hygiene in the cooking area, besides, they taste the cooked food before it is supplied for distribution in the schools. MDM Supervisors check the quantity and quality of MDM and also taste the same before taking delivery of it from the cooking institutes and further deliver the same to the respective schools after getting the quantity, quality, and taste of MDM checked by the teacher-in-charge of MDM. The cooking institutes have a well established system to procure cooking ingredients, devices and appointment of cooking staff. In the schools, Cook-cum-Helpers are engaged by the School Management Committees.

Systems to Ensure Transparency, Accountability

The management of food grains is monitored and supervised by the committee consisting of following members in a systematic manner:-

1. The District Education Officer,
2. The Director Health Services,
3. District Food and Supply Officer,
4. The principal of Government . Sr. Sec. Schools,
5. Representative of FCI.

After inspection by the committee, food-grains will be lifted from the FCI warehouse located at Kurali (Punjab) and stored in the departmental stores. Storekeeper (MDM) maintains the record of the food-grains. He is also responsible for the issue of food grains (rice and wheat flour) to the cooking institutes. Wheat is further supplied from departmental store to the miller. Wheat flour is lifted from miller for delivery to the cooking institute on weekly basis and rice is lifted from the store to cooking institutes on weekly basis and managed smoothly. Record of food-grains received and utilised is also maintained at the cooking institutes, which is inspected regularly by the inspectors. Cooking of MDM and serving is regularly supervised by the inspectors and supervisors of MDM.

Table 4.11: Food Quantity Norm with Effect from 1-12-2009

Items	*Quantity per Day/Child*	
	Primary	*Upper Primary*
Food grains	100 gms	150 gms
Pulses	20 gms	30 gms
Vegetables (leafy also)	50 gms	75 gms
Oil and fat	5 gms	7.5 gms
Salt and condiments	As per need	As per need

Source: District Education Office, UT Chandigarh.

Cooking Cost

Cooking cost fixed by the Government of India i.e. ₹ 3.34 per meal for primary stage children and ₹ 5.00 for upper primary stage children up to 30.6.2014. From 1.7.2014 it is ₹ 3.59 and ₹ 5.38 respectively. W.e.f. 1.7.2015 it has further enhanced to ₹ 3.76 and ₹ 5.64 for primary and upper primary children respectively. Out of this, GOI is contributing per meal cost as ₹ 2.51 for primary and ₹ 3.75 for upper primary up to 30.6.2014 and from 1.7.2014 ₹ 2.69 and ₹ 4.04 and from 1.7.2015 ₹ 2.82 and ₹ 4.23 for primary and upper primary respectively. This cost comprises the cost of components viz pulses, vegetables, oil and fats, salt and condiments and fuel but it does not include the cost of food-grains labour and Administrative charges. Food-grains are provided by the GOI through FCI, the whole cost of which is borne by GOI. In UT, Chandigarh, the work of preparation of MDM has been entrusted to the three reputed agencies (Government . undertakings) viz Chandigarh Industrial and Tourism Development Corporation Ltd (CITCO), Dr Ambedkar Institute of Hotel Management (AIHM), and Chandigarh Institute of Hotel Management (CIHM). The per meal cooking cost being paid to these institutes is as under:-

CITCO ₹ 4.50+VAT @12.50 per cent= ₹ 5.06 (both for primary and upper primary classes)

AIHM ₹ 8.94 including VAT (both for primary and upper primary classes)

CIHM ₹ 7.20 +VAT@ 12.50 per cent = ₹ 8.10 (for primary classes) and ₹ 9.17 +VAT@ 12.50 per cent = ₹ 10.32 (for upper primary classes)

Per meal cooking cost for these institutes has been so devised that it includes the cost of cooking ingredients like pulses, vegetables, oil and fats, salt and condiments and fuel, labour, administrative and other overhead charges ranging from 15 to 20 per cent but it does not include the cost of food grains as the same is provided free of cost to the institutes by the education department.

School-based kitchens at GMSSS-10, 15, 26, 44 and 47 and GMHS-38 and 42 (7 schools) procure cooking ingredients at their own level. Food-grains (wheat and rice) are provided by the department. Per meal, the cooking cost is reimbursed to them as per norms fixed by GOI i.e. ₹ 3.34 for primary and ₹ 5.00 for upper primary up to 30.6.2014. From 1.7.2014 at the rate of ₹ 3.59 and ₹ 5.38, while from 1.7.2015 ₹ 3.76 and ₹ 5.64 respectively. To maintain the records/ documents of MDM, one organizer has also been provided to in-charge of each kitchen.

Monitoring

All the HCS/PCS officers working in Chandigarh Administration and senior officers of Education Department monitor the MDM activities. Senior officers monitor the implementation of MDM programme at the cooking institutes and schools. They check the taste, quality, quantity of MDM and hygiene. School Management committees monitor the implementation of MDM programme in the schools. Four committees consisting of cluster heads, SMC members, and NGOs also monitor the MDM activities at the schools and MDM kitchens. Department has engaged one Inspector for each kitchen for monitoring the cooking of MDM. Twenty Supervisors are engaged who go with the mini trucks to ensure hygienic delivery of cooked Meal in the Schools. The MDM is handed over to the Teacher In-charge of MDM in the school who checks and taste the quantity and quality. The MDM is distributed to the students in the classrooms by the cook-cum-helpers engaged for the purpose, in the presence of teachers. Teachers also taste the MDM in the classrooms before its distribution.

Capacity Building

The staff employed in cooking institutes are having the requisite qualifications and well conversant in the field. Training is given to the persons involved in MDM programme by the cooking institutes. Further, quality and hygiene standard are as per the requirements to be maintained by any accredited food institute. Training to the cook-cum-helpers engaged in the schools for a serving of MDM is given by the experts.

DISCUSSION

Methodology

The study is based on both primary and secondary data sources. Primary data is collected in the year 2015, by conducting a personal interview with the help of structured questionnaire at the place of residence by following clustered systematic random sampling method. Field survey is conducted in all the three administrative regions of the city from 500 sample respondents i.e. 250 households and 250 school going children from these respective households. Chandigarh city is selected for the study because it occupies the third rank in per capita income among the Indian cities, hence it attracts a large number of migrant poor people from different parts of India. Children of these migrant poor people generally study in government schools, having a habit of consuming a mid-day meal, hence it is felt important to know the perceptions of the parents and children on the status of implementation of the scheme, for further improvement.

Geographical Distribution of the Respondents

Table 4.12, shows that total of 250 sample respondent households and 250 Mid-Day Meal beneficiary children (one child from each household) of the respective households were selected from slums and shanties in Chandigarh. More than half (51.6 per cent) of the respondents were selected from EWS colony Dhanas due to concentration of more families, followed by 27.2 per cent from 4 No. Colony Industrial area, while 8.8 per cent respondents were taken from

New Indira Colony Mani Majra, 7.6 per cent taken from Janata Colony Sector 25, the remaining from Sanjay Labour Colony Industrial Area, Kalyan Colony Kudda Jassu and Bhat Colony Mauli Jagra.

Table 4.12: Selection of Sample Respondents (Households and children)

Name of the Cluster	*Number of Respondent Households*	*Percentage*	*Number of Respondent MDM Beneficiary Children*	*Percen-tage*
EWS Colony, Dhanas	129	51.6	129	51.6
4 No. Colony, Industrial Area	68	27.2	68	27.2
New Indira Colony, Mani Majra	22	8.8	22	8.8
Janata Colony, Sector 25	19	7.6	19	7.6
Sanjay Labour Colony, Industrial Area	9	45.0	9	45.0
Kalyan Colony, Kudda Jassu	2	0.8	2	0.8
Bhat Colony, Mauli Jagra	1	0.4	1	0.4
Total	**250**	**100.0**	**250**	**100.0**

Source: Field Survey Data.

Work Status of Respondents (Parents)

The working and living conditions of informal workers are very poor, it influences educating their children. Table 4.13, indicates that the majority (46 per cent) of the respondents are casual labour, while (28.4 per cent) respondents are self-employed, about (20 per cent) are regular workers and the remaining (5.6 per cent) are unemployed.

Table 4.13: Work Status of Respondents (Head of the Households)

Category of Workers	*Number of Respondents*	*Percentage*
Casual Labour	115	46.0
Self-Employed	71	28.4
Regular Workers	50	20.0
Unemployed	14	5.6
Total	**250**	**100.0**

Source: Field Survey Data.

Parents' Permission to Their Wards to Take MDM

Parent's permission determines whether to take MDM or not to take. Table 4.14, indicates that the larger majority (96.8 per cent) of the respondents (parents of the children) have no objection to their children to have a mid-day meal in the school. However, only (3.2 per cent) of the respondents not permitted their wards to have MDM in the school on the probability of becoming ill or due to the existing in health problems.

Table 4.14: Parents' Permission to Their Children to Have MDM at School

Permission	*Number of Respondents*	*Percentage*
Given	242	96.8
Not given	8	3.2
Total	**250**	**100.0**

Source: Field Survey Data.

Parents Perceptions on Health Consequences of MDM

Parent's permission determines the decision to consume a mid-day meal. That the predominant majority (82.8 per cent) of the respondents stated that, there are no ill health consequences of taking MDM by their children, however, (12.8 per cent) respondents felt MDM causes stomach pain, indigestion, and vomiting. The negligible proportion (4.4 per cent) revealed that they aren't sure, that the ill health is due to consuming mid-day meal only (Table 4.15).

Table 4.15: Parents Perceptions on Children Health Consequences by Taking MDM at School

Perception	*Number of Respondents*	*Percentage*
Causes stomach pain, indigestion, vomiting	32	12.8
Don't know	11	4.4
No Problem	207	82.8
Total	**250**	**100.0**

Source: Field Survey Data.

Parents, Preference of MDM vs. Cash Transfer

Table 4.16, indicates that, more than half (62.4 per cent) of the sample respondents preferred cooked MDM over cash transfer of ₹ 300 per month per child, however, (37.6 per cent) of the respondents preferred cash transfer over cooked MDM. Lack of another option compels parents to permit their children to take MDM. The reasons stated for preferring cash transfers are- inadequate quantity, poor quality, children don't take regularly, fear of ill health, repetition of the same type of menu, lack of knowledge about the impact of MDM on socialisation, attention, attendance, and retention.

Table 4.16: Parents, Preference of MDM vs. Cash Transfer.

Preference	*Number of Respondents*	*Percentage*
Cooked Meal	156	62.4
₹ 300 Per Month Per Child	94	37.6
Total	**250**	**100.0**

Source: Field Survey Data.

Note: The maximum number of parents felt that they have no idea about the positive consequences of MDM on weight gain, health improvement, attendance and socialisation. But they felt that there is some positive impact on the above said parameters, but cannot say it is definitely due to MDM only.

PERCEPTIONS OF BENEFICIARY CHILDREN

Gender of the Respondent Children

Table 4.17, indicates that more than half (52 per cent) of the sample respondent children are boys, the remaining (48 per cent) are girls. From each family relatively larger number of boys are having the habit of taking MDM than girls, because girls are more hygienic sensitive than boys. In addition to that, consumption of energy is more in the case of boys than girls due to differences in time spent for play activities.

Table 4.17: Gender of the Respondent Children

Gender	*Number of Respondents*	*Percentage*
Boys	130	52.0
Girls	120	48.0
Total	**250**	**100.0**

Source: Field Survey Data.

Children Levels of Schooling

Higher the class that the children are studying more will be the experience with MDM, hence children studying from class 2nd were considered for this study. Purposively the larger proportion of children studying higher classes were considered for the study to get appropriate feedback. That the predominant majority (28 per cent) of the children are studying 7th class, (26 per cent) 8th class, (18 per cent) 6th class, (12.4 per cent) 5th class, while the remaining are studying 4th, 3rd and 2nd classes (Table 4.18).

Table 4.18: Class-wise Classification of MDM Beneficiary Children

Class Studying	*Number of Respondents*	*Percentage*
2	8	3.2
3	13	5.2
4	18	7.2
5	31	12.4
6	45	18.0
7	70	28.0
8	65	26.0
Total	**250**	**100.0**

Source: Field Survey Data.

Food Menu, Before Going to School

Table 4.19, indicates that, more than half (70.4 per cent) of the children having the habit of taking Tiffin (in the case of day school) / Lunch (in the case of evening school) at home before going to the school. About one quarter (27.2 per cent) of the children having a habit of taking only Tea/ Milk. Precariously only (2.4 per cent) of the

Table 4.19: Food Menu, Children Having Before Going to School

Status	*Number of Respondents*	*Percentage*
Only Tea/Milk	68	27.2
Tiffin/Lunch	176	70.4
Nothing	6	2.4
Total	**250**	**100.0**

Source: Field Survey Data.

children don't take anything, due to parents' inability/have no time to provide food/negligence of children. It reveals that the certain proportion of the children completely depends on MDM.

Weekly Number of Days Consumption of MDM

A weekly number of days children consume MDM indicates the extent of attachment with MDM. Table 4.20, shows, that the majority (70 per cent) of the children consume MDM during all the six working days, relatively a lesser proportion of children consume a lesser number of days per week, while (13.6 per cent) children don't take MDM on any day is the matter of discourse.

Table 4.20: Weekly Number of Days Intake of MDM

Number of Days	*Number of Respondents*	*Percentage*
1	6	2.4
2	11	4.4
3	10	4.0
4	11	4.4
5	3	1.2
6	175	70.0
Not taking at all	34	13.6
Total	**250**	**100.0**

Source: Field Survey Data.

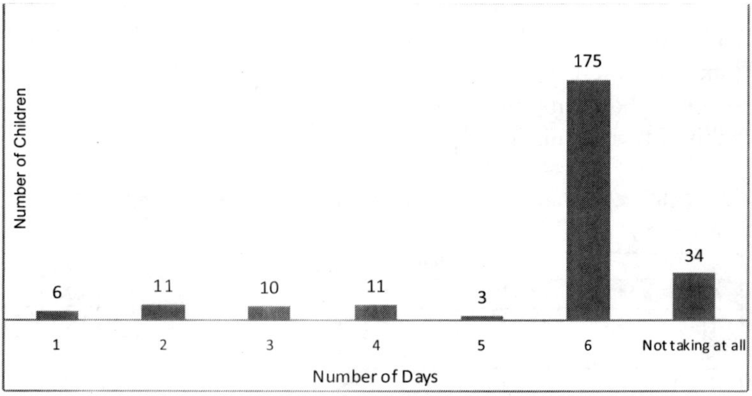

Source: Field Survey Data.

Fig. 4.1: Weekly Number of Days Intake of MDM.

Figure 4.1, demonstrates that, the larger number of children consume MDM during all the working days, while certain number of children don't consume MDM certain days only, while 34 children don't consume at all is the matter of concern.

(c) Reasons for Non-consumption of MDM During All the Working Days

Table 4.21, shows that about the 3/4th majority (70 per cent) of the children felt they like MDM, while the remaining children have not taken MDM during all the days of the week. They stated a number of reasons viz... food not tasty, parents don't allow, insects may be as per newspapers and TV reports, not well cooked, more salt / no salt, not hygienic etc, some of them stated no reason and others stated more than one reason for not taking meal daily.

Table 4.21: Reasons for Not Taking MDM during All the Working Days

Reason	*Number of Respondents*	*Percentage*
Parents Don't Allow	8	3.2
More Salty / No salt	4	1.6
Not Well Cooked	6	2.4
Not Hygienic	2	0.8
Not Tasty	10	3.6
Insects may be as per News Papers and TV	8	3.2
Any of the Above Two Reasons	11	4.4
Any of the Above Three Reasons	10	4.0
Any of the Above Four Reasons	11	4.4
Any of the Above Five Reasons	5	2.0
No Problem	175	70.0
Total	**250**	**100.0**

Source: Field Survey Data.

Adequacy of Quantity of MDM

Availability of adequate quantity will habituate a large number of children depends on MDM. As referred in Table 4.22, that the greater majority (62.4 per cent) of the children felt that, the quantity being served is adequate, while (24 per cent) of the children felt quantity is inadequate, while (13.6 per cent) of the children not taking at all.

Table 4.22: Opinion of Adequacy of Quantity of MDM

Opinion	*Number of Respondents*	*Percentage*
Adequate	156	62.4
Inadequate	60	24.0
Not taking at all	34	13.6
Total	**250**	**100.0**

Source: Field Survey Data.

Figure 4.2, illustrates that, the larger number of children felt that, the given quantity of MDM is adequate, while 60 children stated that the quantity is inadequate, the remaining children don't take MDM.

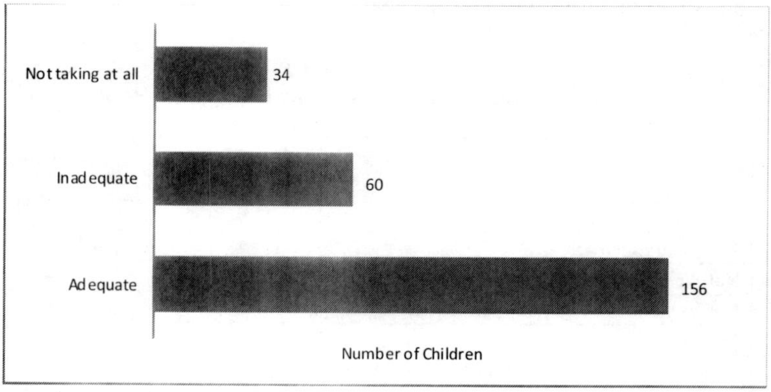

Source: Field Survey Data.

Fig. 4.2: Opinion of Adequacy of Quantity of MDM Served.

Status of Consumption of the Quantity Served

Status of consumption of the given quantity indicates, children interest in taking MDM. As shown in Table 4.23, that the larger majority (67.6 per cent) of the children consumed the given quantity. About (18.8 per cent) of the children threw it out/ take home, while the remaining (13.6 per cent) not taking at all. Some of the children revealed that they consume food in spite of no taste, due to hungry and also pressure from teachers to maintain discipline at meal.

Table 4.23: Status of Consumption of the entitled Quantity of Meal

Experience	*Number of Respondents*	*Percentage*
Eat the whole share	169	67.6
Half quantity threw out/ take home from share	47	18.8
Not taking at all	34	13.6
Total	**250**	**100.0**

Source: Field Survey Data.

Figure 4.3, indicates that, the maximum proportion of the children consume MDM in the school itself, while 19 per cent of the children stated that they consume half of the given quantity, and remaining threw in dustbin or take home.

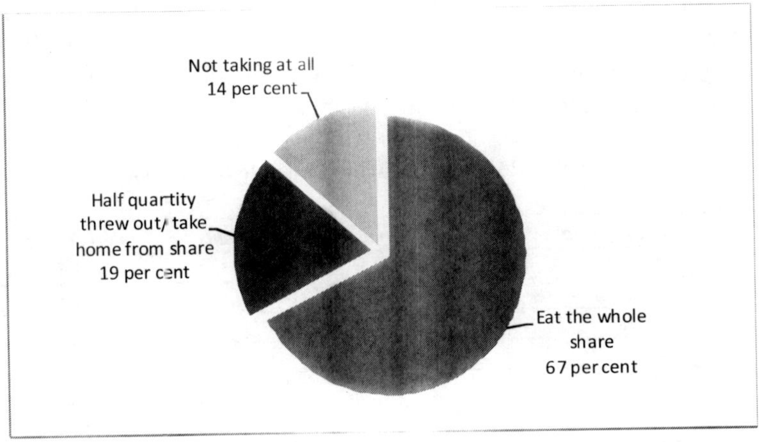

Source: Field Survey Data.

Fig. 4.3: Status of Consumption of the entitled Quantity of MDM.

The Status of Demand for More Quantity of MDM

Table 4.24, indicates that the majority (73.6 per cent) of children don't ask food second time either due to lack of quality or they feel insulted if not given. However, (11.6 per cent) of the children told that, if they ask more will be available, while (1.2 per cent) of the children said that they asked but not available, the remaining (13.6 per cent) not taking at all.

Table 4.24: The Status of Demand for More Quantity of MDM

Experience	*Number of Respondents*	*Percentage*
Ask More Food and They Give	29	11.6
Don't Ask	184	73.6
Ask But Don't serve	3	1.2
Not Taking At All	34	13.6
Total	**250**	**100.0**

Source: Field Survey Data.

Habit to Bring Lunch to the School

Children know the menu in advance so that they decide whether to bring adequate lunch/ certain quantity of lunch / not to bring at all from home. During the days of the favourite food menu, they don't bring lunch, otherwise bring lunch. As referred in Table 4.25, about (48.4 per cent) of the children don't bring lunch at all on any day, while about (35.6 per cent) of the children bring lunch during all the days, the remaining (16 per cent) bring lunch during few days when their favourite food not served.

Table 4.25: Habit to Bring Lunch to the School

Habit to bring	*Number of Respondents*	*Percentage*
All The Days	89	35.6
Not At All	121	48.4
One Day	3	1.2
2 Days	18	7.2
3 Days	14	5.6
4 Days	5	2.0
Total	**250**	**100.0**

Source: Field Survey Data.

Habit to Eat at Home after Coming Back from School

Due to non-availability of adequate quantity of MDM/not interested in taking MDM or limited lunch carried to school, force almost all the children eat after coming back from the school. About (99.2 per cent) of the children eat at home after coming back from the school, while the remaining (0.8 per cent) doesn't eat after coming back from school (Table 4.26).

Table 4.26: Habit to Eat at Home after Coming back from School

Habit	*Number of Respondents*	*Percentage*
Eat	248	99.2
Don't Eat	2	0.8
Total	**250**	**100.0**

Source: Field Survey Data.

Recipe Fond off by the Children from MDM Menu

The per capita income of people living in Chandigarh is more than the other cities in India. There is demonstration effect which makes poor children also habituate the culture of eating modern food / Jung food items irrespective of its nutrition value and health implications. The majority (62.8 per cent) of the children like to eat Kadi pakora and veg pulav, while (6.8 per cent) children like Rajma Rice and Prantha, while the remaining children fond off Dal Rice, Chole Rice, Chana dal. Interestingly (2 per cent) of the children felt that they like the menu during all the days (Table 4.27).

Table 4.27: Recipe Fond off, to Eat that is Being Served at School

Recipe	*Number of Respondents*	*Percentage*
All menu is Good	5	2.0
Chana Dal	4	1.6
Dal Chana, Parantha	6	2.4
Dal Rice, Prantha	13	5.2
Karhi Pakora, Veg Pulav	157	62.8
Karhi Pakora, Parantha	14	5.6
Rajma Rice, Parantha	17	6.8
Don't Eat At All	34	13.6
Total	**250**	**100.0**

Source: Field Survey Data.

Recipe Don't Like to Eat

Tastes of all the children are not similar with regarding consumption of a type of food. Even though the majority (43.2 per cent) of the children don't like Pili dal and Rice, (14.8 per cent) of the children don't like Dal Rice, Black dal Rice, Black dal parantha, while (6.4 per cent) don't like Chana dal Rice, (4 per cent) of the children don't like Kali chana, Rice. Interestingly (2 per cent) of the children like the whole menu, while (1.6 per cent) children dislike the whole menu but take some times occasionally, while the remaining (13.6 per cent) don't take at all (Table 4.28).

Table 4.28: Recipe Don't Like to Eat, That is Being Served at School

Recipe	*Number of Respondents*	*Percentage*
Like the Whole Menu	5	2.0
Dislike the Whole Menu But Take Some Times	4	1.6
Don't Take At All	34	13.6
Chana Dal, Rice	16	6.4
Black Chana, Rice	10	4.0
Dal Chana, Puri	4	1.6
Dal Rice, Black chana Rice, Prantha	37	14.8
Arhar Dal, Rice	108	43.2
Urad Dal/ Gia Dal	3	1.2
Karhi Pakora, Rice	14	5.6
Pulav	3	1.2
Rajma, Rice	13	5.2
Total	**250**	**100.0**

Source: Field Survey Data.

Habit to Bring MDM to Home

The Table 4.29, shows that the majority (66.8 per cent) of the children don't bring MDM from school to home, while (18.8 per cent) of the children bring from their share, only negligible proportion (0.8 per cent) bring other than their share and the remaining (13.6 per cent) don't take at all. Teachers don't allow children to waste

Table 4.29: Experience of Bring Back MDM to Home

Experience	*Number of Respondents*	*Percentage*
Don't Take At All	34	13.6
Bring From Share	47	18.8
Bring other Than Share	2	0.8
Don't Bring	167	66.8
Total	**250**	**100.0**

Source: Field Survey Data.

food also the reason to bring food to their home, even though they have no intention to eat at home by themselves or their family members.

Consumption Pattern of MDM, which Bring Back to Home

The analysis as given in Table 4.30, that the great majority (66.8 per cent) of the children don't bring MDM to their home, about (8.8 per cent) of the children threw food in dustbin at home, (3.2 per cent) children each said that they themselves/ parents eat; whereas (3.6 per cent) stated that their brother/ sister eat, while (13.6 per cent) don't take at all.

Table 4.30: Status of Consumption of MDM at home by Self/Family Members

Experience	*Number of Respondents*	*Percentage*
Don't Take At All	34	13.6
Don't Bring	167	66.8
Self-Consumption	8	3.2
Brother/Sister	9	3.6
Brother /Sister/ Parents	2	0.8
Parents	8	3.2
Threw in Dust Bin	22	8.8
Total	**250**	**100.0**

Source: Field Survey Data.

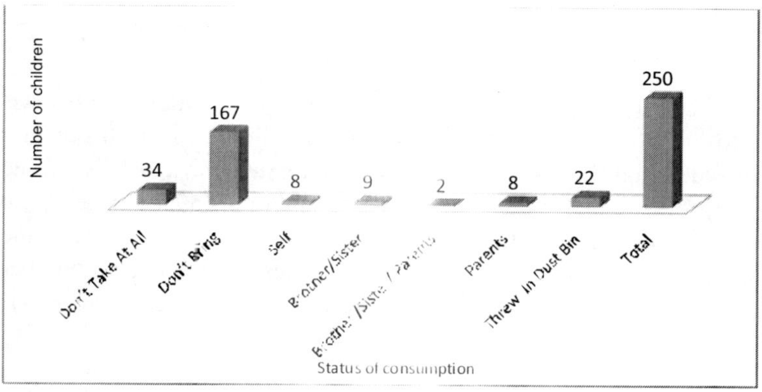

Source: Field Survey Data.

Fig. 4.4: Status of Consumption of MDM, which is bring back to home.

Status of consumption of MDM at home can be known from Fig 4.4, that the larger number of children don't bring MDM from their schools. About 22 children stated that they bring but threw in the dust-bin, while the lesser proportion of the children stated that their family members consume MDM.

IMPACT OF MID DAY MEAL SCHEME

Geographical Distribution of the Sample Respondents

To know the impact of MDM on body mass index of the children, a study is conducted. Based on the concentration of residents and school going children, three larger slum clusters from different parts of the city were chosen for selecting sample respondents. About 200 (40 per cent) respondents from EWS Colony Dhanas, 200 (40 per cent) respondents from 4 No. Colony Industrial Area and the remaining 100 (20 per cent) respondents were selected from Janata Colony sector 25 (please see Table 4.31).

Table 4.31: Selection of Sample Respondents from Clusters of Chandigarh

Name of the Colony	*Number of Children*	*Percentage*
EWS Colony Dhanas	200	40.0
4 No. Colony Industrial Area	200	40.0
Janata Colony sector 25	100	20.0
Total	**500**	**100.0**

Source: Field Survey Data.

Though MDM entitled to all the school going children from class 1 to 8th, the higher end classes studying children were taken into consideration because they have larger experience with MDM. Table 4.32, reflects that the larger number of children (39.4 per cent) are studying 6th class, while 35.4 per cent studying 7th class and the remaining 25.2 per cent are studying 8th class, in total equal number of boys and girls were selected for the study. (Please see Table 4.34).

Table 4.32: Class and Gender of Sample Respondent Children

Class	*Boys*	*Percentage*	*Girls*	*Percentage Children*	*Number of*	*Percentage*
6	104	41.6	93	37.2	197	39.4
7	85	34.0	92	36.8	177	35.4
8	61	24.4	65	26.0	126	25.2
Total	**250**	**100.0**	**250**	**100.0**	**500**	**100.0**

Source: Field Survey Data.

Status of Availing MDM and Gender

Table 4.33, reveals that the predominant majority (87.2 per cent) of the children continued MDM from the date of joining in the respective school, while (5.2 per cent) discontinued and (7.6 per cent) were never taken. Among never taken and discontinued the proportion of girls are more than boys, while among the continuing, the proportion of boys are more than girls. The data reveals that boys are more interested in availing MDM when compared to girls.

Table 4.33: Gender and Availing MDM

Status	*Boys*	*Percentage*	*Girls*	*Percentage*	*Number of Children*	*Percentage*
Never taken	17	6.8	21	8.4	38	7.6
Discontinued	12	4.8	14	5.6	26	5.2
Continued	221	88.4	215	86.0	436	87.2
Total	**250**	**100.0**	**250**	**100.0**	**500**	**100.0**

Source: Field Survey Data.

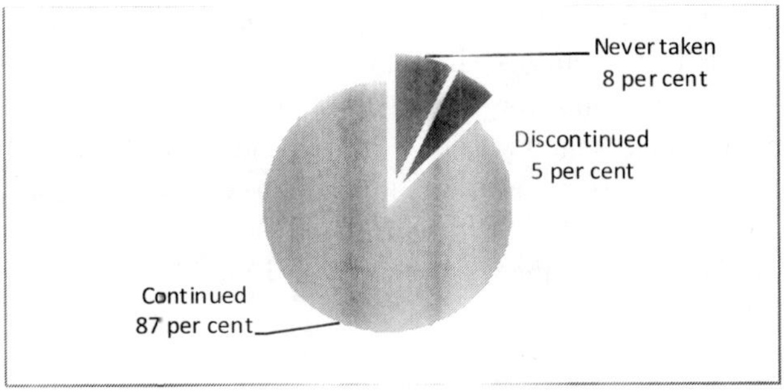

Source: Field Survey Data.

Fig. 4.5: Consumption pattern of MDM by the children.

Figure 4.5, indicates that, the maximum proportion of the children continued MDM, while lesser proportion of the children either discontinued or never taken.

Figure 4.6, indicates that gender and consumption pattern of MDM is concerned, among the never taken and discontinued, the larger proportion are girls, while among the continued the proportion of boys are more than girls.

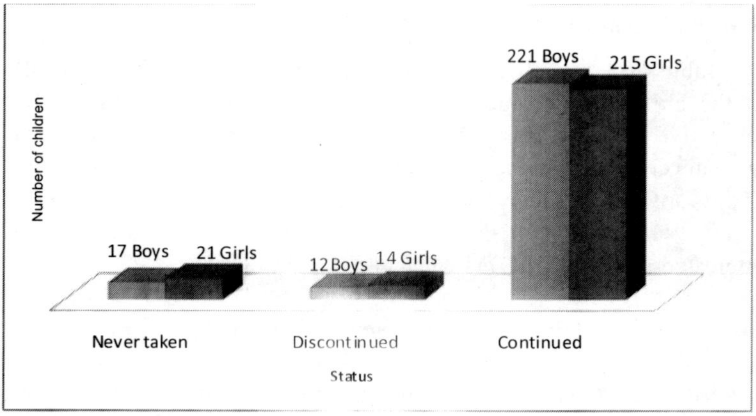

Source: Field Survey Data.

Fig. 4.6: Gender of the Children and Consumption pattern of MDM.

Status of Availing MDM and Classes Studying

Higher the classes that the children are studying lesser the proportion of them availing MDM. With regarding continuation of MDM, the larger proportion of the children studying 6th class are continuing than their seniors. Table 5.34, indicates that (41.0 per cent), (35.77 per cent), (23.16 per cent) of 6th, 7th, 8th class studying children respectively taking MDM. It can be stated that the lower the class children studying, lower the freedom to avoid MDM.

Table 4.34: Class-wise Status of Children Availing MDM

Class	Never Taken	Per cent	Disconti-nued	Per cent	Conti-nuing	Percen-tage	Total	Percentage
6	10	26.31	8	30.76	179	41.00	197	39.4
7	10	26.31	12	46.15	156	35.77	177	35.4
8	18	47.36	6	23.07	101	23.16	126	25.2
Total	**38**	**100.0**	**26**	**100.0**	**436**	**100.0**	**500**	**100.0**

Source: Field Survey Data.

Status of Availing MDM and Income Category

Higher the income level, lesser the probability of availing MDM. Table 4.35, presents that the majority (10.75 per cent) of the children belongs to APL category families never taken MDM when compared to only (5.50 per cent) of BPL and (6.41 per cent) no card children. In the case of continuation of MDM, the larger majority (90.25 per cent) of children belongs to BPL than that of (84.40 per cent) of APL and (84.61 per cent) of cardless children.

Table 4.35: Status of Availing MDM and Possession of Type of Ration Card by the Parents of the Respective Children

Status of Availing MDM	Ration Card Status						Total Number of Children	Percen-tage
	APL	Per cent	BPL	Per cent	No card	Per cent		
Never taken	20	10.75	13	5.50	5	6.41	38	7.6
Discontinued	9	4.83	10	4.23	7	8.97	26	5.2
Continuing	157	84.40	213	90.25	66	84.61	436	87.2
Total	**186**	**100.0**	**236**	**100.0**	**78**	**100.0**	**500**	**100.0**

Source: Field Survey Data.

Status of Weekly Number of Days Availed MDM and Gender

Table 4.36 reveals that more than half (60 per cent) of the boys availed MDM during all the six days of the week when compared to (54 per cent) of girls. In the case of no consumers of MDM, the proportion of girls are more than boys. Weekly (7.6 per cent) children availed MDM for two days, (7.4 per cent) availed three days, (6.2 per cent) availed four days and (5.6 per cent) of children availed five days. The data indicates that the respondent children felt monotony to avail MDM during all the working days, it is due to the repetition of the similar menu and the poor quality of food.

Table 4.36: Weekly Number of Days Availed MDM in the School

Number of Days Per Week	*Boys*	*Per cent*	*Girls*	*Per cent*	*Number of Children*	*Percentage*
0	29	11.6	35	14.0	64	12.8
1	8	3.2	9	3.6	17	3.4
2	20	8.0	18	7.2	38	7.6
3	16	6.4	21	8.4	37	7.4
4	15	6.0	16	6.4	31	6.2
5	12	4.8	16	6.4	28	5.6
6	150	60.0	135	54.0	285	57.0
Total	**250**	**100.0**	**250**	**100.0**	**500**	**100.0**

Source: Field Survey Data.

Continuity in Availing MDM during All the Years of Their Study in the School

Higher the class the children studying, lesser the proportion of them availing MDM. Table 4.37, reflects that, when compared to 7th and 8th class children, that the three-fourth majority (74.09 per cent) of 6th class children stated that they have continuously availed MDM during all the years of their study in the school, while (67.23 per cent) of the 7th class children and (59.9 per cent) of the 8th class children availed MDM. Either fear from the teachers or lack of pocket money in their hands are the reasons for a larger proportion of children studying lower classes, availed MDM.

Table 4.37: Status of Continuity in Availing MDM during All the Years of Their Study in the School

Class	*Number of Children*	*MDM Availed During All The Years of Their Study*	*Percentage*
6	197	143	74.09
7	177	119	67.23
8	126	75	59.59
Total	**500**	**337**	**67.4**

Source: Field Survey Data.

Body Mass Index of Respondent Children (BMI=Weight in Kgs/ Height in Meters Square)

Body Mass Index (BMI) =Weight in Kgs / Height in meters square. BMI measured in accordance with World Health Organisation norms. Underweight (BMI below 18.5), Normal weight (BMI 18.5 to 24.9), Overweight (BMI 25.0-29.9), Obese (BMI 30 and above). Table 4.38, indicates that the larger proportion 211 (42. 2 per cent) of the children BMI is in the range of 16-19, while lesser proportion 9 (1.8 per cent) of the children Body Mass Index (BMI) is in the range of 22-25.

Table 4.38: Body Mass Index (BMI) of Respondent Children (BMI=Weight in Kgs / Height in Meters Square)

BMI Range	*Number of Children*	*Percentage*
10-13	15	3.0
13-16	202	40.4
16-19	211	42.2
19-22	62	12.4
22-25	9	1.8
25 and above	1	0.2
Total	**500**	**100.0**

Source: Field Survey Data.

BMI Status and Gender of the Children

Table 4.39, indicates that the predominant majority (82.8 per cent) of the children are suffering from underweight, only (17 per cent) of the children having normal weight, and (0.2 per cent) having overweight. BMI in accordance with gender is concerned; the larger majority of boys (88.8 per cent) are suffering from underweight when compared to (76.8 per cent) girls. The larger segment (22.8 per cent) of the girls having normal weight when compared to (11.2 per cent) boys, except only one girl is suffering from overweight. Boys are more dependent on MDM when compared to girls, but surprisingly suffering from the problem of low BMI, it indicates that the impact of MDM scheme is positive in reducing classroom hunger, but fails to reduce anemia and malnutrition.

Table 4.39: BMI Status and Gender of the Children

Status of BMI	*Boys*	*Percentage*	*Girls*	*Percentage*	*Number of Children*	*Percentage*
Below 18.5 (Under Weight)	222	88.8	192	76.8	414	82.8
18.5 to 24.9 (Normal Weight)	28	11.2	57	22.8	85	17.0
25.0-29.9 (Over Weight)	0	0.0	1	0.4	1	0.2
30 and Above (Obese)	0	0.0	0	0.0	0	0.0
Total	**250**	**100.0**	**250**	**100.0**	**500**	**100.0**

Source: Field Survey Data.

BMI and Status of Availing MDM

Table 4.40, indicates that, among 38 non-consumers of MDM, 32 of them (84.21 per cent) are facing the problem of underweight, while only (13.15 per cent) having normal weight, (2.63 per cent) having overweight. Among 26 children who discontinued MDM, the larger majority (65.38 per cent) having underweight, while only (34.61 per cent) having normal weight. In totality among those 436 MDM continuing children, the greater majority (83.71 per cent) suffering from underweight, while only (16.29 per cent) having normal weight. MDM have no positive impact on maintaining health standards. Due to increase in economic status some of the children discontinued MDM; but their BMI is better than the other consuming respondents.

Table 4.40: BMI and Status of Availing MDM

BMI Status	*Never Taken*	*Per cent*	*Disconti-nued*	*Per cent*	*Conti-nuing*	*Per cent*	*Number of Children*	*Percen-tage*
Below 18.5 (Under Weight)	32	84.21	17	65.38	365	83.71	414	82.8
18.5 to 24.9 (Normal Weight)	5	13.15	9	34.61	71	16.28	85	17.0
25.0-29.9 (Over Weight)	1	2.63	0	0.0	0	0.0	1	0.2
30 and Above (Obese)	0	0.0	0	0.0	0	0.0	0	0.0
Total	**38**	**100.0**	**26**	**100.0**	**436**	**100.0**	**500**	**100.0**

Source: Field Survey Data.

BMI Status and Number of Days Availed MDM

Table 4.41, reveals that the majority 241 (58.21) of children are the consumers of the mid-day meal during all the six days of the week, but they are suffering from the low body mass index. On the other hand in case of normal weight, a considerable number 44 (51.76 per cent) of children consume mid-day meal during all the six days of the week, they are better than the less number of days mid-day meal availed children. If we compare six days mid-day meal consuming children, the proportion of children suffering from underweight (58.21) are higher than normal weight children (51.76 per cent). It can be concluded that the positive impact of the mid-day meal on body mass index is very negligible.

Status of BMI of Different Classes Studying Children

Table 4.42, shows that in case of normal weighted 85 children, the larger proportion 33 (38.82 per cent) are studying class seventh, whereas in case of 414 underweight children, the larger proportion 174 (42.02 per cent) are studying 6th class, only one student who is studying class 8th, is suffering from overweight. The larger proportion of 6th class studying children are the consumers of mid-day meal, but the larger proportion of them are suffering from the low body mass index when compared to their peers. The data reveals that more the dependency on mid-day meal lesser will be the impact on recovery from anemia and malnutrition.

Table 4.41: BMI Status and Number of Days Availed MDM

Status of BMI	***Number of days availed MDM Per Week***								
	6	***5***	***4***	***3***	***2***	***1***	***0***	***Total no. of Children***	***Per cent***
	Number of Children								
Below 18.5 (Under Weight)	241 (58.21)	25 (6.03)	24 (5.79)	29 (7.0)	30 (7.24)	16 (3.86)	49 (11.83)	414 (100.0)	82.8
18.5 to 24.9 (Normal Weight	44 (51.76)	3 (3.52)	7 (8.23)	8 (9.41)	8 (9.41)	1 (1.17)	14 (16.47)	85 (100.0)	17.0
25.0-29.9 (Over Weight)	0 (0.0)	0 (0.0)	0 (0,0)	0 (0.0)	0 (0.0)	0 (0.0)	1 (100)	1 (100.0)	0.2
Total	**285**	**28**	**31**	**37**	**38**	**17**	**64**	**500**	**100.0**

Source: Field Survey Data.

Note: Figures in parentheses are percentage to horizontal totals.

Table 4.42: BMI of the Sample Children

Class	*BMI < 18.5 (Under Weight)*	*BMI 18.5 to 24.9 (Normal Weight)*	*BMI 25.0 to 29.9 (Over Weight)*	*Total*	*Percentage*
6th	174(88.32)	23(11.67)	0(0)	197(100)	39.4
7th	144(81.35)	33(18.64)	0(0)	177(100)	35.4
8th	96(76.19)	29(23.01)	1(0.79)	126(100)	25.2
Total	**414**	**85**	**1**	**500**	**100.0**

Source: Field Survey Data.
Note: Figures in parentheses are percentage to horizontal totals.

BMI and Economic Status of the Parents

Table 4.43, indicates that among 186 Above Poverty Line (APL) category children, the greater majority (85.48 per cent) are suffering from underweight, while among 236 Below Poverty Line (BPL) category children (84.74 per cent) are suffering from underweight, while among 78 cards less children (70.51 per cent) are suffering from under weight. Irrespective economic status, in spite of consuming mid-day meal, children suffering from low body mass index.

Table 4.43: BMI and Economic Status of the Parents

BMI status	*APL*	*BPL*	*No Card*	*Total*	*Percentage*
Below 18.5 (Under Weight)	159 (85.48)	200(84.74)	55(70.51)	414	82.8
18.5 to 24.9 (Normal Weight)	26(13.97)	36(15)	23(29.48)	85	17.0
25.0-29.9 (Over Weight)	1(0.53)	0(0.0)	0(0.0)	1	0.2
Total	**186(100.0**	**236(100.0)**	**78(100.0)**	**500**	**100.0**

Source: Field Survey Data.
Note: Figures in parentheses are percentage to vertical totals.

Mean Weight and Mean BMI of Children According to the Status of Availing MDM

Table 4.44, demonstrates that the mean weight of all the sample respondents is 34.67, it is not much varying with the mean weight of never taken, discontinued, and continuing children. While there is no much difference between the mean weight of girls and boys. The mean

BMI of all the sample respondents is 16.55, it is not much vary with BMI of never taken, discontinued, and continuing, but the mean BMI of girls is 17.04 and boys it is 16.55, it indicates that even though the proportion of boys availing MDM is higher, but net benefit received by them is lesser in terms of enhancing Body Mass Index.

Table 4.44: Mean Weight and Mean BMI of Children According to the Status of Availing MDM

Status	*Number of*	*Percentage Children*	*Mean Weight Kgs*	*Mean BMI*
Never Taken	38	7.6	34.62	16.43
Discontinued	26	5.2	34.66	16.54
Continued	436	87.2	34.28	16.55
Total	500	100.0	34.67	16.55
Males	250	50.0	34.67	16.55
Females	250	50.0	34.73	17.04
Availed all the 8 years of their study	75	15.0	34.72	16.69
Availed zero years	38	7.6	34.62	16.43
Availed all the six days	285	57.0	34.65	16.54
Availed zero days (Never taken + Discontinued)	64	12.8	34.66	16.54
Availed one day per week	17	3.4	34.76	16.46

Source: Field Survey Data.

Perceptions of the MDM In-Charge Teachers

MDM in-charge teachers are the important stakeholders in implementing MDM scheme. To know the first-hand information about the consumption pattern of the children and status of implementation of the scheme by the Chandigarh administration, a primary level study is conducted among the MDM in-charge teachers in the sample schools.

Geographical Distribution of the Sample Respondent Teachers

Table 4.45, shows there are three clusters (administrative divisions) in the city Chandigarh i.e. East, Central, and South. From East division (34 per cent), Central division (32 per cent) and South division (34 per cent) MDM in-charge teachers, both males and females were selected randomly for the study. Certain proportion of all types of schools i.e. model (English medium); non-model (Hindi medium) primary, secondary and senior secondary schools were selected for the study.

Table 4.45: Administrative Divisions and Number of Sample Respondent MDM in-charge Teachers in Government Schools in Chandigarh

Administrative Divisions	*Sectors and localities in each division*	*Number of Sample Schools Selected*	*Percentage*
East	7, 18, 19, 20, 21, 26, 27, 28, 29, 30, 31, 47, Colony No. 4, Grain Market, Bapudham Colony, Transport Area, Railway Colony, Hallomajra, Industrial Area, Manimajra, Baimajra, Karsan, Behlana, Gagamajra, Jhumu	17	34.0
Central	1, 2, 3, 4, 5, 6, 7, 8, 9, 10, 11, 12, 14, 15, 16, 17, 22, 23, 24, 25, Village Kaimbwala, Khudalohra, Khudajassu, Sarangpur, Dhanas, Khuda Alisher	16	32.0
South	32, 33, 34, 35, 36, 37, 38, 39, 40, 41, 42, 43, 44, 45, 46, 47, 48, 49, 50, 51, Burail, Dadumajra, Khejri, Maloya, Zizanpur, Attwa, Palsora Colony No. 5	17	34,0
Total		**50**	**100.0**

Source: Field Survey Data.

Sample Schools Having Classes

Table 4.46, indicates that the greater majority (52 per cent) of the schools were selected are having classes from I-VIII, (26 per cent) of the schools having VI-VIII classes, while (14 per cent) schools having I–V classes, and the remaining schools having I-VII and VII-VIII classes.

Table 4.46: Sample Schools Having Classes

Classes	*Number of MDM In-charge Teachers (Number of Sample Schools)*	*Percentage*
I-V	7	14.0
I-VII	1	2.0
I-VIII	26	52.0
VI-VIII	13	26.0
VII-VIII	3	6.0
Total	**50**	**100.0**

Source: Field Survey Data.

Administrative Regions and Percentage of Children Avail MDM

Figures in Table 4.47, reveals that, among three administrative divisions, as per school records the larger majority (63.49 per cent) of the children availed MDM from central division, while (60.82 per cent) from south division and (57.29 per cent) availed from east division, whereas among the beneficiaries the larger majority (64.26 per cent) belongs to non-model schools, when compared to (57.22 per cent) beneficiaries from model schools. Children studying in model schools are economically better than those studying in non-model schools are the reason for this gap.

Table 4.47: Percentage of Children Availed MDM According to Administrative Divisions and Model (English Medium) and Non Model (Hindi Medium) Schools

Administrative divisions and Model and Non-Model Schools	*Percentage of children availed MDM*
East	57.29
Central	63.49
South	60.82
Model	57.22
Non Model	64.26

Source: Field Survey Data.

Schools and Percentage of Children Availed MDM

MDM in-charge teachers felt that on an average among the greater majority (32 per cent) of the schools, about 45 to 55 per cent of the children (studying classes I to VIII) consume MDM, while the mean number of children taking MDM is 60.60 per cent (Table 4.48).

Table 4.48: Percentage of Children Consumed MDM in the Sample Schools

Percentage Range	*Number of schools*	*Percentage*
25-35	3	6.0
35-45	3	6.0
45-55	16	32.0

(Contd...)

55-65	9	18.0
65-75	9	18.0
75-85	5	10.0
85-95	4	8.0
95-100	1	2.0
Total	**50**	**100.0**

Source: Field Survey Data.

Supply Source of MDM for Schools

Table 4.49, shows that, among 50 sample schools, the highest majority of the schools (90 per cent) were getting food from three centralised kitchens (hotels) located in Chandigarh, while the remaining five (10 per cent) of the schools had their own kitchens in their respective schools.

Table 4.49: Distribution of Sample Schools According to Source of Getting MDM

Source	*Number of sample schools*	*Percentage*
Centralised Kitchens (Hotels)	45	90.0
Kitchen in the School	5	10.0
Total	50	**100.0**

Source: Field Survey Data.

Rank Given to MDM Supplying Hotels in Chandigarh

Keeping in view the experience of getting food from centralised kitchens (Hotels being managed by the government), based on punctuality, maintenance of hygiene, quality and quantity of food supplied, teachers assigned ranks to the three hotels. A large majority of the MDM in-charge teachers (84.44 per cent) assigned the first rank to Chandigarh Institute of Hotel Management, Sector 42, about (84.44 per cent) teachers assigned the second rank to Ambedkar Institute of Hotel Management, Sector 42, while (86.66 per cent) teachers assigned the third rank to Shivalik Hotel, Sector 17.

Table 4.50: Rank Given to Food Supplying Hotels in Chandigarh by MDM In-charge Teachers

MDM supplying Hotels	*Rank given*			*Total Number of schools getting MDM from centralised kitchens*
	1	*2*	*3*	
	Number of Schools			
Chandigarh Institute of Hotel Mgt, Sector 42	38 (84.44)	7 (15.55)	0 (0.0)	45
Ambedkar Institute of Hotel Mgt, Sector 42	7 (15.55)	38 (84.44)	0 (0.0)	45
Shivalik Hotel, Sector 17	0 (0.0)	6 (13.33)	39 (86.66)	45

Source: Field Survey Data.

Note: Figures in parentheses are percentage of the respective totals.

Reasons for Giving Least Rank to Shivalik Hotel

Teachers stated a number of reasons for assigning rank 3 to Shivalik hotel. The larger majority (51.11 per cent) stated poor quality is the main reason, about (17.77 per cent) teachers stated three reasons i.e. poor quality, lesser quantity, less hygienic, while (15.55 per cent) stated food either overcooked / undercooked, while the remaining teachers stated more than one reason (Table 4.51).

Table 4.51: Reasons for Giving Least Rank to Shivalik Hotel, Sector 17 Chandigarh

Reasons	*Number of MDM In-charge Teachers (Number of Sample Schools)*	*Percentage*
Poor Quality of Food	23	51.11
Poor Quality, Less Quantity, Less Hygienic	8	17.77
Food Either Over Cooked / Under Cooked	7	15.55
No Taste and Not Cooked Properly	3	6.66
Poor Quality and No Punctuality	2	4.44
Poor Quality, Germs, Insects	1	2.22
Poor Quality and Taste Less	1	2.22
Total	**45**	**100.0**

Source: Field Survey Data.

Note: 5 schools having kitchens in the school itself.

Quality of MDM Supplied by Hotels

Table 4.52, reflects that the larger majority (62.2 per cent) of the teachers felt that the food supplied on an average is good in quality, only (37.77 per cent) of the teachers felt the food is normal in quality. Interestingly nobody said that the food quality is poor.

Table 4.52: Opinion of MDM in-charge Teachers on Quality of MDM Supplied by Hotels

Quality of Food Supplied	*Number of MDM In-charge Teachers (Number of Sample Schools)*	*Percentage*
Good	28	62.2
Normal	17	37.77
Poor	0	0.0
Total	45	**100.0**

Source: Field Survey Data.

Impact of MDM on Children Enrollment, Attendance, Attention Towards Studies

The majority of the teachers perceived the positive impact of MDM on increase in enrollment and attendance. Table 4.53, indicates that

Table 4.53: Impact of MDM on Enrollment, Attendance and Attention towards Studies

Impact Status (1)	*Number of MDM in-charge Teachers (Number of Sample Schools) (2)*	*Due to MDM (3)*	*Cannot say due to MDM (4)*	*Indiffe-rent (5)*	*Total (3+4+5)*
	Enrolment Increased?				
Yes	40	22	18	0	40
No	10	NA	NA	0	
Attendance Increased?					
Yes	48	34	14	0	48
No	2	NA	NA	0	
Attention Towards Studies Increased?					
Yes	39	14	23	2	39
No	11	NA	NA	0	

Source: Field Survey Data.

22 teachers said that MDM is the reason for the increase in enrollment, 34 teachers opined that MDM has made a positive impact on the increase in attendance, while 14 teachers stated that MDM is the reason for the increase in attention towards studies.

Figure 4.7, shows that, the maximum proportion of the teachers said that MDM caused to increase in enrollment, while the lesser proportion of the respondent teachers revealed that MDM is not the reason for the increase in enrollment.

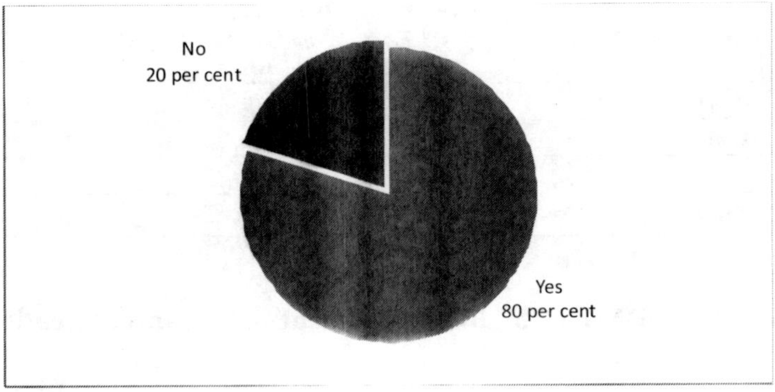

Source: Field Survey Data.

Fig. 4.7: Impact of MDM on increse in Enrollment.

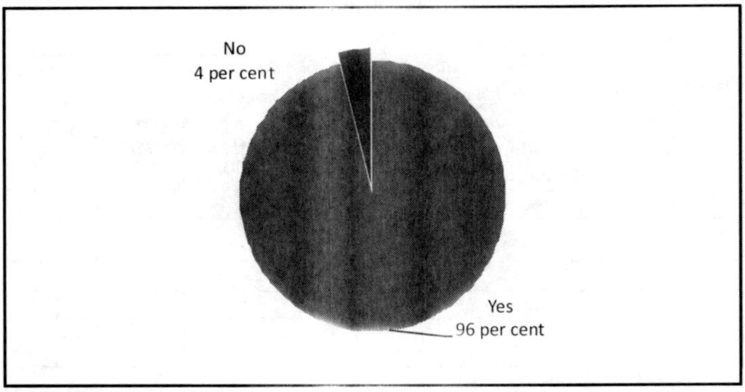

Source: Field Survey Data.

Fig. 4.8: Impact of MDM on increse in Attendance.

Figure 4.8, reveals that, the maximum proportion of the teachers accepted that MDM, has shown a positive impact on the increase in attendance, while meager proportion stated that, it is not the reason for the increase in attendance.

Figure 4.9, indicates that, the larger proportion of the in-charge teachers stated that, MDM caused to increase in attention towards studies, while the lesser proportion of the teachers felt that, MDM has not increased attention towards studies.

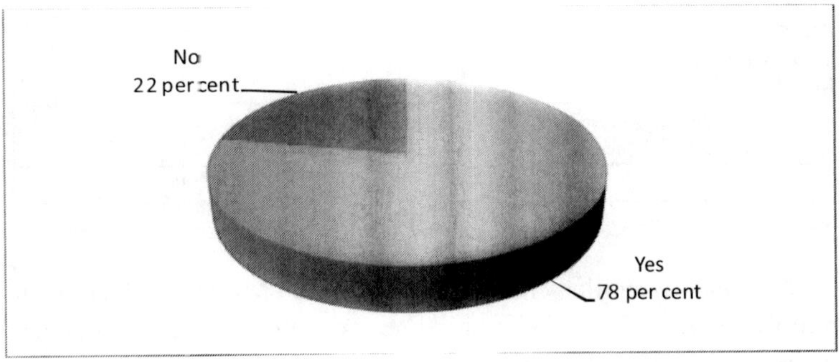

Source: Field Survey Data.

Fig. 4.9: Impact of MDM on Increse in Attention towards studies.

Perception about Consumption and Quality of MDM

The In-charge teachers assigned different reasons for a certain proportion of the entitled school going children not taking the mid-day meal. It is clear from Table 4.54, that the larger majority (36 per cent) of the teachers stated three reasons viz...lack of parents' permission, food not tasty, repetition of the same type of menu, while (26 per cent) of the teachers expressed only one reason, i.e., repetition of the same food. Teachers stated different reasons for students' not taking MDM. About (26 per cent) of teachers revealed that those who attended school takes meal, while about (12 per cent) teachers said that children bring food from their home, children prefer to buy food which is available in the school premises and in the market, food distribution too early i.e. much before than lunch time.

Table 4.54: Reasons for Entitled Children Not Consuming MDM

Reasons	*Number of MDM In-Charge Teachers (Number of Sample Schools)*	*Percentage*
Lack of Parents Permission, Food Not Tasty, Repetition of the Same Food	18	36.0
Repetition of the Same Food	13	26.0
Those Who Attended School, Avail Meal	13	26.0
Bring Food From Home	4	8.0
Preference of Food other Than Being Supplied through MDMS	1	2.0
Food Distribution Too Early i.e. earlier than Lunch Time	1	2.0
Total	**50**	**100.0**

Source: Field Survey Data.

Reasons for entitled children not consumed MDM, can be known from figure 4.10. The maximum number of in-charge teachers stated that, parents did not give permission to their children is the major reason for non-consumption of MDM, about 13 teachers stated that children did not consume due to repetition of the same food every day.

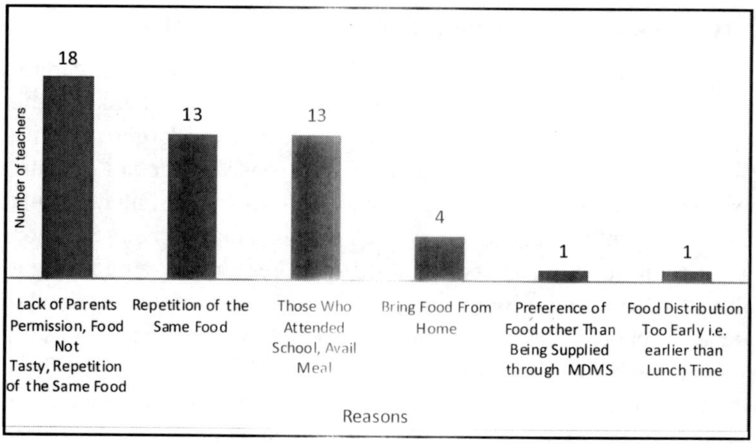

Source: Field Survey Data.

Fig. 4.10: Reasons for Entitled Children Not Consuming MDM.

Level of Satisfaction about Status of Implementation of MDM in Chandigarh

As regards the level of satisfaction on consumption of MDM, about (34 per cent) of the teachers said that they were satisfied with the way in which Chandigarh administration implementing MDMS. In contrast, about (34 per cent) teachers said that the need of improvement of quality and quantity (not satisfied), and about (24 per cent) teachers opined that there is a need to change the menu (not satisfied). Based on the above information it can be concluded that the major proportion of the teachers were not satisfied. Only in-charge teachers of school based kitchens (8 per cent) expressed full satisfaction (Table 4.55).

Table 4.55: In-charge Teachers Level of Satisfaction about Implementation of MDM in Chandigarh

Opinion	*Number of MDM In-Charge Teachers (Number of Sample Schools)*	*Percentage*
Satisfied	17	34.0
Need Improvement of Quality and Quantity (not satisfied)	17	34.0
Change menu (not satisfied)	12	24.0
Fully Satisfied	4	8.0
Total	**50**	**100.0**

Source: Field Survey Data.

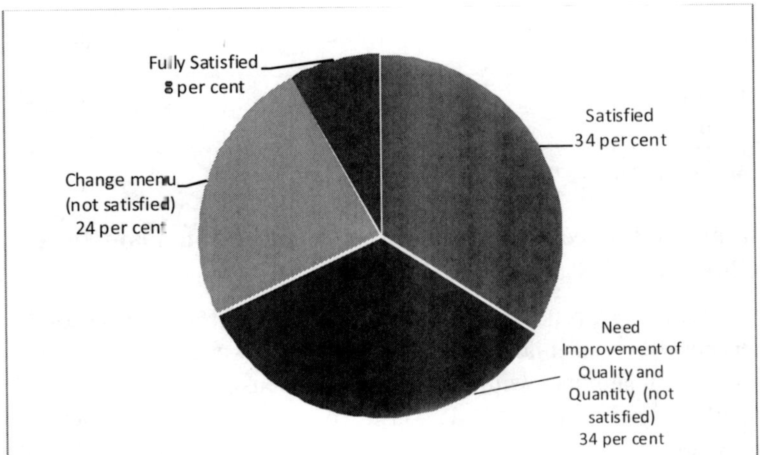

Source: Field Survey Data.

Fig. 4.11: In-charge Teachers Level of Satisfaction about Implementation of MDM.

Figure 4.11, illustrates that the maximum proportion of the respondent teachers stated that, they are not satisfied and needed improvement of the menu, while lesser proportion of the respondents satisfied with the menu.

The Kind of Food, Children Generally Waste

Table 4.56, indicates that the dominant majority (66 per cent) of the teachers felt that, children don't waste food. About (14 per cent) of the teachers said that children waste chana dal, while (6 per cent) teacher stated they don't allow children to waste food, the remaining said that children waste white rice, pulses, Parantha, Yellow Rice, and chapatti.

Table 4.56: The Kind of Food Item (MDM) Children Generally Waste

Type of Food	*Number of MDM In-Charge Teachers (Number of Sample Schools)*	*Percentage*
Arhar Dal	2	4.0
Chana Dal	7	14.0
White Rice	2	4.0
Pulse, White Rice	1	2.0
Don't Allow	3	6.0
Parantha	1	2.0
Yellow Rice, Parantha	1	2.0
Don't Waste	33	66.0
Total	**50**	**100.0**

Source: Field Survey Data.

Reasons for Wastage and Non-Consumption Food by the Children

Table 4.57, reflects that the larger proportion (66 per cent) of the teachers said that children don't waste food. However, all the teachers were not unanimous with regard to the reasons for wastage of food. While (16 per cent) revealed no taste, (6 per cent) teachers stated that they don't allow children to waste, (4 per cent) said food not well-cooked, while the remaining (4 per cent) of the teachers expressed thin consistency of pulses (more water content).

Table 4.57: Reasons for Wastage of MDM by the Children from Their Respective Share

Reasons	*Number of MDM In-charge Teachers (Number of Sample Schools)*	*Percentage*
Don't Waste	33	66.0
No Taste	8	16.0
Don't Allow to Waste	3	6.0
Don't Like	2	4.0
Not Well Cooked	2	4.0
Thin Consistency of Pulses (more water content)	2	4.0
Total	**50**	**100.0**

Source: Field Survey Data.

Figure 4.12, demonstrates that, the maximum number of in-charge teachers stated that certain proportion of the children don't take food due to not well cooked, no taste, thin consistency of pulses, children don't like etc.

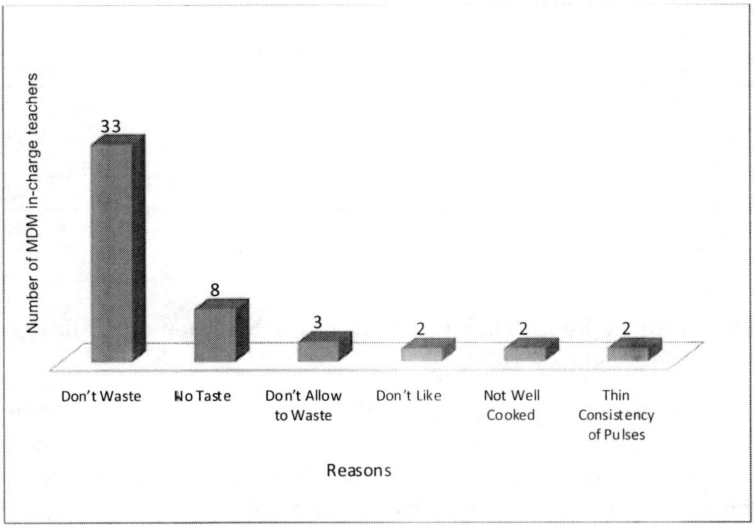

Source: Field Survey Data.

Fig. 4.12: Reasons for Wastage of MDM by the Children from Their Respective Share.

Children Preference of Menu Being Supplied in the Schools

Table 4.58, demonstrates that more than half of the (56 per cent) respondent teachers said that children fond of Karhi pakora and veg pulav, (10 per cent) felt children like White chana and black chana, while (6 per cent) said they like Karhi Rajma and White Chana, (4 per cent) each stated children like Karhi pakora, Pulav, Rajma Rice, White Chana, Parantha, Black Chana, (2 per cent) each said that they like White Chana, Karhi pakora, Mah Dal and White Chana Rice.

Table 4.58: Children Preference of Menu Being Supplied in Schools

Menu	*Number of MDM In-charge Teachers (Number of Sample Schools)*	*Percentage*
Karhi Pakora, Veg pulav	28	56.0
Karhi Pakora, Pulav, White chana, Black chana	5	10.0
Karhi Pakora, Pulav, Rajma Rice, White Chana	2	4.0
Karhi Pakora, Prantha, Black Chana	2	4.0
Karhi pakora, Rajma, White Chana	3	6.0
Karhi pakora, Pulav, Prantha	2	4.0
Rajma Rice, Karhi Rice	4	8.0
Rajma, Karhi pakora, White and Black Chana	3	6.0
White Chana, Karhi Pakora	1	2.0
White Chana, Rice	1	2.0
Total	**50**	**100.0**

Source: Field Survey Data.

The Kind of Food That the Maximum Number of Children Not Interested to Eat

Table 4.59, reveals that the majority (56 per cent) of the children don't like Chana dal, white rice, (12 per cent) don't like Arhar dal, Rice, (10 per cent) don't like mixed dal, Chana dal, while (8 per cent) stated that children are interested in the whole menu, among them 4 teachers are the in-charges of school based kitchens.

Table 4.59: The Type of Food (MDM) Children Not Interested to Eat in the School

Menu	*Number of MDM In-charge Teachers (Number of Sample Schools)*	*Percentage*
Arhar dal, Rice	6	12.0
Chana dal, white rice	28	56.0.
Dal Prantha	1	2.0
Mixed dal, chana dal	5	10.0
Gia dal, prantha	2	4.0
Kichidi	1	2.0
Black chana, Arhar dal	1	2.0
Zeera rice	2	4.0
Interested the whole menu	4	8.0
Total	**50**	**100.0**

Source: Field Survey Data.

Reasons for Non-consumption of MDM

Table 4.60, shows that majority (34 per cent) of the teachers stated that children were not interested in eating MDM due to no-taste, (26 per cent) said children don't like menu, (10 per cent) stated repetition of pulses, and only (10 per cent) teachers said that they like the whole menu. Thin consistency of pulses (more water content), no variety, no vegetables in pulses, not appealing for students, not a good combination of menu, repetition of pulses, eat similar food at home also were the other reasons.

Table 4.60: Reasons for No Interest to Consume MDM

Menu Not Interested	*Number of MDM In-charge Teachers (Number of Sample Schools)*	*Percentage*
Don't Like	13	26.0
No Taste	17	34.0
Repetition of Pulses	5	10.0
Whole Menu Is Good	5	10.0

(Contd...)

Not Properly Cooked	3	6.0
Thin Consistency of Pulses	2	4.0
No Vegetables in Pulses	1	2.0
Not Appealing for Students	1	2.0
Not Good Combination of Menu	1	2.0
Not Stated Any Reason	1	2.0
Same food available at Home Also	1	2.0
Total	**50**	**100.0**

Source: Field Survey Data.

Conclusion

The journey of Implementation of Mid-Day Meal Scheme in Chandigarh is in mid-way, it has to do more to reach a satisfactory level. In addition to the central government grant, UT spending a large amount of money as subsidy. There is much scope for further improvement of quality and service delivery. Involvement of parents is necessary for fixing menu. Reduce infrastructural bottlenecks on war foot basis. Instead of distribution of food from centralised kitchens, it is better to decentralise kitchens for better supervision and to increase nutritional standards. Involvement of NGOs should be a welcome step for better implementation.

5

Rashtriya Swasthya Bima Yojna

Introduction

About 20 per cent of the world's population has adequate social security coverage by virtue of working in the organised sector, while the remaining workings in unorganised sector are not covered under social security benefits. They are vulnerable at the workplace and at the place of residence. Less than 10 per cent of the workers in the least developed nations are covered by social security (International Labour Organisation, 2010). The major challenge facing the world today is how to protect workers working in informal and non-standard employment relationships through social security coverage, Jeemol Unni (2003).

Health is a vital element of social security, it is an absolute responsibility of a welfare state, to be provided to its citizens on a priority basis. Health security can be described as ensuring low exposure to risk and providing access to healthcare services at free of cost/at the subsidised and affordable price to all citizens, Chronic Poverty Report (2008-09). In India less than one-sixth of the total population have access to affordable healthcare, for the rest medical help is often inaccessible and beyond their reach. Too often the cost of staying alive pushes one-quarter of Indians below the poverty line and hospitalisation results in indebtedness, Devadasan, (2011).

In India, the unorganised sector accounts for (92.8 per cent) of the total workforce i.e. of about 460.22 million (NSSO 66th round).

Although there are some state-assisted and/or promoted schemes for social security for workers in the informal sector, but the coverage has not been more than (6 per cent) of the total (NCEUS, 2007). In addition to the breakdown of the joint family system, the incidence of poverty, unable them to made social security arrangements at their own level, moreover informal jobs are temporary, menial and carry low earnings. Neither the state nor the employers take healthcare of the vulnerable working poor because they don't have legal protection. Illness causes an increase in out of pocket expenditure; loss of assets, reduction of earning capacity which thrown into a debt trap, ultimately made them impossible to come out of the vicious circle of poverty. The National Sample Survey Organisation NSSO (2004) had reported that 65 per cent of India's poor get into debt and one per cent fall below the poverty line due to sickness.

The healthy human resource is really a valuable asset for the progressive development of a nation. Provision of healthcare is an absolute responsibility of a welfare state; it is a basic infrastructure to be provided by the government to its citizens. Though after independence healthcare facilities have widely expanded, still public healthcare expenditure is at very low level and not accessible to vulnerable sections. A number of health insurance schemes like Arogya Shree, Yeshashwini schemes etc. have been implemented by state governments but, in addition to limited coverage, there are flaws in design and implementation of these schemes. One of the major insecurities that the informal workers and their families are facing is illness and hospitalisation. Keeping in view the risk and unaffordability of the vulnerable sections to meet the growing healthcare expenditure, the central government thought of health insurance is one of the effective ways of providing protection. Ministry of Labour and Employment, Government of India has started a National Health Insurance Scheme (Public Private Partnership model) in the year 2008 for unorganised sector workers and Below Poverty Line (BPL) population; it is called as Rashtriya Swasthya Bima Yojana.The operation of the scheme involves three stages – enrollment, hospital transactions and monitoring.

The another objective is to provide access and improve utilisation of healthcare services by these households. RSBY is a novel attempt in the country to provide such coverage to the resource-poor families in the entire country. While there have been some evaluations of RSBY in terms of enrollment and utilisation by Nandi *et al* (2012); Devadasan N. (2011); Selvaraj, S. and Karan, A. K. (2009); Selvaraj, S. and Karan, A. K. (2011) and Das and Leino (2011).

As of now, the scheme is operational in 398 districts of 25 states. There are 10116 hospitals empanelled across these states out of which 5941 are private sector hospitals and 4175 are public sector hospitals. A total of 3.75 crore card holders, providing coverage to a total of 11.25 crore beneficiaries at an average premium of approximately ₹ 400. A total of 25 lakh beneficiaries has availed hospitalisation services at an average claim payout of approximately ₹ 5000. About 22 lakh people were treated under the scheme every year. The average cost per treatment is around ₹ 4000 (Government of India, 2014).

The objective of RSBY is to provide protection to BPL households from financial liabilities arising out of health shocks that involve hospitalisation. Beneficiaries under RSBY are entitled to hospitalisation coverage upto ₹ 30,000 for most of the diseases that require hospitalisation. The insurer will get the smart card every year by paying ₹ 30 as registration fee. The smart card is divisible in use, portable and valid all over the country in all the empanelled hospitals; it is more convenient to migrant workers. Family members can get more than one card but total amount not to exceed ₹ 30,000. Insured members need not pay cash payment for treatment of diseases covered under this scheme. Medicines, laboratory tests, food, lodging, etc. are covered at package rates, the payment of which is made by the insurance company to the hospital. Pre-existing conditions are covered from day one and there is no age limit. Insurance coverage extends to five members of the family which include the head of the households, spouse, and up to three dependents. One day pre-hospitalisation and five days post-hospitalisation expenses covered under this scheme. Transport expenses ₹ 100 per hospitalisation and the maximum of 1000 per annum will be paid and the same will be deducted from total package of ₹ 30,000. The premium to the insurer selected by the state government on the basis of a competitive bidding. Premium will be borne by central and state government in the ratio of 75:25 between central and state/UTs and 90:10 in the case of J and K and northeast states.

Enrolled patients of Rashtriya Swasthya Bima Yojna can avail treatment from the empanelled Government/ESI/Private hospitals from anywhere in India based on the package rates fixed. It is the responsibility of the State Government to verify the eligibility of the beneficiary BPL workers and their family members and furnish the details to the insurance provider. Each of the beneficiary family will be issued a smart card and each member included in the card becomes eligible for insured medical care. Existing diseases will also be covered in the schemes. Cashless service is envisaged in the schemes. As regards insurance provider those companies in both public and private sector are to be considered and the selection will be through competitive bidding process.

Rashtriya Swasthya Bima Yojna (RSBY) has been faced with multiple weaknesses from the operational front, which has led to the low accessibility of the scheme by the beneficiaries. Some of the key weaknesses observed are: (1) there is a conflict of interest with the Insurance Company conducting enrollment, empanelment/de-empanelment of hospitals as well as the insurance claims settlements, in some cases through the Third Party Administrators (TPAs), (2) The different software at the field level e.g. Transaction Management Software (TMS), was flawed, leading to no data or inaccurate data being reported, (3) There were no Key Performance Indicators defined for monitoring the scheme, (4) Lack of checks and balances at the operational level have led to multiple frauds in the scheme, (5) The TPA's have been operating the scheme at various states, whereas the contract was signed with the insurance company, this has led to instances where the states had to coordinate with the TPA, who has no stake in RSBY and (6) Inadequate staffing of the SNA is one of the key issues observed in RSBY.

Rashtriya Swasthya Bima Yojna (RSBY) committee final draft report (Government of India, 2014) stated the following weaknesses i.e. Fraudulent admissions, conversion of outpatient cases to inpatient cases, high incidence of day-care procedures, deliberate blocking of higher-priced packages to claim higher amounts, blocking of multiple packages even though not required, connivance with beneficiaries to swipe the cards even without any need for treatment, non-payment of transportation charges, not dispensing post-hospitalisation medication, showing medical management cases as non-invasive surgeries, Impersonation in connivance with cardholder and hospitals, replacing fingerprints fraudulently at district kiosk, addition of outsiders as family members and inclusion of biometrics, irregular or inordinately delayed synching of transactions to avoid investigations, treatment of diseases which a hospital is not equipped for, showing admission in ICU though treatment is given in general/private wards.

Status of RSBY Scheme in Chandigarh

RSBY scheme has started its implementation in Chandigarh w.e.f. 1-4-2009, a total number of five hospitals empanelled (three government and two private). Private hospitals felt it is not a profitable deal to admit RSBY patients, at the package rates decided by the government. A total number of 7865 i.e. 5854 BPL and 2011 Building and other Construction Workers (BOCW) registered under this scheme. BPL households paid a registration fee of ₹ 30 per annum, but on behalf of BOCW, registration fee was paid by the labour department of UT administration Chandigarh. Insurance company pay fee to the service provider Third Party Administrator (TPA), for preparing smart cards, data recording, communicating and registering the UT government identified targeted (eligible) population (Statistical Abstract, 2015).

Premium amount of ₹ 387 per annum per person is fixed on the basis of competitive bidding, National insurance company is the lowest bidder, hence contract is given to this company, thereby medical claims including transport expenses of not more than ₹ 30,000 per family per annum will be paid by the insurance company to the hospitals on behalf of the enrolled (if RSBY card holder admitted as inpatient). A total number of 48 patients admitted, a total amount of ₹ 37,45,706 paid to the national insurance company as a premium by the government for 15 months.

Table 5.1: Statement of Accounts of RSBY Scheme in Chandigarh since its inception

Year	*Number of enrolled units* (₹)	*Premium per household (card)* (₹)	*Total Premium paid by the government* (₹)	*Number (Patients admitted) of Claims settled by the insurance company*	*Amount paid by the insurance company to the hospitals* (₹)	*Fee paid to TPA by the insurance company* (₹)	*Profit* (₹)
2009-2010	5407	501.02	27,09,028	NA	NA	NA	NA
2010-2011	4913	537.63	26,41,398	NA	NA	NA	NA
2011-2012 2012-2013	Scheme suspended	Scheme suspended	Scheme suspended	Scheme suspended	Scheme suspended	Scheme suspended	Scheme suspended
1-10-2013 to 31-12-2014 (for 15 months)	5854 BPL +2011 (Building and Other Construction Workers)=7865	476.25 (Rs 387 per annum+ for 3 months)	37,45,706 (To the National Insurance Company)	48	2,54,000	1,051,944 (Good Health plan limited)	24,98,750 (To the National Insurance Company)
W.e.f. 1-1-2015 Scheme suspended	NA	NA	NA	NA	NA	NA	NA

Source: Office of the National Insurance Company, and Labour Commissioner.

DISCUSSION

Methodology

This study is based on both primary and secondary data sources. Field survey is conducted in the year 2015 among 250 sample respondent households (first time registered 138, second time registered 112) who are residing in slums and shanties in UT Chandigarh (in all the three administrative regions). Households interviewed by following clustered, systematic random sampling method by using structured questionnaire by personal visit at the place of residence. Information also acquired from nodal officers of the empanelled hospitals, officials of insurance companies and labour department.

Geographical Selection of the Sample Respondents

Table 5.2, shows that, total of 250 sample respondents selected from different slum areas based on the systematic random sampling method. The larger majority 129 (51.6 per cent) of the respondents were selected from EWS colony, Dhanas, 68 (27.2 per cent) taken from 4 No. Colony, Industrial Area, while 22 (8.8 per cent) respondents taken from New Indira Colony, Mani Majra, 19 (7.6 per cent) taken from Janata Colony Sector 25, the remaining from Sanjay Labour Colony Industrial Area, Kalyan Colony Kudda Jassu and Bhat Colony Mauli Jagra.

Table 5.2: Geographical Distribution of the Sample Respondents

Name of the Cluster (Slum)	*Number of Respondents*	*Percentage*
EWS Colony, Dhanas	129	51.6
4 No. Colony, Industrial Area	68	27.2
New Indira Colony, Mani Majra	22	8.8
Janata Colony, Sector 25	19	7.6
Sanjay Labour Colony, Industrial Area	9	45.0
Kalyan Colony, Kudda Jassu	2	0.8
Bhat Colony, Mauli Jagra	1	0.4
Total	**250**	**100.0**

Source: Field Survey Data.

Categories of the Workers (Respondents)

Table 5.3, indicates that the greater segment (46 per cent) of the respondents are casual labour. while (28.4 per cent) respondents are self-employed, about (20 per cent) are regular workers and the remaining (5.6 per cent) are unemployed.

Table 5.3: Number and Category of Workers (Head of the Households / Respondents)

Category of Workers	*Number of Respondents*	*Percentage*
Casual Labour	115	46.0
Self-Employed	71	28.4
Regular Workers	50	20.0
Unemployed	14	5.6
Total	**250**	**100.0**

Source: Field Survey Data.

Figure 5.1, reveals that, all the RSBY respondents are informal labour, the maximum proportion of them are casual labour, while lesser proportion of them are unemployed.

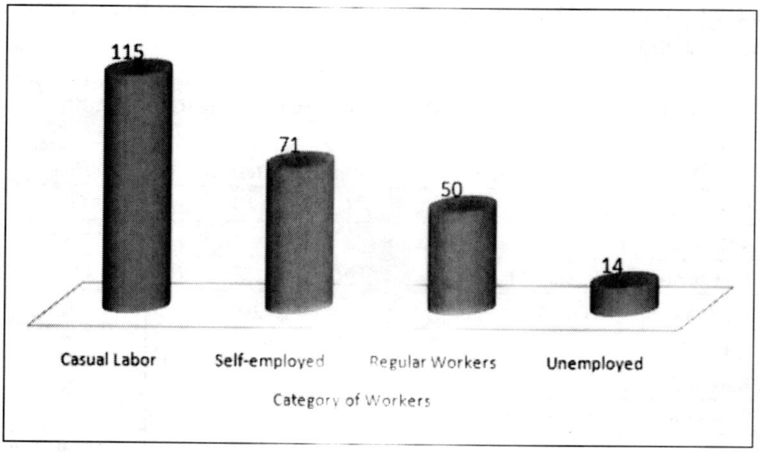

Source: Field Survey Data.

Fig. 5.1: RSBY respondents and their Category of work.

Status of Availing Benefits under RSBY

Information about the names and location of the empanelled hospitals are essential to rush the hospital during emergencies without facing hurdles and wastage of time. That the larger segment (65.2 per cent) of the respondents secured the names of the hospitals at the time of registration which is supplied by the TPAs, the remaining (34.8 per cent) respondents did not get any information about the hospitals. There are three government hospitals and two private hospitals empanelled in Chandigarh. Private hospitals don't treat RSBY patients because the amount of packages fixed by the government is very less when compared to market rates. Inaccurate/ no availability of information caused wastage of time and money of the poor patients. Most of the respondents are illiterates; they approached PGI and got disappointment because PGI is not an empanelled one.

Mere enrollment doesn't serve any purpose. Among the registered respondents, the predominant majority (66.4 per cent) of the respondents not admitted to any hospital as inpatients, about (30.4 per cent) respondents admitted as inpatients during the card validity period but not availed benefits under this scheme, while only (3.2 per cent) of the respondents admitted and availed benefits under this scheme. Sample respondents stated a number of reasons for not availing benefits under this scheme. Table 5.4, indicates that (14.4 per cent) respondents stated that staff in the hospital not co-operative to get treatment under this scheme, about (7.6 per cent) respondents said that their cards expired, about (5.6 per cent) of the sample respondents revealed that, hospital staff asked BPL card instead of RSBY card for free treatment (reasons unknown). Precariously (1.6 per cent) respondents said that they have no adequate knowledge about how to avail benefits by using RSBY card, three respondents stated card lost/forget to bring/card not opened in the hospital counter due to software/hardware problems.

Table 5.4: Reasons for Benefits Not Availed Under RSBY

Reasons	*Number of Respondents*	*Percentage*
Card is expired	19	7.6
Staff in the hospital not co-operated	36	14.4
Card lost/Forget to bring	2	0.8

(Contd...)

Card not opened due to software/ hardware problems	1	0.4
Hospital staff asked BPL card instead of RSBY card for free treatment	14	5.6
Not having adequate knowledge about the use of RSBY card	4	1.6
Benefits availed	8	3.2
Not admitted as inpatient	166	66.4
Total	**250**	**100.0**

Source: Field Survey Data.

Figure 5.2, illustrates that about 65 respondents/ family members admitted as inpatients in the hospital during their card validity period, among them, the maximum number of respondents stated that, staff in the hospital are not co-operated to avail the benefits under the scheme. Only eight respondents/ family members availed benefits under the scheme.

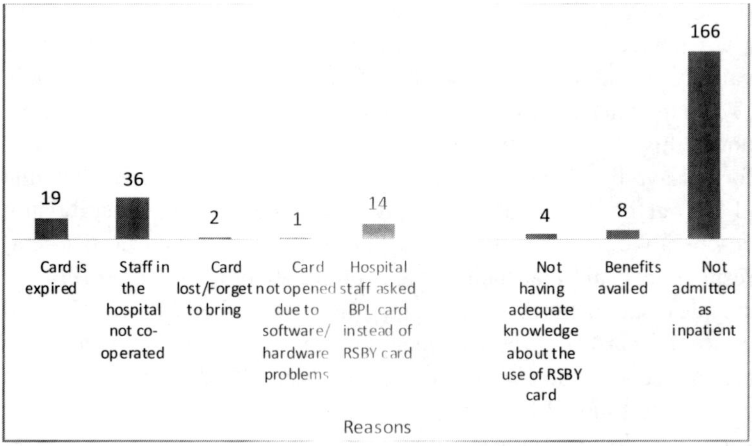

Source: Field Survey Data.

Fig. 5.2: Reasons for Benefits Not Availed Under RSBY.

The interested and eligible residents can register every year by paying ₹ 30 as registration fee. Though the larger proportion of the respondents not secured benefits under this scheme, but they want to register again hoping to get benefits under this scheme in future. More than half (56 per cent) of the respondents said they are willing to register again, while (44 per cent) said that they don't want to register again because (1) Hospital staff says that "RSBY card has no value, you go and meet those people who gave this card to you", (2) it is the wastage of registration fee, (3) lost one day wage and time by standing in queue for registration and (4) don't know to whom do we meet in the hospital for treatment under this scheme.

Expenditure Incurred as Inpatients

Out Of Pocket (OOP) health expenditure which makes poor people in the grip of the vicious circle of poverty. Table 5.5, indicates that during the validity period of the card (46.05 per cent) of the respondent in patients spent money for treatment in the range of ₹ 1000-5000, while (28.94 per cent) spent ₹ 5001 to 10,000, about (26 per cent) of the respondents spent ₹ 10001-15000, this kind of forced expenditure causes debt trap or distress sale of assets thereby further causes destitution.

Table 5.5: Expenditure Incurred As Inpatients Due to Not Availing Benefits under This Scheme

Expenditure Incurred (₹)	*Number of Respondent card holders (admitted as inpatients)*	*Percentage*
1000-5000	35	46.05
5001-10000	22	28.94
10001-15000	4	5.26
15001-20000	2	2.63
20001-25000	3	3.94
25001-30000	4	5.26
50001-55000	2	2.63
55001-60000	1	1.31
1 lakh	2	2.63
2 lakhs	1	1.31
Total	**76**	**100.0**

Source: Field Survey Data.

Knowledge on Guidelines of the Scheme

Possession of knowledge about guidelines of this scheme will make easy to get benefits. That the predominant majority (74.4 per cent) of the respondents know free treatment available in the hospital up to ₹ 30,000 only, about (16.4 per cent) respondents know free treatment available in the hospital but don't know the amount; the remaining respondents know more than one guidelines of the scheme. Interestingly only one card holder knows all the guidelines of the scheme i.e. free treatment available in the hospital up to ₹ 30,000, transport cost ₹ 100 per admit, one day pre-hospitalisation and five days post-hospitalisation expenses, card is valid for one year only, the month of beginning and month of expiring card, benefit only for inpatient etc.

Perceptions of the Admitted Patients (RSBY Card Holders)

Among the 250 households (RSBY card holders) only eight respondents received benefits as a result of admitted as inpatients. Among the admitted patients only (37.5 per cent) got transport charges, the remaining (62.5 per cent) denied this opportunity. Except two patients admitted on the spot; the remaining waited minimum of one hour and a maximum of three hours for getting admission under this scheme. The great majority (87.5 per cent) of the respondents said that information about the cost involved for treatment is not disclosed by the hospital staff to the family members, while only one patient stated that information is disclosed by the staff. Neither the patients nor the family members got information about the money balance left in the smart card account, though it is the right of the patients to know. Hospital staff said that "your work is over, what is the need of knowing it, you go"; this type of attitude of the staff nullifies the very objectives of the scheme.

The majority (62.5 per cent) of the respondent patients said that staff at the RSBY help desk in the hospital not polite and helpful, while (37.5 per cent) revealed that they are polite and helpful. Interestingly almost all the patients said that hospital supplied food at free of cost during the stay in the hospital, it can be appreciated. As per the provision of this scheme, the hospital is supposed to pay one-day pre- and five days post-hospitalisation expenses to the admitted patients. Almost all the patients said no such expenses paid to them, is the index of not taking a serious note about the guidelines of the scheme. A great majority (62.5 per cent) of the patients said that medicines not given and tests not conducted at free of cost, while three patients felt that these things are done at free of cost. Almost (100 per cent) patients stated that post-treatment their health has improved is a positive sign of availability of good treatment in the hospitals. About three-fourth majority (75 per cent) of the patients said that they are satisfied with the implementation of the scheme, while (25 per cent) patients revealed that they are not satisfied with the implementation of the scheme.

(vi) Impact of RSBY

The impact of RSBY on the reduction of institutional and non-institutional medical expenditure is not optimistic; these expenses are still quite high. Medical expenses seem to be catastrophic for the poor families. For the resource poor households, any amount of money which is going for their healthcare threatens their households' basic needs. A number of respondents stated that this scheme causes loss of registration fee, loss of one or two man days for standing in the queue for registration. The very negligible number of respondents secured some of the benefits (but not full benefits) under this scheme. A reasonable proportion of registered RSBY card holders even though admitted as inpatients, failed to utilise services under this scheme, which caused to incur Out Of Pocket (OOP) expenditure. Insurance companies cropped huge profits by way of premium paid to them by the government on behalf of registered RSBY card holders is the matter of great concern.

Conclusion

Providing health security to informal labour will reduce out of pocket expenditure and increases per head productivity. In Chandigarh, insurance providers secured more benefit than the intended beneficiaries. Create awareness about different provisions of the scheme for better utilisation of benefits. There are exclusion and inclusion errors in identification of eligible beneficiaries. If RSBY scheme applicable to outpatients we can reduce out of pocket expenditure and indebtedness, thereby poor people can spend their hard earnings on education, communication, transport and nutritious food.

6

Policy Initiatives

Public Distribution System

On the basis of various findings and observations, the following recommendations have been made in the effective implementation of this scheme.

- There should be strict supervision by the external body other than food supply department on the functioning of Fair Price Shops in the city.
- Fix living wages equivalent to wages of class IV employees / timely pay commission to the Fair Price Shops owners on the sale of the quantity and also increase the commission to nullify price raise and to stop leakages.
- Travel and transport costs can be reduced by decentralisation of ration depots at different places in the city.
- Leakages, fear of uncertainty and wastage of time in standing longer hours in the queue will be minimised by fixing distribution to a fixed number of households per day and by fixing a time for distribution.
- If the implementation of the newly proposed direct cash transfer system is warranted, there should be a mechanism which is operated by the government to make available these essential commodities at reasonable prices.

- If the implementation of the newly proposed direct cash transfer system is warranted, there should be a proper control on prices and black marketing of the essential commodities.
- Ensure monthly payment of the subsidy amount by making an adjustment in the subsidy amount at the current rate of inflation.
- Distribution of goods irregularly and distributing backlog causes more burdens on the consumers because their earning capacity is limited, they cannot save such an amount.
- During school hours school going children should not be allowed to stand in queue.
- Sometimes migrants have to rush to their home town due to any reason, in such cases backlog ration should be given if he/ she turned up within three months.
- Ration cards which are given 15 to 20 years back are on mutilation stage, hence new ration cards should be issued in the place of old by maintaining proper columns.
- Every month concerned columns in the ration cards should be filled properly; otherwise action should be taken on the FPS owners.
- Unique numbered smart card should be given to get ration anywhere in India from any FPS, will be useful to the migrant poor.
- Computerise all Fair Price Shops by giving proper training to reduce leakages (what it is prevailing in Kerala and Karnataka).
- There should be proper check by weights and measures department on machines being used by FPS owners.
- Mixing good and bad quality grains can be avoided by making frequent checks and return back poor quality grains to FCI, in this connection transport cost and labour costs should be borne by the government.
- By distributing all the entitled items on the same day wastage of time can be stopped.
- Married people should be given ration cards, even though they are living with their parents.

- There is mixing of Gamaxin and other types of preservatives in food grains, it should be avoided to stop health implication on females and children.
- There should be an option to refuse poor quality of ration by the beneficiaries, in such case backlog should be given during next month otherwise subsidy amount should be given.
- There should be PDS adalat once per every month at concerned FPS to solve the problems of customers; otherwise customers have to run around the offices by wasting their man-days and money.
- Date and time of distribution of ration should be written properly on the notice boards of FPS by the FPS owners at least before three days, it should be made mandatory to avoid uncertainty and fear among poor people.
- Distribute ration every month before 15th because during these days people have money to buy items.
- There should be parity in quantity of PDS items distributed and actually made an entry in the ration card.
- Ration should be properly stored, instead of keeping in open air.
- Net subsidy amount available to consumers can be enhanced by reducing waiting time in queue, time for travel (reduce opportunity cost foregone) and expenditure for travel and transport.
- Jan Dhan Yojna, Aadhar and Mobile numbers (JAM) trinity technologies can be used to combat illegal diversion of goods and strengthen the present food security system.
- SMS should send at free of cost by the banks to the beneficiaries about the amount of subsidy money credited in their accounts, if direct benefit scheme implemented.
- There should be a clear mention about the subsidy amount for the concerned month, through SMS and print on bank pass book to avoid any confusion.

Mid-Day Meal Scheme

On the basis of various findings and observations, the following recommendations have been made in the effective implementation of this scheme.

- Repetition of one or other type of pulses should be avoided on a consequent day.
- Inculcate habits of washing hands before and after the meal by providing liquid soup to the children in the school.
- On special days a special menu should be provided.
- Sweet dish and seasonal fruits and dairy items should be given at least once per week.
- Seasonal green vegetables should be given every day.
- Food should not be undercooked/overcooked.
- If food is not proper, MDM in-charges should have freedom to send back to the concerned hotel.
- There should be part-time employees to handle the activities of MDM scheme in the school so that he or she can involve more.
- By increase in quality of food, more children will be attracted towards MDM and they consume the whole entitled quantity thereby wastages can be averted.
- At least one south Indian food should be introduced to love the food culture of other states.
- Distribution of quantity of same food to a large number of students than it is ordered for is taking place, it implies each child is taking less than the entitled quantity, hence by an increase in quality, this problem can be solved.
- There should be weighing of food in the school at the time of delivery, hence it should be done to plug loopholes if any.
- Girls are more health sensitive than boys, the larger proportion of girls bring lunch from their home than boys, hence their proportion of taking MDM can be enhanced by increasing quality and hygiene.

- There are no separate rooms constructed in any school (not having a school-based kitchen) to store the food which is received from hotels, the present rooms are not hygienic hence it is suggested to construct standard all-weather rooms for this purpose.
- By the time food distribution starts, it becomes cold because preparation end every day before 6 am at centralised kitchens, hence facilities should be provided to keep food in hot condition.
- Preparation of food at school-based kitchens having good features like good quality, timely availability, and supervision by the principal, flexibility in the menu. The proportion of children availing MDM will be more if food is in hot condition/ hygienic and nutritious.
- If school-based kitchens construction is not possible in every school, at least one kitchens for a cluster of three schools should be maintained and entrust kitchen responsibilities to a full-time employee, not to the teachers.
- Food menu composition should be changed at least once per year.
- The maximum number of children doesn't like pili dal and white rice, hence it should be avoided.
- Food distribution should start from 12 noon instead of 11 am, because children who had their breakfast at home cannot eat the entitled quantity.
- There should be a rotation of MDM in-charge post once per every three or five years and pay remuneration of a certain amount to feel it is not an extra burden.
- Parents' suggestion should be taken into account while fixing menu, timings of food etc.
- Contract should be cancelled to those hotels not up to the mark in maintaining quality, punctuality and hygiene.
- The maximum number of children likes Karhi Pakora, Veg Pulav; hence its frequency should be increased.

- The monthly wages of MDM workers should be fixed at least by paying minimum wages, If so they will work with dedication. At least one paid holiday per month should be given to them.
- MDM workers should not be entrusted duties other than related to MDM, like cleaning of school premises and classrooms, peon duties, maintain discipline in the classes when the teacher is on leave etc.
- Create confidence among the parents by maintaining taste, hygiene, and quality, then only the proportion of children intake of MDM can be increased.
- MDM facility can be extended to those children studying 9th class in non-model (Hindi medium) schools located nearby slum areas.
- Per head expenditure allocation should be increased keeping growing prices under consideration.
- Reputed NGOs expect no profit or less profit, hence food preparation and supply responsibility should be entrusted to one NGO per every 10 schools for decentralisation and to increase the quality of food.

Rashtriya Swasthya Bima Yojana

The findings from this study strongly recommend that

- Knowledge regarding the scheme should be adequately imparted to the registered intended beneficiaries through various mass media channels.
- Staff in government hospital feel treating RSBY patients involved some procedure, also a reason to avoid RSBY patients; hence incentives should be given to the concerned hospital staff to take proper care.
- It should be mentioned on the top of every card, that the date of starting and date of expiry of the card to avoid confusion.
- Non-functioning of the machine causes some of the patients loose the chance of getting the benefit, hence proper care should be taken for infrastructure.

- After issuing cards, the government should conduct camps to get feedback and to solve the problems if any being encountered by the registered intended beneficiaries.
- Some of the respondents complained that TPAs threatened them "if not registered under RSBY your ration cards will be cancelled", hence no such coercive measures adopted to increase the number of registered people.
- Total premium amount paid by the government is proportionately larger than the number of beneficiaries got the benefit (amount of money paid to hospitals by the insurance company) under this scheme, hence there should be facilitation/information centres in each primary health care centre/ anganwadi to avail the benefit.
- There should be awareness among the doctors and the supporting staff about the provisions of this scheme; hence proper training should be given.
- Maximum numbers of patients visit PGI for inpatient treatment; hence PGI also should be empanelled under this scheme.
- After issuing cards, due to administrative problems, if government suspend the operationalisation of this scheme/ if extension period is given, the same should be widely informed to the registered intended beneficiaries.
- Instances of charging registration fee more than ₹ 30, reported by some of the respondents, it should be stopped further.
- Transport charges of ₹ 100, pre- and post-hospitalisation charges should be paid to the inpatients under this scheme.
- The amount of money utilised and the balance amount of money left in the smart card should be informed to the inpatients or family members.
- Inspite of having a valid card, the number of patients spent money on treatment beyond their capacity; hence proper care should be taken by the hospital administration to treat patients under this scheme.

- Instead of registering every year to get benefits under this scheme, the validity should be increased to three years to stop loss of man-days and reduce expenditure for registration.
- Benefits under this scheme should be extended to outpatients also.
- In every empanelled hospital at registration counter 'Help Desk for RSBY Patients' should be written in English, Hindi and local language.
- TPAs should be available in need to help the patients to get benefits under this scheme.

Conclusion

Poverty anywhere is a danger to prosperity and peace everywhere. Speedy economic growth and macroeconomic stability may not be sufficient, but necessary for reduction of poverty in the long run. In addition to accountability of the administrative machinery, political commitment and transparency are essential. Information and communication technology should be used to reduce leakages in implementing anti-poverty programmes. Implementing safety nets with better urban governance is a necessary condition for empowering the urban poor and improving their opportunities and security. Poor people should be allowed to participate in the decision-making, on the matters related to them. Reduce procedural formalities to get credit from public sector banks, to achieve financial inclusion. Low priced houses should be constructed and allotted to slum dwellers at free of cost by dismantling slums to improve living standards. Prices of essential goods should be stabilised while guaranteeing minimum earnings. Urban labour market unfavourable to informal workers due to their oversupply, hence strengthen the present employment generation programmes in rural areas to reduce rural–urban distress labour migration, thereby equilibrium in the urban labour market can be achieved. Introduce low skill-based labour intensive techniques to absorb unemployed job seekers. Enhance the productive capacity of the workers by imparting training for skill formation, which will increase earning capacity, thereby economic growth will be more inclusive, transformative and sustainable.

Bibliography

Afridi, F. (2005), "Mid-Day Meals in Two States; Comparing the Financial and Institutional organisation of the Programme", *Economic and Political Weekly*, Vol. 40, No. 5, April 9, pp. 1528-1534.

Ahuja, Ram (1997), *Social Problems in India*. New Delhi: Rawat Publications.

Ahmad, E. (1991), Social Security and the Poor: Choice for Developing Countries, *World Bank Research Observer* 6 (1),

Alagh, Y.K. (2002), *Globalisation and Agricultural Crisis in India,* Deep and Deep Publishers (P) Ltd, New Delhi.

Amartya Sen .(1995), "Radical Needs and Moderate Reforms" in Jean Dreze and Amartya S, (ed) *Indian Development Selected Regional Perspectives*, Oxford University Press, Mumbai, pp. 1-27.

Amitab, Kundu, Alak N, Sharma (2001), *Informal Sector in India Perspectives and Policies*. Institute of Human Development and Institute of Applied Manpower Research. New Delhi.

Asian Development Bank (2003), Social Protection: Reducing Risks and Increasing Opportunities, Manila: ADB.

Bagai, S. B. (1956), Trends *in Rural Urban Migration in India*, 1901-1951, Indian Economic Conference, Number 15-29.

Bandyopadhyay, D. (1998), "Direct Intervention Programmes For Poverty Alleviation: An Appraisal", *Economic and Political Weekly* 23(26): A77-A88, 24 January.

Bandyopadhyay, K.R. (1997), Poverty alleviation and pro-poor growth in India, *Asian Institute of Transport Development,* New Delhi.

Bhagwati, J. (1988), "Poverty and Public Policy", *World Development* 16(5): 539-55.

Baulch, Bob. (1996), The New Poverty Agenda: A Disputed Consensus. *IDS Bulletin,* 27 (1):1-10.

Bird, K and Deshingkar, P. (2009), '*Circular Migration in India*', ODI Policy Brief No. 4 http://www.odi.org.uk/resources/download/2506.pdf

Bose, Ashish. (1967), "Migration Streams in India", *Population Review* 11: 39-45.

Breman, J. and C. Jerry (eds.) (1979), *Casual Work and Poverty in Third World Cities.* Chichester: John Wiley.

Breman, J. (1996), *Footloose labor- Working in India's Informal Economy*, University Press, Cambridge.

Breman, Jan. (2004), 'The Labouring Poor in India: Patterns of exploitation, Subordination, and Exclusion', Oxford University Press, New Delhi, pp. 194-220.

Cannel, J., B. Dasgupta, R. Balaishley and M. Liptan. (1976), *Migration from Rural Areas: The Evidences from Village Studies.* New Delhi: Oxford University Press.

Carynnyk-Sinclair, N. (1974). *Rural Urban Migration in Developing Countries, 1950-1970. A Survey of the Literature.* Geneva: ILO.

CART (2006), *Measuring Effectiveness of Mid-day Meal Scheme in Rajasthan*, CUTS Centre for Community Action, Research, and Training, Jaipur.

Chen, M., Vanek, J. and Carr, M. (2004), *Mainstreaming Informal Employment and Gender in Poverty Reduction: A Handbook for Policy Makers and Other Stakeholders,* Commonwealth Secretariat, London.

Chelliah, R. J. and Sudarshan, R. (1999), *Income Poverty and Beyond: Human Development in India* (New Delhi, Social Science Press).

Chronic Poverty Research Centre (2008-09), 'Scope for Increasing the Participation of the Chronically Poor in Economic Growth', *Chronic Poverty Report 2008-09,* University of Manchester, Manchester; UK.

Clyde, Mitchel J. (1959), "The Causes of Labour Migration", *Bulletin of the Inter African Labour Institute:* 12-47.

Cornia, G.A. (ed). (2004), *Inequality, growth and poverty in an era of liberalisation and globalisation* (Oxford, Oxford University Press/

United Nations University, World Institute for Development Economics Research). Dasgupta, S. (2002), Organising for Socio-Economic Security in India, Geneva: International Labour Office.

Council for Social Development (2008), *India Social Development Report 2008*. New Delhi: Oxford University Press.

Dantwala, M.L. (1993), Agricultural Policy: Prices and Public Distribution System, *Indian Journal of Agricultural Economics*, Vol. 48, No. 2, April-June.

Das, J., and Leino, J. (2011), Evaluating the RSBY: Lessons from an Experimental Information Campaign. *Economic and Political Weekly*, *46*(32), 85-93.

Davis, M. (2006), *Planet of Slums* (London: Verso).

De Haan, Arjan. (2011), "Inclusive Growth? Labour Migration and Poverty in India", *Working Paper* No. 513. International institute of Social Studies.

Deaton, Angus. (2002), "Is World Poverty Falling?", *Finance and Development*, 39(2): 4-7, June.

Deshingkar, P. and J. Farrington. (2009), Circular Migration and Multi Locational Livelihood Strategies in Rural India. New Delhi: Oxford University Press.

Devadasan, N. (2011), Review of the Rashtriya Swasthya Bima Yojna. *Economic and Political Weekly*, *45*(29), 13-18.

Department for International Development, DFID (2009), 'Eliminating World Poverty: Building Our Common Future.' London: DFID.

Dreze, J. and Sen, A. (1989), *Hunger and Public Action*, Clarendon Press, Oxford.

Dreze, Jean and Geeta Gandhi Kingdon. (2001), "School Participation in Rural India". *Review of Development Economics*, 5(1): 1-24.

Dreze, J. and A. Sen. (1998), *Hunger and Public Action*. Oxford: Oxford University Press.

Eames, Edwin. (1965), "Urbanisation and Rural-Urban Migration in India", *Population Review*, January.

Everett, S. Lee (1966), "A Theory of Migration", *Demography* 3: 47-57.

Gaunde, J. (1976), *Causes and Repercussions of Rural Migration in Developing Countries: A Critical Analysis.* Geneva: World Employment Programme Research, ILO, p.10.

Government of India. (1991). National Commission on Rural Labour, Ministry of Labor and Employment.

————.(2006), *Report on Conditions of Work and Promotion of Livelihoods in Unorganised Sector* (National Commission for Enterprises in the Unorganised Sector), New Delhi.

————.(2008), *Eleventh five-year plan 2007-2012*, Vol. 1, Planning Commission, Oxford University Press, New Delhi.

————.(2009), Report of the expert group to review the methodology for estimation of poverty, Planning Commission, New Delhi.

————.(2009), *India Urban Poverty Report 2009*, Oxford University Press, New Delhi.

————.*2009-2010,* 2010-11, 2011-12, 2012-13, *Economic Survey,* Ministry of Finance, Oxford University Press, New Delhi.

————.(2011), Census Commissioner, New Delhi.

————.(2012), Report of the expert group to recommend the detailed methodology for identification of families living below poverty line in urban areas, Planning Commission of India, S.R. Hashim committee report.

————.(2012), Press note on poverty estimates 2009-10, Planning Commission, New Delhi.

————.(2013), *India Rural Development Report 2012/13*, Ministry of Rural Development (MoRD), New Delhi.

————.(2013), National Food Security Act, Ministry of Law and Justice.

————.(2014), *RSBY Committee Final Draft Report*, New Delhi.

————.(2016), Ministry of school education, Mid Day Meal division.

Gupta, S.P. (1995), "Economic Reforms and its Impact on the Poor", *Economic and Political Weekly* 1188-94, 3 June.

Jain, Jyotsna and Mihir Shah (2005), Mid-day Meal in Madhya Pradesh, *Samaj Pragati Sahyog,* Bagli.

J. Ayeni and M. A. Adelabu, "Improving Learning Infrastructure and Environment for Sustainable Quality Assurance Practice in Secondary Schools in Ondo State, South-West, Nigeria," *International Journal of Research Studies in Education*, Vol. 1, No. 1, 2012, pp. 61-68.

Jayati Ghosh. (2013), 'The strange case of the jobs that did not appear: structural change, employment and social patterns in India' *Presidential address delivered at the Indian Society of Labour Economics 55th annual conference*, held at Jawaharlal Nehru University, New Delhi.

Jha, Pravin. (2010), Less for the Poor, Cover Story, Frontline, March 26.

Joshi, S C. (1994), *Migration to Metropolis*, RBSA Publishers, Raipur, pp. 23-151.

Halfani, Mohamed. (2007), The Urban Face of Poverty: Innovation and New Approaches. Presentation at the conference, *Why Is Urban Assistance Important? Inserting Urban Issues into the Development Agenda*, Comparative Urban Studies Project, and Woodrow Wilson International Center for Scholars, Washington, DC.

Harris, J.R. and M. Todaro. (1970), "Migration Unemployment and Development : A Two Sector Analysis", *American Economic Review* 60: 126-42.

High-Powered Expert Committee. (2011), "Report on Indian Urban Infrastructure and Services", *National Institute of Urban Affairs*, New Delhi.

Institute of Human Development. (2012), *Social and Economic Change in Rural Bihar and the Emerging Policy Framework.* Project sponsored by United Nations Development Programme. New Delhi.

International Labour Organisation. (2005), Growing out of Poverty: How Employment Promotion Improves The Lives of the Urban Poor. *SEED Working Paper No. 74*. International Labour Office Geneva.

————.(2004), *Cities at Work- Employment Promotion to Fight Urban Poverty*. Geneva.

————.(2010), *World Social Security Report 2010–11: Providing coverage in times of crisis and beyond* (Geneva).

————.(2013), International Labour Office, Geneva.

India Development Report. (1999), Kirit S. Parikh (ed). Oxford University Press. New York.

Johri, C.K. and S.M. Pandey. (1978), "Dimensions of Poverty and Incomes Policy", *Indian Journal of Industrial Relations* 14(1): 87-130 (July).

Jeemol Unni. (2003), Informal Employment in India. *Indian Journal of Labour Economics* 50(3).

Jayati Ghosh and C.P. Chandrasekhar. (2006), 'Employment Growth; The Latest Trends, the results of the latest survey of the 61st round covering 2004-05'(17th November 2006 *Business Line*).

Kannan, K.P. (1994), "Leveling Up or Leveling Down? Labour Institutions and Economic Development in India", *Economic and Political Weekly,* 23 July to 29 July.

————.(2008), "Dualism, Informality and Social Inequality", *Presidential Address* at 50th Annual Conference ISLE. Lucknow.

Kannan, K. P. and Pillai N. (2007), 'Social Security in India: The Long Lane Treaded and the Longer Road Ahead towards Universalisation', *MPRA Paper No. 9601*, June 2007, posted on 16 July 2008, online at http://mpra.ub.uni-muenchen.de/9601/.

Karen Coelho, Anant Maringanti. (2012), Urban Poverty in India Tools, Treatment, and Politics at the Neoliberal Turn. *Economic and Political Weekly,* December 1, 2012, Vol. xlviI, nos. 47 and 48.

Kuznets, Simon. (1955), 'Economic Growth and Income Inequality', *American Economic Review* 45:1-28.

Kundu, Amitabh, and Shalini Gupta. (1996), Migration, Urbanisation and Regional Inequality, *Economic and Political Weekly*, Vol. 31, No. 52, Dec. 28.

Kundu, A. and N. Sarangi. (2007), "Migration, Employment Status and Poverty: An Analysis Across Urban Centres," *Economic and Political Weekly*, Vol. 42, No. 4, pp. 299-307.

Kuznets, Simon. (1955), "Economic Growth and Income Inequality", *American Economic Review* 45: 1-28.

Kundu, Amitab and Alak N. Sharma. (2001), *Informal Sector in India Perspectives and Policies*. New Delhi: Institute of Human Development and Institute of Applied Manpower Research.

Kundu, A. (2012), 'Migration and Exclusionary Urbanisation in India', *Economic and Political Weekly*, Vol. 47, No. 26 and 27, pp. 219-227.

Mathur, Beena. (2005), *Situation Analysis of Mid-day Meal Programme in Rajasthan. University of Rajasthan* and UNICEF.

Mahendra Dev, S. (2000), "Economic Reforms Poverty Income Distribution and Employment", *Economic and Political Weekly*, 4-10 March.

Mishra, S.N. (2005*), Poverty and Its Alleviation.* Deep and Deep Publications Pvt Ltd., New Delhi.

Mohan, Rakesh, and Dasgupta, Shubhagata (2005), 'The 21st Century: Asia Becomes Urban', *Economic and Political Weekly*, 40(3), 213-23.

Murthy, KSRK, 'Organic Farming and Food Security", *Business Line*, July 11, 2008.

Mohan, Rakesh and Shubhagato Dasgupta. (2005), "The 21st Century: Asia Becomes Urban", *Economic and Political Weekly* 40(3): 213-23 (15-21 January).

Mukhergi, Sekhar. (2006), *Migration and Urban Decay: Asian Experience* New Delhi: Rawat Publications.

Nandi *et al.* (2012), *A study of Rashtriya Swasthya Bima Yojana in Chhattisgarh, India.* Biomed Central Proceedings, 6 (Suppl 1):o5. Doi: 10.1186/1753-6561-6-S1-O5

National Commission on Rural Labour (1991), Government of India.

Narasimha Reddy D. (2005), 'Challenges of Decent Work in the Globalising World'. *Indian Journal of Labour Economics* . Vol. 48. No.1.

NCEUS (2007), *Report on Conditions of Work and Promotion of Livelihoods in the Unorganised Sector.* The government of India, New Delhi. Also published by academic foundation, New Delhi, www.RSBY.gov.in

Nirathron, Narumol. (2006), *Fighting Poverty from the Street: A Survey of Street Food Vendors in Bangkok,* International Labour Office.

NSSO (2001). *Employment-Unemployment Situation in India 1999-2000*, Round 55th, Report No. 458 – I and II (55/10/2), Ministry of Statistics and Programme Implementation, Government of India, New Delhi.

————.(2002), Unorganised Manufacturing Sector in India; 2000-01- Key Results, *NSSO* 56th *Round (July 2000-June 2001), Report No. 477*, Government of India, New Delhi.

————.(2004-05), on employment and unemployment, Ministry of Statistics, Government of India, New Delhi.

————.(2007-08, 64th round), *Migration in India*, New Delhi: Ministry of Statistics and Programme Implementation, Government of India.

————.(2009-10, 55th and 66th rounds), on employment and unemployment, Ministry of Statistics, Government of India, New Delhi.

————.(2010-11), Employment and unemployment situation in India, report no. 537(66/10/1), *National Statistical Organisation*. Ministry of Statistics and programme implementation, the Government of India, New Delhi.

Overseas Development Institute (2002), Safety Nets and Opportunity Ladders: Addressing Vulnerability and Enhancing Productivity in South Asia, Working Paper 159, and London.

Pratichi Trust. (2005), *Cooked Mid-day Meal Programme in West Bengal – A study in Birbhum District*, Kolkata.

Popola,T S. (1986), *Urbanisation, Rural-Urban Migration and Growth of Informal Sector*. Working Paper No. 51 Giri Institute of Development Studies.

Popola, T. S. (2004), Globalisation Employment and Social Protection, Emerging Perspectives for the Indian Workers, *Indian Journal of Labour Economics* 47 (3).

Rangarajan, C. (2006), "*Employment and growth*", Monograph 2/2006, Madras School of Economics, Chennai.

Ranga Rao, K. and M.S.A. Rao. (1984), *Cities and Slums*. New Delhi: Concept Publishing Company.

Ravallion, M. (1996), "Issues in Measuring and Modeling Poverty", *Economic Journal*. Vol. 106, No. 438, pp. 1328-43.

Ravallion, Martin. (2007), Urban poverty. *Finance and Development* 44 (3).

Ravallian Martin, Shaohua Chen and Prem Sangraula. (2007), *New Evidence on The Urbanisation of Global Poverty'*, policy research paper No. 4199, World Bank, Washington DC.

Rao, V.M. (1998), "Economic Reforms and Poor: Emerging Scenario", *Economic and Political Weekly,* Xxxiii (29 and 30), July 18.

Ravenstein, E G. (1985), the Laws of Migration, *Journal of Royal Statistical Society*.

Rogaly, B., *et al.* (2001), Seasonal migration, social change and migrants rights, lessons from West Bengal. *Economic and Political Weekly*, pp. 4547-58.

Saxena, O.P. (1978), *Rural Urban Migration in India: Causes and Consequences.* Bombay: Popular Prakashan.

Sethuraman, S.V. (1978), 'The Urban Informal Sector: Concept, Measurement, and Policy'. *International Labour Review*, 114 (1): 69-81.

Sen, Abhijit. (1996), "Economic Reforms Employment and Poverty Trends and Options", *Economic and Political Weekly*. Vol. 31, No. 35.

Shenggen Fan. (2008), *Public Expenditures, Growth, and Poverty.* Oxford University Press, New Delhi.

Srinivas, M.N. (1992), *Social Change in Modern India.* New Delhi: Orient Longman.

Subramanian, S (2015), Once More unto the Breach. The World Bank's latest assault on global poverty. *Economic and Political Weekly*, Nov 7, Vol. L No. 45, pp. 35-40.

Sukhadeo Thorat and Amaresh Dubey, 'How inclusive growth has been during 1993/94 -2009/10 implications for 12th plan Strategy', paper presented at the workshop organised by UNDP and Planning Commission during October 24-25, 2011 in New Delhi.

Srinivasan, T.N. (1999), "Poverty and Reforms in India". Paper Presented in the Conference on Reforms. Organised by NCEAR, December 14-15, Rajasthan.

Sundaram, K and Tendulkar Suresh D. (2003), Poverty among Social and Economic Groups in India in the 1990s, *Economic and Political Weekly*, Vol. 38, No. 50 (Dec. 13-19, 2003), pp. 5263-5276.

Sundaram, K. (2001), "Employment and Poverty in 1990s: Further Results from NSS 55th Round Employment–Unemployment Survey, 1999-2000", *Economic and Political Weekly* 36(32), 11 August.

Tendulkar, S.D., K. Sundaram and L.R. Jain. (1996), *Macro Economic Policy and Poverty in India, 1966-67 to 1993-94*. Paper Presented for ILO, New Delhi.

Thakur, C.P and Venkat Ratnam C. S. (2000), Conditions of Work in the Unorganised Sector in India. *Indian Journal of Labour Economics* 50(4).

Todaro, M. (1970), A Model of Labour Migration and Urban Unemployment in Less Developed Countries, *American Economic Review*, Vol. 59, pp. 138-148.

United Nations Organisation. (2001), *Human Rights Watch 2001*, Washington D.C.

United Nations Development Programme (2011), *Human Development Report 2011*, New York.

————.(2007), World Population Trends and Policies, p. 117.

UN-HABITAT, (2006),'State of the World's Cities 2006/2007'. *The Millennium Development Goals and Urban Sustainability*, London, UK.

UT Administration (2015), Statistical Abstract, Chandigarh.

————.(2015), Statistical Abstract.

————.(2016), Department of School Education, Chandigarh

U.S Agency for International Development. (2007), Washington, D.C.

UNDP. (2011), "Sharing Innovative Experiences: Successful Social Protection Floor Experiences" Vol.18, Global South- South Development Academy, New York.

UNFPA. (2007), United Nations Fund for Population Activities, *United Nations Organisation*, New York.

World Bank. (2001), *World Development Report. Attacking Poverty*. Oxford University Press, New York.

————.(2003), *World Development Report,* India Sustaining Reforms, Reducing Poverty. Oxford University Press, New Delhi.

———.(2008), Urban Poverty: A Global View, *The World Bank Group*, Washington, D.C.

———.(2008), *World Development Report.,* Washington D C.

———.(2010), 'India's Employment Challenge, Creating Jobs, Helping Workers'. Oxford University Press, New Delhi.

———.(2014), *World Development Report,* Washington D C.

———.(2014-15), Ending Poverty and Sharing Prosperity, Global Monitoring Report, Washington, DC.

Yunus, Muhammad (1998), "Poverty Alleviation: Is Economics Any Help? Lessons from the Grameen Bank Experience", *Journal of International Affairs* 52: 47-65.

Websites

http://www.rsby.in/about_rsby.html

"Mid-Day Meal Scheme," http://education-.nic.in/elementary/mdm/index.htm,

http://www.rsby.in/about_rsby.html

www.ministry of hrd .govt. India

Annexure

Annexure -1

The National Food Security Act, 2013

An Act to provide for food and nutritional security in human life cycle approach, by ensuring access to adequate quantity of quality food at affordable prices to people to live a life with dignity and for matters connected therewith or incidental thereto.

Chapter I

Preliminary

1. (*1*) This Act may be called the National Food Security Act, 2013.

(*2*) It extends to the whole of India.

Definitions.

(*1*) "*anganwadi*" means a child care and development centre set up under the Integrated Child Development Services Scheme of the Central Government to render services covered under section 4, clause (*a*) of sub-section (*1*) of section 5 and

(*2*) "central pool" means the stock of food grains which is,—

(*i*) procured by the Central Government and the State Governments through minimum support price operations;

(*ii*) maintained for allocations under the Targeted Public Distribution System, other welfare schemes, including calamity relief and such other schemes;

(*iii*) kept as reserves for schemes referred to in sub-clause (*ii*);

(*3*) "eligible households" means households covered under the priority households and the Antyodaya Anna Yojana referred to in sub-section (*1*) of section 3;

(*4*) "fair price shop" means a shop which has been licensed to distribute essential commodities by an order issued under section 3 of the Essential Commodities Act, 1955, to the ration card holders under the Targeted Public Distribution System;

(*5*) "food grains" means rice, wheat or coarse grains or any combination thereof conforming to such quality norms as may be determined, by order, by the Central Government from time to time;

(*6*) "food security" means the supply of the entitled quantity of food grains and meal specified under Chapter II;

(*7*) "food security allowance" means the amount of money to be paid by the concerned State Government to the entitled persons under section 8;

(*8*) "local authority" includes Panchayat, municipality, district board, cantonment board, town planning authority and in the States of Assam, Manipur, Meghalaya, Mizoram, Nagaland and Tripura where Panchayats do not exist, the village council or committee or any other body, by whatever name called, which is authorised under the Constitution or any law for the time being in force for self-governance or any other authority or body vested with the control and management of civic services, within a specified local area;

(*9*) "meal" means hot cooked or pre-cooked and heated before its service meal or take home ration, as may be prescribed by the Central Government;

(*10*) "minimum support price" means the assured price announced by the Central Government at which food grains are procured from farmers by the Central Government and the State Governments and their agencies, for the central pool;

(*11*) "notification" means a notification issued under this Act and published in the Official Gazette;

(*12*) "other welfare schemes" means such Government schemes, in addition to the Targeted Public Distribution System, under which food grains or meals are supplied as part of the schemes;

(*13*) "person with disability" means a person defined as such in clause (*t*) of section 2 of the Persons with Disabilities (Equal Opportunities, Protection of Rights and Full Participation) Act, 1995;

(*14*) "priority households" means households identified as such under section 10.

(*15*) "prescribed" means prescribed by rules made under this Act;

(*16*) "ration card" means a document issued under an order or authority of the State Government for the purchase of essential commodities from the fair price shops under the Targeted Public Distribution System;

(*17*) "rural area" means any area in a State except those areas covered by any urban local body or a cantonment board established or constituted under any law for the time being in force;

(*18*) "Schedule" means a Schedule appended to this Act;

(*19*) "senior citizen" means a person defined as such under clause (*h*) of section 2 of the Maintenance and Welfare of Parents and Senior Citizens Act, 2007;

(*20*) "social audit" means the process in which people collectively monitor and evaluate the planning and implementation of a programme or scheme;

(*21*) "State Commission" means the State Food Commission constituted under section 16;

(*22*) "State Government", in relation to a Union Territory, means the Administrator thereof appointed under article 239 of the Constitution;

(*23*) "Targeted Public Distribution System" means the system for distribution of essential commodities to the ration card holders through fair price shops;

(*24*) "Vigilance Committee" means a committee constituted under section 29 to supervise the implementation of all schemes under this Act;

(*25*) the words and expressions not defined here but defined in the Essential Commodities Act, 1955, or any other relevant Act shall have the meaning respectively assigned to them in those Acts.

Chapter II

Provisions for Food Security

3. (*1*) Every person belonging to priority households, identified under sub-section (*1*) of section 10, shall be entitled to receive five kilograms of food grains per person per month at subsidised prices specified in Schedule I from the State Government under the Targeted Public Distribution System:

Provided that the households covered under Antyodaya Anna Yojana shall, to such extent as may be specified by the Central Government for each State in the said scheme, be entitled to thirty-five kilograms of food grains per household per month at the prices specified in Schedule I: Provided further that if annual allocation of food grains to any State under the Act is less than the average annual off take of food grains for last three years under normal Targeted Public Distribution System, the same shall be protected at prices as may be determined by the Central Government and the State shall be allocated food grains as specified in Schedule IV.

Explanation.— For the purpose of this section, the "Antyodaya Anna Yojana" means, the scheme by the said name launched by the Central Government on the 25th day of December, 2000; and as modified from time to time.

(*2*) The entitlements of the persons belonging to the eligible households referred to in sub-section (*1*) at subsidised prices shall extend up to seventy-five per cent. Of the rural population and up to fifty per cent. Of the urban population.

(*3*) Subject to sub-section (*1*), the State Government may provide to the persons belonging to eligible households, wheat flour in lieu of the entitled quantity of food grains in accordance with such guidelines as may be specified by the Central Government.

4. Subject to such schemes as may be framed by the Central Government, every pregnant woman and lactating mother shall be entitled to—

(*a*) meal, free of charge, during pregnancy and six months after the child birth, through the local *anganwadi*, so as to meet the nutritional standards specified in Schedule II; and (*b*) maternity benefit of not less than rupees six thousand, in such installments as may be prescribed by the Central Government: Provided that all pregnant women and lactating mothers in regular employment with the Central Government or State Governments or Public Sector Undertakings or those who are in receipt of similar benefits under any law for the time being in force shall not be entitled to benefits specified in clause (*b*).

5. (*1*) Subject to the provisions contained in clause (*b*), every child up to the age of fourteen years shall have the following entitlements for his nutritional needs, namely:–

(*a*) in the case of children in the age group of six months to six years, age appropriate meal, free of charge, through the local *anganwadi* so as to meet the nutritional standards specified in Schedule II: Provided that for children below the age of six months, exclusive breast feeding shall be promoted;

(*b*) in the case of children, up to class VIII or within the age group of six to fourteen years, whichever is applicable, one mid-day meal, free of charge, everyday, except on school holidays, in all schools run by local bodies, Government and Government-aided schools, so as to meet the nutritional standards specified in Schedule II.

(*2*) Every school, referred to in clause (*b*) of sub-section (*1*), and *anganwadi* shall have facilities for cooking meals, drinking water and sanitation: Provided that in urban areas facilities of centralised kitchens for cooking meals may be used, wherever required, as per the guidelines issued by the Central Government.

6. The State Government shall, through the local *anganwadi*, identify and provide meals, free of charge, to children who suffer from malnutrition, so as to meet the nutritional standards specified in Schedule II.

7. The State Governments shall implement schemes covering entitlements under sections 4, 5 and section 6 in accordance with the guidelines, including cost sharing, between the Central Government and the State Governments in such manner as may be prescribed by the Central Government.

Chapter III

Food Security Allowance

8. In case of non-supply of the entitled quantities of food grains or meals to entitled persons under Chapter II, such persons shall be entitled to receive such food security allowance from the concerned State Government to be paid to each person, within such time and manner as may be prescribed by the Central Government.

Chapter IV

Identification of Eligible Households

9. The percentage coverage under the Targeted Public Distribution System in rural and urban areas for each State shall, subject to sub-section (*2*) of section 3, be determined by the Central Government and the total number of persons to be covered in such rural and urban areas of the State shall be calculated on the basis of the population estimates as per the census of which the relevant figures have been published.

10. (*1*) The State Government shall, within the number of persons determined under section 9 for the rural and urban areas, identify—

(*a*) the households to be covered under the Antyodaya Anna Yojana to the extent specified under sub-section (*1*) of section 3, in accordance with the guidelines applicable to the said scheme;

(*b*) the remaining households as priority households to be covered under the Targeted Public Distribution System, in accordance with such guidelines as the State Government may specify: Provided that the State Government may, as soon as possible, but within such period not exceeding three hundred and sixty-five days, after the commencement of the Act, identify the eligible households in accordance with the guidelines framed under this sub-section: Provided further that the State Government shall continue to receive the allocation of food grains from the Central Government under the existing Targeted Public Distribution System, till the identification of such households is complete. (*2*) The State Government shall update the list of eligible households, within the number of persons determined under section 9 for the rural and urban areas, in accordance with the guidelines framed under sub-section (*1*).

11. The State Government shall place the list of the identified eligible households in the public domain and display it prominently.

Chapter V

Reforms in Targeted Public Distribution System

12. (*1*) The Central and State Governments shall Endeavour to progressively undertake necessary reforms in the Targeted Public Distribution System in consonance with the role envisaged for them in this Act.

(*2*) The reforms shall, *inter alia*, include— (*a*) doorstep delivery of food grains to the Targeted Public Distribution System outlets;

(*b*) application of information and communication technology tools including end-to-end computerisation in order to ensure transparent recording of transactions at all levels, and to prevent diversion;

(c) leveraging "aadhaar" for unique identification, with biometric information of entitled beneficiaries for proper targeting of benefits under this Act;

(*d*) full transparency of records;

(*e*) preference to public institutions or public bodies such as Panchayats, self help groups, co-operatives, in licensing of fair price shops and management of fair price shops by women or their collectives;

(*f*) diversification of commodities distributed under the Public Distribution System over a period of time;

(*g*) support to local public distribution models and grains banks;

(*h*) introducing schemes, such as, cash transfer, food coupons, or other schemes, to the targeted beneficiaries in order to ensure their food grain entitlements specified in Chapter II, in such area and manner as may be prescribed by the Central Government.

Chapter VI

Women Empowerment

13. (*1*) The eldest woman who is not less than eighteen years of age, in every eligible household, shall be head of the household for the purpose of issue of ration cards.

(*2*) Where a household at any time does not have a woman or a woman of eighteen years of age or above, but has a female member below the age of eighteen years, then, the eldest male member of the household shall be the head of the household for the purpose of issue of ration card and the female member, on attaining the age of eighteen years, shall become the head of the household for such ration cards in place of such male member.

Chapter VII

Grievance Redressal Mechanism

14. Every State Government shall put in place an internal grievance redressal mechanism which may include call centres, help lines, designation of nodal officers, or such other mechanism as may be prescribed.

15. (*1*) The State Government shall appoint or designate, for each district, an officer to be the District Grievance Redressal Officer for expeditious and effective redressal of grievances of the aggrieved persons in matters relating to distribution of entitled food grains or meals under Chapter II, and to enforce the entitlements under this Act.

(*2*) The qualifications for appointment as District Grievance Redressal Officer and its powers shall be such as may be prescribed by the State Government.

(*3*) The method and terms and conditions of appointment of the District Grievance Redressal Officer shall be such as may be prescribed by the State Government.

(*4*) The State Government shall provide for the salary and allowances of the District Grievance Redressal Officer and other staff and such other expenditure as may be considered necessary for their proper functioning.

(*5*) The officer referred to in sub-section (*1*) shall hear complaints regarding nondistribution of entitled food grains or meals, and matters relating thereto, and take necessary action for their redressal in such manner and within such time as may be prescribed by the State Government.

(*6*) Any complainant or the officer or authority against whom any order has been passed by officer referred to in sub-section (*1*), who is not satisfied with the redressal of grievance may file an appeal against such order before the State Commission.

(*7*) Every appeal under sub-section (*6*) shall be filed in such manner and within such time as may be prescribed by the State Government.

16. (*1*) Every State Government shall, by notification, constitute a State Food Commission for the purpose of monitoring and review of implementation of this Act.

(*2*) The State Commission shall consist of—

(*a*) a Chairperson;

(*b*) five other Members; and

(*c*) a Member-Secretary, who shall be an officer of the State Government not below the rank of Joint Secretary to that Government: Provided that there shall be at least two women, whether Chairperson, Member or Member-Secretary: Provided further that there shall be one person belonging to the Scheduled Castes and one person belonging to the Scheduled Tribes, whether Chairperson, Member or Member-Secretary.

(*3*) The Chairperson and other Members shall be appointed from amongst persons—

(*a*) who are or have been member of the All India Services or any other civil services of the Union or State or holding a civil post under the Union or State having knowledge and experience in matters relating to food security, policy making and administration in the field of agriculture, civil supplies, nutrition, health or any allied field; or

(*b*) of eminence in public life with wide knowledge and experience in agriculture, law, human rights, social service, management, nutrition, health, food policy or public administration; or (*c*) who have a proven record of work relating to the improvement of the food and nutrition rights of the poor.

(*4*) The Chairperson and every other Member shall hold office for a term not exceeding five years from the date on which he enters upon his office and shall be eligible for reappointment: Provided that no person shall hold office as the Chairperson or other Member after he has attained the age of sixty-five years.

(*5*) The method of appointment and other terms and conditions subject to which the Chairperson, other Members and Member-Secretary of the State Commission may be appointed, and time, place and procedure of meetings of the State Commission (including the quorum at such meetings) and its powers, shall be such as may be prescribed by the State Government.

(*6*) The State Commission shall undertake the following functions, namely:—

(*a*) monitor and evaluate the implementation of this Act, in relation to the State;

(*b*) either *suo motu* or on receipt of complaint inquire into violations of entitlements provided under Chapter II;

(*c*) give advice to the State Government on effective implementation of this Act;

(*d*) give advice to the State Government, their agencies, autonomous bodies as well as non-governmental organisations involved in delivery of relevant services, for the effective implementation of food and nutrition related schemes, to enable individuals to fully access their entitlements specified in this Act;

(*e*) hear appeals against orders of the District Grievance Redressal Officer;

(*f*) prepare annual reports which shall be laid before the State Legislature by the State Government.

(*7*) The State Government shall make available to the State Commission, such administrative and technical staff, as it may consider necessary for proper functioning of the State Commission.

(*8*) The method of appointment of the staff under sub-section (*7*), their salaries, allowances and conditions of service shall be such, as may be prescribed by the State Government.

(*9*) The State Government may remove from office the Chairperson or any Member who—

(*a*) is, or at any time has been, adjudged as an insolvent; or

(*b*) has become physically or mentally incapable of acting as a member; or

(*c*) has been convicted of an offence which, in the opinion of the State Government, involves moral turpitude; or

(*d*) has acquired such financial or other interest as is likely to affect prejudicially his functions as a member; or

(*e*) has so abused his position as to render his continuation in office detrimental to the public interest.

(*10*) No such Chairperson or Member shall be removed under clause (*d*) or clause (*e*) of sub-section (*9*) unless he has been given a reasonable opportunity of being heard in the matter.

17. The State Government shall provide for salary and allowances of Chairperson, other Members, Member-Secretary, support staff, and other administrative expenses required for proper functioning of the State Commission.

18. The State Government may, if considers it necessary, by notification, designate any statutory commission or a body to exercise the powers and perform the functions of the State Commission referred to in section 16.

19. Notwithstanding anything contained in sub-section (*1*) of section 16, two or more States may have a Joint State Food Commission for the purposes of this Act with the approval of the Central Government.

20. (*1*) The State Commission shall, while inquiring into any matter referred to in clauses (*b*) and (*e*) of sub-section (*6*) of section 16, have all the powers of a civil court while trying a suit under the Code of

Civil Procedure, 1908, and, in particular, in respect of the following matters, namely:—

(*a*) summoning and enforcing the attendance of any person and examining him on oath;

(*b*) discovery and production of any document;

(*c*) receiving evidence on affidavits;

(*d*) requisitioning any public record or copy thereof from any court or office; and

(*e*) issuing commissions for the examination of witnesses or documents.

(*2*) The State Commission shall have the power to forward any case to a Magistrate having jurisdiction to try the same and the Magistrate to whom any such case is forwarded shall proceed to hear the complaint against the accused as if the case has been forwarded to him under section 346 of the Code of Criminal Procedure, 1973.

21. No act or proceeding of the State Commission shall be invalid merely by reason of—(*a*) any vacancy in, or any defect in the constitution of, the State Commission; or (*b*) any defect in the appointment of a person as the Chairperson or a Member of the State Commission; or (*c*) any irregularity in the procedure of the State Commission not affecting the merits of the case.

Chapter VIII

Obligations of Central Government for Food Security

22. (*1*) The Central Government shall, for ensuring the regular supply of food grains to persons belonging to eligible households, allocate from the central pool the required quantity of food grains to the State Governments under the Targeted Public Distribution System, as per the entitlements under section 3 and at prices specified in Schedule I.

(*2*) The Central Government shall allocate food grains in accordance with the number of persons belonging to the eligible households identified in each State under section 10.

(*3*) The Central Government shall provide food grains in respect of entitlements under sections 4, 5 and section 6, to the State Governments, at prices specified for the persons belonging to eligible households in Schedule I.

(*4*) Without prejudice to sub-section (*1*), the Central Government shall,—

(*a*) procure food grains for the central pool through its own agencies and the State Governments and their agencies;

(*b*) allocate food grains to the States;

(c) provide for transportation of food grains, as per allocation, to the depots designated by the Central Government in each State;

(*d*) provide assistance to the State Government in meeting the expenditure incurred by it towards intra-State movement, handling of food grains and margins paid to fair price shop dealers, in accordance with such norms and manner as may be prescribed by the Central Government; and

(*e*) create and maintain required modern and scientific storage facilities at various levels.

23. In case of short supply of food grains from the central pool to a State, the Central Government shall provide funds to the extent of short supply to the State Government for meeting obligations under Chapter II in such manner as may be prescribed by the Central Government.

Chapter IX

Obligations of State Government for Food Security

24. (*1*) The State Government shall be responsible for implementation and monitoring of the schemes of various Ministries and Departments of the Central Government in accordance with guidelines issued by the Central Government for each scheme, and their own schemes, for ensuring food security to the targeted beneficiaries in their State.

(*2*) Under the Targeted Public Distribution System, it shall be the duty of the State Government to—

(*a*) take delivery of food grains from the designated depots of the Central Government in the State, at the prices specified in Schedule I, organise intra-State allocations for delivery of the allocated food grains through their authorised agencies at the door-step of each fair price shop; and

(*b*) ensure actual delivery or supply of the food grains to the entitled persons at the prices specified in Schedule I.

(*3*) For food grain requirements in respect of entitlements under sections 4, 5 and section 6, it shall be the responsibility of the State Government to take delivery of food grains from the designated depots of the Central Government in the State, at the prices specified in Schedule I for persons belonging to eligible households and ensure actual delivery of entitled benefits, as specified in the aforesaid sections.

(*4*) In case of non-supply of the entitled quantities of food grains or meals to entitled persons under Chapter II, the State Government shall be responsible for payment of food security allowance specified in section 8.

(*5*) For efficient operations of the Targeted Public Distribution System, every State Government shall,—

(*a*) create and maintain scientific storage facilities at the State, District and Block levels, being sufficient to accommodate food grains required under the Targeted Public Distribution System and other food based welfare schemes;

(*b*) suitably strengthen capacities of their Food and Civil Supplies Corporations and other designated agencies;

(*c*) establish institutionalised licensing arrangements for fair price shops in accordance with the relevant provisions of the Public Distribution System (Control) Order, 2001 made under the Essential Commodities Act, 1955, as amended from time to time.

Chapter X

Obligations of Local Authorities

25. (*1*) The local authorities shall be responsible for the proper implementation of this Act in their respective areas.

(*2*) Without prejudice to sub-section (*1*), the State Government may assign, by notification, additional responsibilities for implementation of the Targeted Public Distribution System to the local authority.

26. In implementing different schemes of the Ministries and Departments of the Central Government and the State Governments, prepared to implement provisions of this Act, the local authorities shall be responsible for discharging such duties and responsibilities as may be assigned to them, by notification, by the respective State Governments.

Chapter XI

Transparency and Accountability

27. All Targeted Public Distribution System related records shall be placed in the public domain and kept open for inspection to the public, in such manner as may be prescribed by the State Government.

28. (*1*) Every local authority, or any other authority or body, as may be authorised by the State Government, shall conduct or cause to be conducted, periodic social audits on the functioning of fair price shops, Targeted Public Distribution System and other welfare schemes, and cause to publicise its findings and take necessary action, in such manner as may be prescribed by the State Government.

(*2*) The Central Government may, if it considers necessary, conduct or cause to be conducted social audit through independent agencies having experience in conduct of such audits.

29. (*1*) For ensuring transparency and proper functioning of the Targeted Public Distribution System and accountability of the functionaries in such system, every State Government shall set up Vigilance Committees as specified in the Public Distribution System

(Control) Order, 2001, made under the Essential Commodities Act, 1955, as amended from time to time, at the State, District, Block and fair price shop levels consisting of such persons, as may be prescribed by the State Government giving due representation to the local authorities, the Scheduled Castes, the Scheduled Tribes, women and destitute persons or persons with disability.

(*2*) The Vigilance Committees shall perform the following functions, namely:—

(*a*) regularly supervise the implementation of all schemes under this Act;

(*b*) inform the District Grievance Redressal Officer, in writing, of any violation of the provisions of this Act; and

(*c*) inform the District Grievance Redressal Officer, in writing, of any malpractice or misappropriation of funds found by it.

Chapter XII

Provisions for Advancing Food Security

30. The Central Government and the State Governments shall, while implementing the provisions of this Act and the schemes for meeting specified entitlements, give special focus to the needs of the vulnerable groups especially in remote areas and other areas which are difficult to access, hilly and tribal areas for ensuring their food security.

31. The Central Government, the State Governments and local authorities shall, for the purpose of advancing food and nutritional security, strive to progressively realise the objectives specified in Schedule III.

Chapter XIII

Miscellaneous

32. (*1*) The provisions of this Act shall not preclude the Central Government or the State Government from continuing or formulating other food based welfare schemes.

(*2*) Notwithstanding anything contained in this Act, the State Government may, continue with or formulate food or nutrition based plans or schemes providing for benefits higher than the benefits provided under this Act, from its own resources.

33. Any public servant or authority found guilty, by the State Commission at the time of deciding any complaint or appeal, of failing to provide the relief recommended by the District Grievance Redressal Officer, without reasonable cause, or willfully ignoring such recommendation, shall be liable to penalty not exceeding five thousand rupees: Provided that the public servant or the public authority, as the case may be, shall be given a reasonable opportunity of being heard before any penalty is imposed.

34. (*1*) For the purpose of adjudging penalty under section 33, the State Commission shall authorize any of its member to be an adjudicating officer for holding an inquiry in the prescribed manner after giving any person concerned a reasonable opportunity of being heard for the purpose of imposing any penalty.

(*2*) While holding an inquiry the adjudicating officer shall have power to summon and enforce the attendance of any person acquainted with the facts and circumstances of the case to give evidence or to produce any document which in the opinion of the adjudicating officer, may be useful for or relevant to the subject matter of the inquiry and if, on such inquiry, he is satisfied that the person has failed to provide the relief recommended by the District Grievance Redressal Officer, without reasonable cause, or willfully ignored such recommendation, he may impose such penalty as he thinks fit in accordance with the provisions of section 33.

35. (*1*) The Central Government may, by notification, direct that the powers exercisable by it (except the power to make rules), in such circumstances and subject to such conditions and limitations, be exercisable also by the State Government or an officer subordinate to the Central Government or the State Government as it may specify in the notification.

(*2*) The State Government may, by notification, direct that the powers exercisable by it (except the power to make rules), in such circumstances and subject to such conditions and limitations, be exercisable also by an officer subordinate to it as it may specify in the notification.

36. The provisions of this Act or the schemes made thereunder shall have effect notwithstanding anything inconsistent therewith contained in any other law for the time being in force or in any instrument having effect by virtue of such law.

37. (*1*) If the Central Government is satisfied that it is necessary or expedient so to do, it may, by notification, amend Schedule I or Schedule II or Schedule III or Schedule IV and thereupon Schedule I or Schedule II or Schedule III or Schedule IV, as the case may be, shall be deemed to have been amended accordingly.

(*2*) A copy of every notification issued under sub-section (*1*), shall be laid before each House of Parliament as soon as may be after it is issued.

38. The Central Government may, from time to time, give such directions, as it may consider necessary, to the State Governments for the effective implementation of the provisions of this Act and the State Governments shall comply with such directions.

39. (*1*) The Central Government may, in consultation with the State Governments and by notification, make rules to carry out the provisions of this Act.

(*2*) In particular, and without prejudice to the generality of the foregoing power, such rules may provide for all or any of the following matters, namely:—

(*a*) scheme including cost sharing for providing maternity benefit to pregnant women and lactating mothers under clause (*b*) of section 4;

(*b*) schemes covering entitlements under sections 4, 5 and section 6 including cost sharing under section 7;

(*c*) amount, time and manner of payment of food security allowance to entitled individuals under section 8;

(*d*) introducing schemes of cash transfer, food coupons or other schemes to the targeted beneficiaries in order to ensure their food grains entitlements in such areas and manner under clause (*h*) of sub-section (*2*) of section 12;

(*e*) the norms and manner of providing assistance to the State Governments in meeting expenditure under clause (*d*) of sub-section (*4*) of section 22;

(*f*) manner in which funds shall be provided by the Central Government to the State Governments in case of short supply of food grains, under section 23;

(*g*) any other matter which is to be, or may be, prescribed or in respect of which provision is to be made by the Central Government by rules.

(*3*) Every rule made by the Central Government under this Act shall be laid, as soon as may be after it is made, before each House of Parliament, while it is in session, for a total period of thirty days which may be comprised in one session or in two or more successive sessions, and if, before the expiry of the session immediately following the session or the successive sessions aforesaid, both Houses agree in making any modification in the rule or both Houses agree that the rule should not be made, the rule shall thereafter have effect only in such modified form or be of no effect, as the case may be; so, however, that any such modification or annulment shall be without prejudice to the validity of anything previously done under that rule.

40. (*1*) The State Government may, by notification, and subject to the condition of previous publication, and consistent with this Act and the rules made by the Central Government, make rules to carry out the provisions of this Act.

(*2*) In particular and without prejudice to the generality of the foregoing power, such rules may provide for all or any of the following matters, namely:—

(*a*) guidelines for identification of priority households under sub-section (*1*) of section 10;

(*b*) internal grievance redressal mechanism under section 14;

(*c*) qualifications for appointment as District Grievance Redressal Officer and its powers under sub-section (*2*) of section 15;

(*d*) method and terms and conditions of appointment of the District Grievance Redressal Officer under sub-section (*3*) of section 15;

(*e*) manner and time limit for hearing complaints by the District Grievance Redressal Officer and the filing of appeals under sub-sections (*5*) and (*7*) of section 15;

(*f*) method of appointment and the terms and conditions of appointment of Chairperson, other Members and Member-Secretary of the State Commission, procedure for meetings of the Commission and its powers, under sub-section (*5*) of section 16;

(*g*) method of appointment of staff of the State Commission, their salaries, allowances and conditions of service under sub-section (*8*) of section 16;

(*h*) manner in which the Targeted Public Distribution System related records shall be placed in the public domain and kept open for inspection to public under section 27;

(*i*) manner in which the social audit on the functioning of fair price shops, Targeted Public Distribution System and other welfare schemes shall be conducted under section 28;

(*j*) composition of Vigilance Committees under sub-section (*1*) of section 29;

(*k*) schemes or programmes of the Central Government or the State Governments for utilisation of institutional mechanism under section 43;

(*l*) any other matter which is to be, or may be, prescribed or in respect of which provision is to be made by the State Government by rules.

(*3*) Every rule, notification and guidelines made or issued by the State Government under this Act shall, as soon as may be after it is made or issued, be laid before each House of the State Legislature where there are two Houses, and where there is one House of the State Legislature, before that House.

41. The schemes, guidelines, orders and food standard, grievance redressal mechanism, vigilance committees, existing on the date of commencement of this Act, shall continue to be in force and operate till such schemes, guidelines, orders and food standard, grievance redressal mechanism, vigilance committees are specified or notified under this Act or the rules made thereunder: Provided that anything done or any action taken under the said schemes, guidelines, orders and food standard, grievance redressal mechanism, or by vigilance committees shall be deemed to have been done or taken under the corresponding provisions of this Act and shall continue to be in force accordingly unless and until superseded by anything done or by any action taken under this Act.

42. (*1*) If any difficulty arises in giving effect to the provisions of this Act, the Central Government may, by order, published in the Official Gazette, make such provisions, not inconsistent with the provisions of this Act, as appear to it to be necessary or expedient for removing the difficulty: Provided that no order shall be made under this section after the expiry of two years from the date of commencement of this Act.

(*2*) Every order made under this section shall be laid, as soon as may be after it is made, before each House of Parliament.

43. The services of authorities to be appointed or constituted under sections 15 and 16 may be utilised in the implementation of other schemes or programmes of the Central Government or the State Governments, as may be prescribed by the State Government.

44. The Central Government, or as the case may be, the State Government, shall be liable for a claim by any person entitled under this Act, except in the case of war, flood, drought, fire, cyclone or earthquake affecting the regular supply of food grains or meals to such person under this Act: Provided that the Central Government may, in consultation with the Planning Commission, declare whether or not any such situation affecting the regular supply of food grains or meals to such person has arisen or exists.

45. (*1*) The National Food Security Ordinance, 2013 is hereby repealed.

(*2*) Notwithstanding such repeal,—

(*a*) anything done, any action taken or any identification of eligible households made; or

(*b*) any right, entitlement, privilege, obligation or liability acquired, accrued or incurred; or (*c*) any guidelines framed or directions issued; or

(*d*) any investigation, inquiry or any other legal proceeding initiated, conducted or continued in respect of such right, entitlement, privilege, obligation or liability as aforesaid; or

(*e*) any penalty imposed in respect of any offence, under the said Ordinance shall be deemed to have been done, taken, made, acquired, accrued, incurred, framed, issued, initiated, conducted, continued or imposed under the corresponding provisions of this Act.

Subsidised Prices Under Targeted Public Distribution System

Eligible households shall be entitled to food grains under section 3 at the subsidised price not exceeding rupees 3 per kg for rice, rupees 2 per kg for wheat and rupee 1 per kg for coarse grains for a period of three years from the date of commencement of this Act; and thereafter, at such price, as may be fixed by the Central Government, from time to time, not exceeding,—the minimum support price for wheat and coarse grains; and (*ii*) the derived minimum support price for rice, as the case may be.

Nutritional Standards

Nutritional standards: The nutritional standards for children in the age group of six months to three years, age group of three to six years and pregnant women and lactating mothers required to be met by providing "Take Home Rations" or nutritious hot cooked meal in accordance with the Integrated Child Development Services Scheme and nutritional standards for children in lower and upper primary classes under the Mid Day Meal Scheme are as follows:

Table 1. Nutritional standards for children in lower and upper primary classes

Sl. No.	*Category*	*Type of meal*	*Calories*	*Protein*
1.	Children (6 months to 3 years)	Take Home Ration	500	12-15
2.	Children (3 to 6 years)	Morning Snack and Hot Cooked Meal	500	12-15
3.	Children (6 months to 6 years) who are malnourished	Take Home Ration	800	20-25
4.	Lower primary classes	Hot Cooked Meal	450	12
5.	Upper primary classes	Hot Cooked Meal	700	20
6.	Pregnant women and Lactating mothers	Take Home Ration	600	18-20

Provisions for Advancing Food Security

(*1*) Revitalisation of Agriculture—

(*a*) agrarian reforms through measures for securing interests of small and marginal farmers;

(*b*) increase in investments in agriculture, including research and development, extension services, micro and minor irrigation and power to increase productivity and production;

(*c*) ensuring livelihood security to farmers by way of remunerative prices, access to inputs, credit, irrigation, power, crop insurance, etc.;

(*d*) prohibiting unwarranted diversion of land and water from food production.

(*2*) Procurement, Storage and Movement related interventions—

(*a*) incentivizing decentralised procurement including procurement of coarse grains;

(*b*) geographical diversification of procurement operations;

(*c*) augmentation of adequate decentralised modern and scientific storage;

(*d*) giving top priority to movement of food grains and providing sufficient number of rakes for this purpose, including expanding the line capacity of railways to facilitate food grain movement from surplus to consuming regions.

(*3*) Others: Access to—

(*a*) safe and adequate drinking water and sanitation;

(*b*) healthcare;

(*c*) nutritional, health and education support to adolescent girls;

(*d*) adequate pensions for senior citizens, persons with disability and single women.

Food Security Through Mid-Day Meal Scheme (rules revised in 2015)

In exercise of the powers conferred by sub-section (1) read with clause (b) of sub-section (2) of section 39 of the National Food Security

Act, 2013 (20 of 2013), the Central Government hereby makes the following rules, namely:-

1. Short title and commencement.–(1) These rules may be called the Mid-Day Meal Rules, 2015.

(2) They shall come into force on the date of their publication in the official Gazette.

2. Definitions.–In these rules, unless the context otherwise requires,-

(a) "Act" means the National Food Security Act, 2013 (20 of 2013);

(b) "food grains" means rice, wheat, coarse grains or any combination thereof conforming to such quality norms as may be determined, by order, by the Central Government from time to time;

(c) "food security allowance" means the food grain and money to be paid by the concerned State Government to the entitled person under section 8 of the Act;

(d) "meal" means hot cooked meal;

(e) "School" includes any school run by Local Bodies, Government or aided by the Government including madrasas and maqtabs supported under Sarva Shiksha Abhiyan;

(f) "section" means the section of the Act; and

(g) words and expressions used herein and not defined but defined in the Act shall have the meanings respectively assigned to them in the Act.

3. Entitlement for nutritional meal.–Every child within the age group of six to fourteen years studying in classes I to VIII who enroll and attend the school, shall be provided meal having nutritional standards as specified in Schedule II of the Act, free of charge every day except on school holidays.

4. Place of serving meal.–The meal shall be served to children at school only.

5. Preparation of meals and maintenance of standards and quality.–(1) The meal shall be prepared in accordance with the

Mid-Day Meal guidelines issued by the Central Government from time to time and in accordance with the provisions of Schedule II of the Act.

(2) Every school shall have the facility for cooking meal in hygienic manner. Schools in urban area may use the facility of centralised kitchens for cooking meals wherever required in accordance with the guidelines issued by the Central Government and the meal shall be served to children at respective school only.

6. State Steering-cum-Monitoring Committee for Mid-Day Meal Scheme.–The State Steering-cum-Monitoring Committee (SSMC) shall oversee the implementation of the scheme with a view to ensure implementation of the Act including establishment of a mechanism for maintenance of nutritional standards and quality of meals.

7. Role of School Management Committee (SMC) for monitoring Mid-day Meals Scheme.–(1) The School Management Committee mandated under Right to Free and Compulsory Education Act, 2009 shall also monitor implementation of the Mid-day Meal Scheme and shall oversee quality of meals provided to the children, cleanliness of the place of cooking and maintenance of hygiene in implementation of Mid-day Meal Scheme.

(2) The Headmaster or Headmistress of the school shall be empowered to utilise any fund available in school for the purpose of continuation of Mid Day Meal Scheme in the school in case of temporary unavailability of food grains, cooking cost etc. in the school. The utilised fund shall be reimbursed to the school account immediately after receipt of mid day meal funds.

8. Testing of Meals by accredited Labouratories.–(1) Hot cooked meal provided to children shall be evaluated and certified by the Government Food Research Labouratory or any laboratory accredited or recognised by law, so as to ensure that the meal meets with the nutritional standards and quality specified in Schedule II to the Act. The Food and Drugs Administration Department of the State may collect samples to ensure the nutritive value and quality of the meals.

(2) The Department referred to in sub-rule (1) shall collect the samples at least once in a month ***from randomly selected schools or***

centralised kitchens and send such samples for examination to the laboratories referred to in sub-rule (1).

9. Food Security Allowance.–(1) If the Mid-Day Meal is not provided in school on any school day due to non-availability of food grains, cooking cost, fuel or absence of cook-cum-helper or any other reason, the State Government shall pay food security allowance as defined in clause (c) of rule 2 to every child referred to in rule 3 by 15th of the succeeding month in the manner provided herein below:-

(a) Quantity of Food grains as per entitlement of the child; and

(b) Cooking cost prevailing in the State.

(2) In case of non-supply of meal by the Centralised Kitchen, the Food Security Allowance shall be realised from the Centralised Kitchen as per sub-rule (1): Provided that in case a child has not taken food on offer for whatever reasons, no claim of food security allowance shall lie with the State Government or Centralised Kitchens: Provided further that no claim shall lie with State Government or Centralised Kitchen for reasons of quality of food grains and meal.

(3) The State Government shall take action to fix responsibility on the person or agency in accordance with the procedure laid down, if mid-day meal is not provided in school on school days continuously for three days or at least for five days in a month.

(4) Wherever an agency of Central Government is involved, the State Government shall take up the matter with Central Government which shall resolve the matter within a month.

10. Saving.–Nothing in these rules shall affect the guidelines issued in this behalf or likely to be issued by the Central Government regarding the activities relating to Mid Day Meal Scheme.

Index

Q

R

S

Disclaimer

The aim of this publication is to supply information taken from sources believed to be valid and reliable. This is not an attempt to render any type of professional advice or neither analysis nor it is too treated as such. While much care has been taken to ensure the veracity and accuracy of the information presented with in. Neither the publisher nor the author bears any responsibility for any damage arising from inadvertent omissions, negligence or inaccuracies (typological or factual) that may have found their way intc this book.